Evaluating Hedge Fund Performance

To Paul Schatz

with Best Wishes

Vardy J. Tean

Nov 2, 2009

Founded in 1807, John Wiley & Sons is the oldest independent publishing company in the United States. With offices in North America, Europe, Australia, and Asia, Wiley is globally committed to developing and marketing print and electronic products and services for our customers' professional and personal knowledge and understanding.

The Wiley Finance series contains books written specifically for finance and investment professionals as well as sophisticated individual investors and their financial advisors. Book topics range from portfolio management to e-commerce, risk management, financial engineering, valuation, and financial instrument analysis, as well as much more.

For a list of available titles, visit our Web site at www.WileyFinance.com.

Evaluating Hedge Fund Performance

VINH Q. TRAN

WILEY

John Wiley & Sons, Inc.

Published by John Wiley & Sons, Inc., Hoboken, New Jersey.
Published simultaneously in Canada.

For general information on our other products and services or for technical support, please
contact our Customer Care Department within the United States at (800) 762-2974,
outside the United States at (317) 572-3993 or fax (317) 572-4002.

Wiley also publishes its books in a variety of electronic formats. Some content that appears
in print may not be available in electronic books. For more information about Wiley
products, visit our web site at www.wiley.com.

Library of Congress Cataloging-in-Publication Data:
Tran, Vinh Quang, 1946-
 Evaluating hedge fund performance / Vinh Q. Tran.
  p. cm.—(Wiley finance series)
  ISBN-13 978-0-471-68171-7 (cloth)
  ISBN-10 0-471-68171-7 (cloth)
  1. Hedge funds—United States. I. Title. II. Series.
 HG4930.T73 2006
 332.64'5—dc22

            2005026226

Printed in the United States of America.

10 9 8 7 6 5 4 3 2 1

In loving memory of my beloved mother

Contents

Foreword

Many misconceptions exist about hedge funds and the hedge fund industry. Few investors know that hedge funds have now existed for almost 60 years. Few investors know that the term *hedge fund* refers more to the legal vehicle (private pool of capital) that houses the underlying strategy than the strategy itself. Most investors view hedge funds primarily as "absolute return" investments in which managers seek to obtain extreme positive returns in all market environments. Often the press has portrayed hedge funds as extremely risky investments.

In *Evaluating Hedge Fund Performance*, Dr. Tran attempts to remove these misconceptions. Instead, he emphasizes the risk reduction role of hedge funds when combined with traditional stock and bond investments. Dr. Tran points out that for most of the past 15 years, most hedge fund strategies have underperformed the S&P 500. This should come as little surprise to investors. The lower return achieved by most hedge fund strategies is consistent with their lower risk. Most investors fail to realize that return variability of the typical hedge fund is less than that of the typical equity investment.

The role of hedge funds as a risk diversifier is a primary focus of this book. The last free lunch of investment rests not in hedge fund investment per se but in combining hedge funds with other traditional assets. The first chapters remind investors that long-term investment does not necessarily remove investment risk. For long time periods, individual asset classes often provide minimal returns. To the degree that a free lunch still exists in investment, it is the result of combining assets with similar return and similar risk but with low correlation. This results in a portfolio with the same return but with lower variance. Just as important, for two assets with similar return, the one with the lower variance will achieve the higher long-term return.

Hopefully, Dr. Tran's argument for concentrating on lower risk instead of concentrating solely on higher return will capture the reader's interest. In the core chapters, hedge fund returns are not presented as providing a higher-return substitute for traditional assets. In contrast, hedge funds are shown often to underperform traditional assets in many market environments. However, the reader is also introduced to the concept of hedge fund alpha (to the degree that hedge funds remove their exposure to equity risk, their return may be compared to that of zero-equity-exposure investments). As important, the reduction in market sensitivity also results in hedge funds that have a low correlation with traditional investments and provide true portfolio risk reduction benefits.

Since this book's primary emphasis is on the risk and return behavior of hedge funds, the final chapters emphasize various aspects of hedge fund construction as well as performance analysis and portfolio construction. Dr. Tran reviews some of the basic concepts in performance analysis and portfolio construction and examines the role of hedge funds within an investor's portfolio. While many of the concepts discussed have been reviewed in other books, the overview of fundamental risks (management and market based) of hedge fund investment reminds investors that there is no substitute for understanding both the hedge fund strategy and the manager behind the strategy.

As hedge funds have grown, the number of books attempting to explain the industry and the strategy has also increased. Each book offers a unique view into the hedge fund world. Many of these books review the return potential of hedge funds. Dr. Tran reminds investors that while return is a fundamental part of any investment, return is fundamentally related to risk. Moreover, while investors must understand the fundamental risks of any investment, risk is not rewarded at the asset class level but only at the portfolio level. As a result, assets such as hedge funds that provide diversification are a necessary ingredient to the long-only equity investor.

For investors who are looking for an introductory view of the hedge fund industry, this book provides a refreshing look at the pros and cons of investment in general and of hedge funds in particular. Hedge funds are, of course, an evolving industry. As markets evolve, so does our understanding. While more advanced readers may wish to spend some time in the footnote sections, individuals wishing an honest introduction to the pros and cons of hedge fund investing will find this book worthwhile.

THOMAS SCHNEEWEIS
Michael and Cheryl Philipp Professor of Finance
Isenberg School of Management
University of Massachusetts

Director, Center for International Securities
    and Derivatives Research
Managed Futures Association

Editor, *Journal of Alternative Investments*

Acknowledgments

T his book would not have been completed without the contributions of so many people. I wish to extend special thanks to Thomas Schneeweis at the Center for International Securities and Derivatives Research; David Brown at Sabrient Systems; Joseph Pignatelli Jr. at The Archstone Partnerships; Greg N. Gregoriou at the State University of New York (Plattsburgh); Vikas Agarwal at Georgia State University; Joel Press and Lawrence M. Statsky at Ernst & Young; Marc S. Goodman at Kenmar; Duane Roberts at Atlantic Asset Management Partners; William J. Crerend at Evaluation Associates Capital Markets; and Scott Beyer at Northern Illinois University. They have read and offered constructive suggestions on the original manuscript. Any remaining errors, however, are mine. My editors, Pamela van Giessen, who encouraged me to write the book, and Bill Falloon, whose patience has sustained me, and the editorial staff, especially Laura Walsh and Mary Daniello, have been most helpful and cooperative.

And I am blessed with the love and support from my wife, Nhung; our son, Thuy; and daughter, Heather. Their patience and encouragement have urged me on.

VINH Q. TRAN

Introduction

Alfred Winslow Jones started a hedge fund in 1949, pioneering the concept and strategy of using hedges to protect his portfolios against market declines. Though hugely successful and producing handsome returns for his investors, and imitated by others in the subsequent decades, Jones' idea did not gain much recognition among the investing public in the 1980s and 1990s, who were fixated by the bull market and the popularity of mutual funds. In fact, TASS Research identified only 68 hedge fund managers when it began collecting data on hedge funds in 1984. But all of that changed with the bear market of 2000–2002, which witnessed unrelenting stock market declines for the longest period since the crash of 1929. While mutual fund and other traditional investors were reeling in losses, investors in many hedge funds suffered little and sometimes stacked up double-digit percentage gains. As a result, assets under management by hedge funds soared from about $200 billion in 2000 to over $500 billion in 2003, and have reached over $1 trillion by 2005—still small compared to about $8 trillion managed by approximately 8,300 U.S.-based mutual funds but nevertheless representing dramatic growth.

But even now, reports about hedge funds remain largely negative. Press headlines such as "Hedge-Fund Follies,"[1] "Hedge Funds May Give Colleges Painful Lessons,"[2] and "A Health Warning on Hedge Funds"[3] clearly are not intended to soothe.

The reality is that hedge funds are investments with risk and return characteristics different from traditional stock and bond investments. Many hedge funds have failed miserably. Others have survived and prospered, and have provided superior rewards to their investors. Some hedge funds have produced returns that are simply unmatched by mutual funds and other more traditional investments. But the spectacle of the demise of the prominent hedge fund Long-Term Capital Management and similar debacles lingers on to taint the overall image of hedge funds.

Hedge funds are complicated trading strategies with high turnover and often use complex derivatives structured by financial engineers and math wizards. They also employ leverage to enhance returns, which at the same time exposes them to greater risks. As a result of all these complexities, they require laborious research and in-depth understanding. Investing in hedge funds without commitment of time and resources is like driving blind in a storm.

Like any other business, the hedge fund industry is sometimes infected with charlatans and mediocrity. But it is also an industry populated by many talented and insightful portfolio managers. As Timothy Geithner, president of the Federal Reserve Bank of New York, remarked, "[hedge funds] can play a beneficial role in the U.S. financial system. They contribute to one of the defining strengths of our financial system: the ease with which we match capital to ideas and innovation."[4]

In writing this book on evaluating hedge fund performance, Dr. Tran has addressed a difficult topic. But the result is an important and needed work that should be of great value to both individual and institutional investors to have a good understanding of the potential benefits and pitfalls of hedge funds. In this book, Dr. Tran presents a balanced assessment of hedge funds and an evaluation of the returns and risks to be expected from them. In other words, what can investors really anticipate from hedge funds? What methods are used to evaluate them? What characteristics distinguish good funds from bad funds? How does an investor assemble a hedge fund portfolio to achieve target investment goals? Importantly, Dr. Tran discusses in great detail the need to investigate thoroughly a hedge fund before investing with it and to continue to monitor and evaluate it after the investment is made. He also points out the hidden risks of hedge funds that are not adequately measured by the usual statistics such as standard deviation or volatility of returns.

Dr. Tran draws on his work and extensive interviews with hedge fund managers and funds of hedge funds, as well as their investors, and from his 20 years of experience in managing hedge fund strategies. In the process, he examines hedge funds in the context of the tenets of modern portfolio theory because it is the foundation on which hedge funds have claimed to possess benefits unobtainable from traditional long-only investments. He also reviews a great deal of research by academics and industry practitioners, which provide analyses and insight on the track records and long-term prospects of hedge funds.

The result of all this research is a tightly structured book with excellent documentation along with sound and well-supported conclusions on investing in hedge funds.

DAVID BROWN
Chairman and Chief Market Strategist
Sabrient Systems, Inc.
Santa Barbara, California

Evaluating Hedge Fund Performance

One

A Primer on Hedge Funds

Though separated by some 70 years, the crash of 1929 and the bubble burst of 2000 shared some similarities. In the five years between the low in May 1924 and the monthly high in August 1929, the Dow Jones Industrial Average, which represented the stocks of the companies of America's fast-growing industrial economy, had risen by 31.8 percent a year. Half a century later, the NASDAQ was the index that captured the imagination of the investing public with its constituent stocks of the companies in the computer, Internet, and information technology sectors. It, too, had risen by an average of 32.8 percent annually during the nearly six years prior to the burst, from the monthly low in June 1994, which had been brought on by the Federal Reserve's aggressive raising of interest rates, to the high in February 2000. The subsequent decline in the NASDAQ was only marginally less severe, 78 percent as compared to 88 percent in the 1929 crash, and lasted almost as long, 31 months versus 34 months starting in 1929.

No one knows how long it will take the NASDAQ to recover to the preburst level of 5,132, although after a year-end rally in 2004 it has gained some 95 percent from the bottom in 2002. However, we do know that two years after the bottom in July 1932, the Dow Jones Industrial Average had risen by 136 percent, and yet it took more than 25 years for the Dow to recover to the precrash level. Twenty-five years is a long time to wait, even for patient and committed long-term investors.

Long-term investment horizon and diversification to reduce risks are two key concepts in investing. They will be analyzed in Chapter 1 of the first part of the book, a primer on hedge funds. It will be shown how these sound principles have been misapplied and how hedge fund strategies can be positioned as long-term investments to reduce portfolio risks. In Chapter 2, the discussion is focused on the potential of hedge funds in reducing risks, not in producing outsized returns. Also, the benefits of hedge funds as a diversification investment and as an alternative investment strategy in bearish and volatile market environments will be discussed in detail. Chapter 3 is a review of the hedge fund industry, its investors, the main hedge fund strategies, and how they have performed in past market conditions.

CHAPTER 1

The Market Goes Up Forever?

The Paradox of Long-Term Investing

J eremy J. Siegel, professor of finance at the Wharton School, started his seminal work *Stocks for the Long Run* by recounting the investment scheme recommended by John J. Raskob, a senior financial executive at General Motors.[1]

FLAWS OF LONG-TERM INVESTING

According to Professor Siegel, Raskob "maintained that by putting just $15 a month into good common stocks, investors could expect their wealth to grow steadily to $80,000 over the next 20 years."[2] Unfortunately for Raskob, Siegel remarked, his timing was a bit off. Raskob made his recommendation two months before the crash in 1929 and was blamed by Senator Arthur Robinson of Indiana "for the stock crash by urging common people to buy stock at the market peak."

A Get-Rich Scheme

So, did Raskob provide "foolhardy advice [that] epitomizes the mania that periodically overruns Wall Street"?[3] No, according to Siegel. In fact, Siegel postulates, "After 20 years, his or her stock portfolio would have accumulated to almost $9,000, and after 30 years, over $60,000. Although not as high as Raskob had projected, $60,000 still represents a fantastic 13 percent return on invested capital, far exceeding the returns earned by conservative investors who switched their money to Treasury bonds or bills at the market peak."[4]

The logic is unassailable and the math is immaculate.

It has become the accepted wisdom for a generation of investors and certainly the progenitors of mutual funds and such financial schemes for the masses. This analysis has been used time and time again by the investment industry to urge investors to buy stocks even when the market was overvalued and poised for a decline, or when the market was just simply tumbling down. Many experts say even buying stocks at a market peak will make you rich. While such a statement may sound appealing, the logic of the scheme rests on two key assumptions that may not always be realistic.

A Discipline Few Can Follow

The first assumption is that one must invest preset amounts of "$15 a month" every month. The critical consequence of this assumption is that the investors who follow this discipline, which is otherwise known as dollar cost averaging, would buy stocks every month without fail, month after month, regardless of the market condition, even when stocks are falling. Such investors therefore would be buying stocks at lower and lower prices as the market weakens, or higher prices as the market strengthens.

What if an investor does not or can not? A retiree, for instance, might not put aside funds for additional investments after retirement. Other investors, such as endowments and foundations, whose sources of funds available for new investments are unpredictable or simply not available, might not be able to make additional investments in the face of continuing lower stock prices. Perhaps they simply exercise prudence by not committing additional funds amid uncertainty in the market.

Investors who had made a one-time investment of $15 in August 1929 would have seen their investments decrease in value to less than $2 in less than three years, assuming that they had invested in the Dow Jones Industrial Average. If these investors managed to hold on to their investments for another 17 years, until 1949, they would have seen their net worth reduced to a mere half of what they had in 1929. Unbelievably, and counter to traditional thinking, they would have suffered a loss of 50 percent for 20 years of long-term investing! Even if any investors had had the wherewithal to double their initial investments just after the crash by putting another $15 in the market in 1932, which was the year when the Dow hit its lowest point, they would still have had a net loss on their $30 investment after 20 years.

In contrast, consider Siegel's "conservative investors who switched their money to Treasury bonds or bills." These conservative individuals would have seen their investments more than triple over the course of those same 20 years.

The second critical assumption is that investors do not take any money out. That is, the initial investments and subsequent investment gains, from both dividends and price appreciation, are left invested in the market. The gains from dividends would be reinvested and the entire proceeds from any stocks that were sold with profits or losses would be plowed back into the market. Since investors did not take the money out, they would not sell into lower prices as the market declines.

But what if investors must sell part of their holdings to meet expenses or other obligations while the market goes lower? The reality is that many individuals need income from their investments to live or to maintain their lifestyles. Institutional investors such as endowments, foundations, and pension plans have spending commitments that they must fulfill. They in turn rely on investment returns to meet these financial commitments.

Consider what would have been left over if after the initial investment of $15 was made in August 1929, the investors had to take out 5 percent of whatever was left at the end of each year to meet daily living expenses or ongoing spending obligations! Well, for the "conservative" investors who had invested in Treasury bonds, the answer would be the initial $15 capital and more! However, those who had invested in the Dow would have been left with practically nothing.

Of course, the market history of the United States has not always been like that of the 1929 crash, although those who invested in NASDAQ stocks in March 2000 might take exception with this statement. In fact, after the crash of 1929, the U.S. stock market embarked on a 70-year expansion, punctuated by periods of one- or two-year declines or lackluster performance. During this expansion nothing like the 1929 disaster occurred until the bubble of 2000 burst.

In this collapse the Dow did not decline as much as it did in 1929. From the top in January 2000 to the bottom in October 2002, the index lost 38.75 percent. As the rally had been fueled by the Internet craze, resembling the stock market hype that preceded the 1929 crash, it was the NASDAQ that took the brunt of the selling. From the intraday high in March 2000, the NASDAQ index lost nearly 78 percent, while displaying the hysteria not unlike the Dow in 1929. In fact, as the collapse progressed, the NASDAQ posted new lows for several months in a row, without respite in between. Then, one- or two-month consolidations were followed by months-long declines without intermediate stops. Near the end, there was a losing streak that lasted for five months with progressively lower lows.

This time, although there was no soup line like in 1929, the unemployment rate almost doubled to over 6 percent, before posting a moderate decline three years later. Three million jobs were lost and at the same time many retirees whose investment savings had vanished were seeking to return to work. In the meantime, endowments and foundations cut their spending, and pension plans' unfunded liabilities soared while corporations posted losses or profit declines due to rising contributions to their pension plans to make up for the losses in their equity investments.

As long as the market keeps going up, investing in stocks is a winning strategy. The bull market starting in 1982 brought wealth to many investors with relatively little volatility. A small market decline along the way was even desirable, for it would allow investors who had been left out to participate. For those who were fortunate to have been in the market, the pullbacks were opportunities to increase their investments, which in fact many people did. Many so-called experts maintain that if you buy on the dips, invest for the long term, you can still make money even if you buy at the peak of the market. How? Because the Dow would rise to 36,000, as a couple of authors went on national television to propagate and to promote their best-selling book.[5] In fact, Siegel's book was first published in 1994 and the professor became a much-sought-after market prognosticator.

A look back, as many investors now realize, reveals that the 1982–1999 period was the most exceptional in U.S. financial history. Between 1982 and 1999, there was only one losing year, 1990, in the entire 18-year duration; and it was a puny loss at that, a mere −3.1 percent registered by the S&P 500, tucked in between two years of stupendous gains, each exceeding 30 percent. For the entire period, the S&P 500 averaged a rate of return of 19.08 percent a year, and volatility of annual returns was 12.14 percent. This 1982–1999 period's average return was more than twice the average return of the preceding 18-year duration, and 40 percent less volatile.

Despite the strong recovery in 2003, few investors believe that the stock market will see the returns produced in the halcyon years before the Internet bubble burst. Though dismissed as "much too pessimistic" by some experienced investors, such as the head of investments of a $1 billion endowment,[6] a number of respected market practitioners believe that stocks will return no more than the mid- to high-single-digit gains going forward. This rate of return range would consist of dividend yield of 1.5 percent, plus 1 to 3 percent due to expansion of price-earnings multiples, and 2 to 4 percent of risk premium.[7] As valuation has returned to the prebubble levels following the strong 2003 recovery,[8] such predictions of more modest gains seem more likely than expectations of double-digit profits. A greater concern is the likelihood that volatility of returns is bound to increase, if only to the level that had been normal in the prebubble years.

WEALTH-REDUCING EFFECTS OF VOLATILITY

The 20-year period prior to the takeoff in 1982 was such a period. There were several years of gains exceeding 20 percent. And the winning streaks typically lasted two or three years in a row. Except for the years of 1973 and 1974, the down years recorded fairly modest losses, 10 percent or less. Certainly this was neither the crash of 1929 nor the bull market of the 1980s. In fact, annually the S&P 500 registered a high-single-digit average return of 8 percent. The volatility of annual returns was 17 percent, exactly its long-run historical average.

Investors who started putting money in the market in 1962 would have seen a $100 investment rising to $364.77 at the end of 1981, a compound annual return of 6.54 percent, certainly not a bad investment compared to bonds.

Volatility, Wealth, and Income

However, the picture becomes a bit more complicated for investors who had to take money out of the market regularly. Table 1.1 provides data helpful in dissecting this period.

Column 2 shows the rate of return, including reinvested dividends, of the S&P 500 in each of the 20 years between 1962 and 1981. In column 3, "Nominal Wealth," the $100 investment in the S&P 500 at the beginning of 1962 is shown to grow to $364.77 in 1981. However, in column 4, it is assumed that at the end of every year, 5 percent of the ending balance is taken out. Thus, at the end of 1962, $4.56 is subtracted from the capital balance of $91.26 (which was the result of the market's decline of –8.74 percent during 1962; likewise, $5.32 was sold out at the end of 1963). Thus, the capital balance at the end of 1962 was $86.70, as shown in column 5. It then rose to $101.03 due to the market's gain in 1963, after deducting the cash-out of $5.32. In this scenario whereby the investor did not add any new investments after the initial amount in 1962, while regularly taking out 5 percent of the capital at the end of each year, the wealth at the end of the 20-year holding period was $130.76, for a rise of 1.35 percent per year. The inflation rate during this period averaged 6 percent. Thus, in real terms, the growth of the initial investment did not keep pace with inflation, although the return on the S&P 500 outstripped the rate of inflation during this 20-year period of generally rising stock prices.

Now, notice how the amounts under column 4, "Available Income," changed from year to year. Every year, the amounts taken out for spending changed with the investment return. In 1966, the available income was cut by 14.5 percent, even though the investment loss was only –10.05 percent.

TABLE 1.1   Stock Returns, Wealth, and Income

End of Year	Rate of Return	Nominal Wealth	Available Income	Accumulated Wealth	Average Available Income
1962	−8.74%	$ 91.26	$4.56	$ 86.70	$4.56
1963	22.66	111.94	5.32	101.03	4.94
1964	16.32	130.21	5.88	111.64	5.25
1965	12.35	146.29	6.27	119.15	5.82
1966	−10.05	131.59	5.36	101.82	5.84
1967	23.88	163.01	6.31	119.83	5.98
1968	10.98	180.91	6.65	126.33	6.10
1969	−8.42	165.68	5.78	109.91	6.25
1970	3.93	172.19	5.71	108.52	6.05
1971	14.56	197.26	6.22	118.11	5.90
1972	18.90	234.54	7.02	133.41	6.32
1973	−14.77	199.90	5.69	108.02	6.31
1974	−26.39	147.14	3.98	75.54	5.56
1975	37.16	201.82	5.18	98.42	4.95
1976	23.57	249.39	6.08	115.54	5.08
1977	−7.42	230.89	5.35	101.62	5.54
1978	6.38	245.62	5.41	102.70	5.61
1979	18.20	290.32	6.07	115.32	5.61
1980	32.27	384.01	7.63	144.91	6.37
1981	−5.01	364.77	6.88	130.76	6.86

After the peak in 1968, available income would not return to this level until four years later, even though the loss in 1969 was relatively modest compared to the gains during the previous two years and the gains in the following three years. In 1974, available income dropped to $3.98, which is 20.4 percent less than the planned amount of $5, and a drastic decrease of 43.3 percent from the peak in 1972. Importantly, the two-year bear market of 1973–1974 depressed available income such that the peak in 1972 would not be seen again until eight years later, in 1980, despite the market's stupendous gain of 37.16 percent in 1975 followed by an impressive return of 23.57 percent in 1976. Overall, the S&P produced an admirable annualized gain of 14.56 percent in the five years 1975–1979 following the 1973 to 1974 decline. But, following the outsized gain in 1980, the S&P took only a slight pullback in 1981, and available income again dropped below the 1972 peak. In comparison, the gain of 28.69 percent in 2003 following the worst bear market in 70 years seems relatively ordinary. The question is, in the next five years will the stock market be so kind as to produce returns in the mid-teens similar to those seen in post-1974?

Similarly, accumulated wealth, shown in column 5, declined to a disastrous $75.54 in 1974, which was 24.46 percent below the initial capital. Remember that all of this happened during the intervening 13 years in which the S&P 500 rose by 47.14 percent.

Faced with declining spending availability, what would investors do? Sell some of the holdings to make up for the shortfall? In a declining market? What if investors must sell regardless of the price levels?

Investors can moderate the fluctuations in the levels of available income from year to year by using some sort of averaging mechanism. Column 6 of Table 1.1 shows the amounts of available income of each year calculated as the simple average of the preceding three years. This averaging mechanism reduces the variability in available income, but it does not prevent spending from dropping off unless capital is drawn on.[9] It merely delays the day of reckoning.

Overall, the high volatility of returns in equity investments, using the S&P 500 as the proxy, leads to consequences that are not wholly palatable to investors who rely on investment returns for future spending, and need a certain level of income to meet periodic spending obligations. One moderately down year such as the loss of −8.42 percent in 1969 may cause available income to drop off, taking several years to recover to the previous highs. After a more severe market decline of greater magnitude and length, available income may take many years to return to the previous peak levels. Such was the period following the 1973–1974 losses, and should be expected in the aftermath of the 2000 bubble burst.

The prospect of continuing declines in available income in many years to come is not fully understood. For example, although the $2.3 billion Duke University Endowment performed better in 2003, its grants fell 6.8 percent from the 2002 level.[10] As the president of the endowment complained, "The thing a lot of nonprofits don't understand is that 2003 being a good year doesn't translate instantly into more money."[11] She continued, "It's hard to explain how you had a good year but you're not giving away an equivalently larger amount." Readers only need to refer to Table 1.1 to see that although the S&P rose 37.16 percent in 1975, users of an averaging scheme, which most institutions are, would see average available income decline by 10.97 percent.

As illustrated in Table 1.1, the recovery of 37.16 percent in 1975 and 23.57 percent in 1976 did not bring available income back to the 1972 level until 1980. As the rally in 2003 was weaker than in 1975, the bubble's losses lasted longer and were more severe, and NASDAQ stocks were surely a part of many investment portfolios, it will take longer for available income to recover to the prior peak levels. This is the issue brought up by Richard E. Anderson, a tenured professor in education finance at

Columbia University, who has been a consultant to college endowments and other institutional investors. He remarked, "College administrators who agonize over the endowment revenue shortfall in the current '03 and the coming '04 budget years, simple math shows that without new gifts *the spending shortfall could continue for decades* [emphasis in the original]."[12] He explained why in Table 1.2.

TABLE 1.2 Endowment Value and Spending: The Future

March	Annual Return[a]	Endowment's Value[b]	Amount Available for Spending[c] (Annual)	Required Spending[d] (Inflation-Adjusted)	Spending Shortfall[e] (Inflation-Adjusted)
2001	18.0%	$111	$5.00	$5.00	0%
2002	−16.4	88	4.93	5.13	3.90
2003	3.6	86	4.73	5.25	9.90
2004	−17.8	66	3.98	5.38	26.02
2005	10.5	69	3.67	5.52	33.51
2006	10.5	72	3.44	5.66	39.22
2007	10.5	76	3.62	5.8	37.59
2008	10.5	81	4.04	5.94	31.99
2009	10.5	85	4.28	6.09	29.72
2010	10.5	90	4.52	6.24	27.56
2011	10.5	101	4.78	6.4	25.31
2012	10.5	107	5.06	6.56	22.87
2013	10.5	113	5.35	6.72	20.39
2014	10.5	120	5.66	6.89	17.85
2015	10.5	126	5.99	7.07	15.28
2016	10.5	134	6.33	7.24	12.57
2017	10.5	141	6.70	7.42	9.70
2018	10.5	150	7.08	7.61	6.97
2019	10.5	158	7.49	7.8	3.97
2020	10.5	167	7.92	8.19	3.30
2021	10.5	177	8.38	8.4	0.23

[a]Assuming a portfolio of 75 percent in equities and 25 percent in bonds, and 12 percent return on stocks and 6 percent on bonds.
[b]After spending.
[c]Five percent of the three-year average of the endowment's value.
[d]Amount of spending required if indexed to inflation assumed at 2.5 percent.
[e]Difference of the preceding two columns.
Source: Richard E. Anderson, "Endowment Spending: The Problem Will Be with Us for a While," *Commonfund Commentary*, May 2003.

Anderson remarked, *"Therefore, it is not until FY '13 that budgeted endowment spending reaches the peak '01 FY spending levels in nominal terms* [emphasis is in the original]. . . . Remember, this simulation is using return assumptions that are purposefully and excessively optimistic."[13] He then noted, "The three-year moving average of asset values, shown in the fourth column, does not regain its March '01 value until March of 2012."[14] If spending is indexed to inflation, assumed at 2.5 percent, the shortfall would last for 20 years, until 2021. Going back to Table 1.1, the average return during 1975–1981 was 13.85 percent. Yet the accumulated wealth declined year after year until 1980 only to decline, in the following year, again below the 1972 peak.

All of this may be an exercise in number crunching, but the spending cuts experienced by charitable foundations, the classrooms that were not repaired, the tuition increases, the professors who could not be hired, all of these impacts of the return volatility are very real and have great social and economic consequences. Certainly these impacts are being felt at the nation's endowments and foundations, in pension plans, and by individual retirees.

Effects on Retirees, Endowments, and Pension Plans

In the report "Foundation Growth and Giving Estimates: 2003 Preview," the Foundation Center stated that the nearly 65,000 U.S. foundations cut their grants by 2.5 percent in 2003 to $29.7 billion from $30.4 billion in 2002.[15] The 902 large and midsize foundations actually reported a larger reduction, 3.2 percent. At the same time, foundation assets lost 6.9 percent between 2002 and 2001, for a cumulative loss of 10.5 percent since 2000. Gifts received by foundations also recorded a sharp drop, nearly 23 percent in 2002, from $28.7 billion to $22.2 billion, "reaching the lowest level recorded since 1997."[16]

College endowments experienced similar setbacks. According to an annual survey by the National Association of College and University Business Officers,[17] the average endowment's assets, at $321.5 million, declined by more than 5 percent between 2002 and 2003 fiscal years, and 23 percent since 2000. However, the median endowment experienced larger drops, to $70 million in 2003 from $80 million in 2002 and $109 million in 2000. At the same time, spending levels as a percentage of endowment assets remained essentially unchanged, typically around 5.4 percent. This is because "Once universities get used to a certain amount of money coming from the endowment, it's really hard to squeeze that back. It's very painful on campus."[18]

Painful as it may be, endowments and educational foundations have seen much better investment returns than the overall stock market. While on average these institutional investors recorded losses of −6 percent in fiscal year 2002 (typically ending in June) and −3 percent in the prior year, according to the Commonfund Benchmark Study,[19] the broad market indexes fared much worse. This was clearly attributable to the significant allocations to alternative investments, including allocations to hedge funds that have evolved at these institutions. Indeed, alternative investments increased from 23 percent in 2000 to 32 percent of endowments' assets in 2002. This shift came entirely at the expense of U.S. equities, which saw their share drop to 32 percent from 41 percent.[20]

The impact of market volatility and negative investment returns manifests itself in a different way on retirement plans for corporate and public sector employees.

When public sector pension plans suffer investment losses, it is the taxpayers who are called on to make up for any resulting unfunded pension liabilities. For corporate pension plans, negative investment returns hit the bottom line of a corporation's income statement as well as reduce the value of its pension plan assets.

Just before Christmas 2003, General Electric (GE) again came out with a prediction that higher pension costs would dampen earnings to below the target of double-digit rate of growth that GE shareholders were used to in the past. This was not the first time in the past few years that GE disappointed shareholders because of pension costs. And GE was not the only corporation that has been presented with this problem of negative returns. General Motors (GM) has watched its pension plan become drastically underfunded during the three-year bear market.[21] By December 2002, GM had experienced a 23 percent or $19 billion shortfall. In comparison, a typical big corporation's plan was 18 percent underfunded, according to the actuarial firm Milliman & Robertson. As a result, "the pension burden weighed on GM like a rock. Between June 2002 and March 2003, its share price tumbled 60 percent to $30, in no small measure because investors were worried that the tab for shoring up the pension plan would cut deeply into GM's revenue and profits."[22] At times, a stock market collapse coupled with financial distress may wreak havoc on an entire industry, such as the airlines.

Thus, the costs of volatility of investment returns on endowments and pension plans are borne by different groups and are manifested differently.

For the endowments, it is the beneficiaries of endowment spending, including the students who might otherwise receive the hoped-for scholarships to attend the colleges of their choice and the professors who might have been hired if endowment spending was not cut. For the private pension plans, the corporations themselves must foot the bills for shortfalls in investment returns. This creates volatility in earnings over and beyond the uncertainty attributable to the normal conduct of the business. The market does not like volatility. Stocks of companies that exhibit higher earnings volatility are discounted by the market with lower multiples. Thus, the costs to a corporation that have volatile pension returns are not necessarily limited to a one-time occurrence when charges to the income statement are made. As its stock price is discounted because of volatile pension returns by the market relative to its competitors that have lower earnings volatility, a company's stock price underperformance tends to persist. To the extent that its operating efficiency and profitability are otherwise competitive or superior, its shareholders are unduly punished by its pension investment strategies. And, not least of all, the efficient allocation of resources in the economy to the most efficient producers may be impaired by pension investment policies that embrace a high level of volatility.

Thus, an investment perspective that is focused on high equity returns, with the attendant high volatility, will likely be unable to meet the future investment needs of many institutional and individual investors alike.

For most investors, the results of Raskob's scheme of taking on equity risks in long-term investing, endorsed by finance professors and mutual fund propagators, are anything but steady.

The assumptions are flawed and the math is incomplete.

The issue of investment volatility and its effects on investors has gained attention on the heels of the bear market. A veteran of the investment business with more than 30 years of experience complained that "it's hard not to get jittery when stocks start gyrating wildly."[23]

He continued, "Few would deny that traditional money management has worked well in the past. But faced with this new order of things, it isn't working so well anymore. Old tenets such as 'buy and hold' and 'there's safety in diversification,' once held as gospel truth, no longer can be counted on to carry the day."[24] He also quoted another investment veteran: "Much of the multitrillion-dollar investment industry is built on half-truths, incorrect interpretations, flawed data, unrealistic expectations, and absolute contradictions. No wonder portfolios based on accepted doctrines have not produced the results intended."[25]

If these critics expect the investment industry to change its long-held beliefs, they might have to wait a while.

Pure Equity Risk Is Unacceptable

The belief in equities and the superior long-term returns of the stock market reigns supreme. Thus, as posited by a senior investment executive, "Any institution—be it a college, a foundation or a hospital—that intends to be in place to meet the needs of future generations must take investment risk."[26] What kind of investment risk? The answer is equities, although "compared to the two percent real return currently available on 10-year TIPS,[27] an equity premium of two percent was insufficient compensation for the risk . . . , [because] . . . [a]bandoning equities in favor of bonds today when interest rates are at 40-year lows could prove to be very costly to the long-term financial health of our investors. The opportunity costs of not owning stocks could be very large."[28]

It is reasonable enough to assume that stocks will outperform bonds, because they have done so in the past over long periods of time. In *Stocks for the Long Run*, Siegel calculated the returns of stocks versus bonds over different time periods. As shown in Table 1.3, historically, over the long term, stocks have outperformed bonds by wide margins, even in relatively low-inflation periods. However, stocks' outperformance tended to be more pronounced in times of higher inflation.

Is equity risk acceptable? This issue can be looked at from a couple of perspectives. One is the risk premium or the reward for risk taking.

Equity returns of mid to high single digits were the averages of the stock market for most periods prior to the takeoff in 1982. Table 1.4 shows the returns on equities over nonoverlapping five-year periods from 1926 to 1980 and for 1982–1999. It is obvious from these data that single-digit returns have been the norms while the 1980s and 1990s have been unusual for equity returns. Assuming that equity returns range about 7 percent over the next 10 years and inflation average 3 percent, real return on equity would be about 4 percent.[29] As current real return on 10-year TIPS is already 2 percent, a 2 percent equity risk premium is simply too low. In fact, it is way below the average of 6.5 percent since 1926.[30]

Would an equity-laden strategy work? Even if stocks outperform

TABLE 1.3 Returns on Stocks and Bonds

Period	Stocks			Long-Term Government Bonds		
	Nominal	Real	Dividend Yield	Nominal	Real	CPI
1926–2001	10.2%	6.9%	4.1%	5.3%	2.2%	3.1%
1946–2001	11.6	7.1	3.8	5.5	1.3	4.1
1966–1981	6.6	–0.4	3.9	2.5	–4.2	7.0
1982–1999	17.3	13.6	3.1	12.0	8.4	3.3
1982–2001	14.1	10.5	2.9	12.0	8.5	3.2

Source: Jeremy J. Siegel, *Stocks for the Long Run: The Definitive Guide to Financial Market Returns and Long-Term Investment Strategies*, 3rd ed. (New York: McGraw-Hill, 2002), p. 13 and p. 15.

TABLE 1.4 Stock Returns in the Long Run

Period	Nominal	Real
1926–1930	5.49%	8.33%
1931–1935	3.13	5.46
1936–1940	1.11	0.71
1941–1945	16.76	11.23
1946–1950	9.41	2.67
1951–1955	20.84	19.14
1956–1960	9.78	7.58
1961–1965	13.25	11.85
1966–1970	3.34	–0.50
1971–1975	3.21	–3.14
1976–1980	14.01	5.50
1982–1999[a]	17.30	13.60

[a]1982–1999 data from Jeremy J. Siegel, *Stocks for the Long Run: The Definitive Guide to Financial Market Returns and Long-Term Investment Strategies*, 3rd ed. (New York: McGraw-Hill, 2002), p. 13.
Source: Charles P. Jones and Jack W. Wilson, "The Changing Nature of Stock and Bond Volatility," *Financial Analysts Journal*, January/February 2004, p. 102.

bonds as they historically have, it is most unlikely that the endowments that rely on equities producing 7 percent returns would achieve their objective of "meeting the needs of future generations." Equity volatility was much lower during the bull market of the 1980s and 1990s than it had been in the past. Between 1982 and 1997, equity volatility was 13.1 percent, a mere two-thirds of the volatility experienced during the 25 years prior to the bull market. If equity returns are in the single digits coupled with volatility returning to the historical norms in the high teens, endowments and pension plans that rely on equities are likely to be in much worse shape in the future than Anderson's calculations may indicate.

Remember that in Anderson's calculations shown in Table 1.2, stocks are assumed to produce 12 percent annually year in, year out. If endowments and pension plans remain heavily exposed to equities, whose returns are likely to be stuck in the single digits, and total portfolio return is reduced to 6 percent, or less than three-fifths of Anderson's assumptions, without new funding endowments' spending and asset values will be unlikely to return to the 2001 level for decades to come. These results are even more astonishing considering that in these calculations, out of 21 years 18 have stellar returns, and in only 2 years does the investment portfolio experience a loss in value.

For an endowment, a higher volatility of return implies that there is a greater risk that the endowment might have to sell holdings at lower prices to raise cash in order to meet its spending needs. For a pension plan, the greater volatility of returns implies that there is a lesser predictability in the amount of contributions that a corporation would have to make every year to its pension plans. Higher earnings volatility implies higher volatility of stock prices. The resulting market discount of price-earnings multiples would have a long-lasting depreciative effect on the corporation's stock prices, therefore undermining shareholders' value.

Thus, from the perspective of investors who have periodic commitments, be it that they are retirees or wealthy families who need investment income to maintain their lifestyles, or endowments and foundations that have committed spending, or pension plans whose yearly contributions affect companies' corporate profits, the question is how to reduce the volatility without sacrificing the returns that they have been used to. The answer clearly does not lie with pure equity risks. Fortunately, investors have rediscovered an alternative investment strategy that is designed to reduce investor portfolio risks and provide protection in market downturns while at the same time being capable of generating returns competitive with equities in the long run. It has been pioneered and practiced for more than 50 years and it is called hedge funds. Unlike traditional investment strategies, hedge funds engage in short selling in order to partly or fully offset their long positions in stocks and bonds. As such, they seek protection against market declines that potentially may bring losses to their investments on the long side, and thereby reduce volatility of returns.

DIVERSIFICATION TO REDUCE RISKS

Investors are aware of the volatility of equity-only portfolios. To reduce risks, the traditional strategy is diversification. Thus, institutional portfolios typically include both stocks and bonds. Within the equity sectors, portfolios are diversified in terms of market capitalization of individual securities, or in terms of styles such as value versus growth, as well as with international stocks.

However, it is commonly overlooked that the degree of correlation of the assets in a diversified portfolio is critical to achieving the objective of reducing risks by diversification. In general, if two assets have similar standard deviation and perfect correlation—that is, the correlation coefficient is equal to 1—diversification with these two assets does not reduce risks in any way. If one of the two assets has higher volatility, risk-averse investors would be better off investing all capital in the lower-volatility asset; adding the higher-volatility asset would only increase the risk. If the two assets have perfect negative correlation—that is, they move in opposite directions and their correlation coefficient is equal to minus 1—it is possible to create a riskless portfolio combining these two assets, even though the two assets may be highly volatile. As the correlation coefficient, which has a range from minus 1 to plus 1, increases, the risk-reducing benefits of diversification decline. At a value of plus 1, risk-reducing benefits of diversification disappear.

Not with Correlated Assets

This has been what happened with traditional long-only equity portfolios in recent history. Though they contained stocks in different equity sectors, diversification neither reduced volatility nor increased returns.

Table 1.5 shows the correlation matrix, volatility, and returns of the various stock indexes, including small-cap and mid-cap stocks as well as growth and value styles, during January 1979–May 2004. Except for the Morgan Stanley Capital International (MSCI) index, they all showed very high degrees of correlation. All of these indexes also had similarly high volatility. Due to near-perfect correlation, diversification among these equity sectors would not reduce portfolio risks. Furthermore, during this 25-year period, the S&P, MSCI, Russell 3000, and Russell Mid Cap produced very similar returns. Also, all the Russell indexes produced similar return ranges between June 1995 and May 2004.

Overall, a strategy of diversification among highly correlated equity sectors with the objectives of reducing risks and/or achieving higher returns was futile during the past 25 years. Depending on the exact allocation strategies with different weightings in different equity sectors, diversification not only did not lower volatility, but it could have reduced returns as well. This would be especially painful if large allocations were made to international stocks.

In Table 1.5, the MSCI World ex-U.S. index represents international stocks. Its correlation with the S&P 500, Russell 3000, and Russell Mid Cap was about 0.6 during the period from January 1979 to May 2004, somewhat lower than the correlations of the domestic indexes among themselves. Taken at face value, this would suggest some benefit in international diversification in terms of risk reduction, though not in enhancing returns. Closer scrutiny, however, reveals a different picture. During the three-year bear market from April 2000 to March 2003, correlation between the S&P and the MSCI went up sharply to 0.85. At the same time,

TABLE 1.5 Equity Correlations

Index	S&P 500	MSCI World Ex-U.S.	Russell 3000	Russell Mid Cap	Russell Growth	Russell Value	Volatility	Annualized Return 1/1979– 5/2004	Annualized Return 6/1995– 5/2004
S&P 500[a]	1						15.35%	10.14%	8.60%
MSCI World ex-U.S.[a]	0.60	1					15.54	10.12	4.10
Russell 3000[a]	0.99	0.60	1				15.58	10.15	8.60
Russell Mid Cap[a]	0.93	0.58	0.96	1			16.59	11.95	10.76
Russell 3000 Growth[b]	0.94	0.77	0.95	0.95	1		20.49	NA	7.08
Russell 3000 Value[b]	0.89	0.72	0.89	0.85	0.71	1	14.79	NA	9.18

[a]Period between January 1979 and May 2004.
[b]Period June 1995 and May 2004.
Source: PerTrac.

volatility of MSCI remained at the 25-year level of 15.5 percent. Particularly painful was the fact that during the global bear market, the MSCI lost 47 percent compared to 43 percent by the S&P. Thus, international diversification in the bear market did not help reduce volatility nor protect investors from sharp declines.

The failure of international diversification to reduce risks has gained attention in the popular press. In a *New York Times* column, Mark Hulbert commented that "academic studies have found that the performance of foreign stocks and domestic stocks tends to be more highly correlated—more closely linked—when domestic stocks are declining than when they are rising. This dual relationship has several unfortunate consequences. It means that foreign stocks provide relatively little risk reduction to a portfolio when it needs it the most: when most of the holdings are declining. It also means that international diversification provides the bulk of its risk reduction when domestic stocks are rising, when investors don't really need it."[31]

Diversification with Fixed Income

Another diversification strategy is mixing stocks and bonds. Since bonds have less volatility and a low correlation with stocks, a stock-and-bond portfolio would have lower volatility than a stock-only portfolio.

In Table 1.6, for the period between January 1979 and May 2004, the Lehman Aggregate Bond index showed a correlation of 0.24 with the S&P (its correlation with the MSCI World index ex-U.S. was also a low 0.17). Its volatility was 6.3 percent, significantly lower than those of the two stock indexes. If the Lehman index and S&P had perfect correlation, combining equal portions of these two indexes in one portfolio would result in a portfolio volatility of 10.82 percent. However, because their correlation was only 0.24, the volatility of this 50/50 portfolio was reduced to 8.4 percent,

TABLE 1.6 Correlations of Stocks and Bonds, January 1979–May 2004

Index	Lehman Aggregate Bond	S&P 500	MSCI World ex-U.S.	Standard Deviation	Annualized Return
Lehman Aggregate Bond	1			6.30%	9.28%
S&P 500	0.24	1		15.35	10.14
MSCI World ex-U.S.	0.17	0.60	1	15.54	10.12

Source: PerTrac.

or 22.4 percent lower. Interestingly enough, there is a minimum-risk portfolio consisting of 92.8 percent in the Lehman index and 7.2 percent in the S&P. This portfolio has a volatility of 6.05 percent, which is lower than that of the Lehman index. However, return is higher than that of the Lehman index by a fractional 0.04 percent to 9.34 percent. Such are the diversification benefits with low-correlation assets.

During the January 1979–May 2004 period, the equity bear market and the simultaneous drops in interest rate allowed the bond index to produce returns that were only slightly lower than those of the two stock indexes. However, in the 20 years between January 1980 and 1999, the Lehman index underperformed the U.S. and international stock indexes by almost 4 percent per annum. In this period, the MSCI and S&P 500 indexes generated 13.7 and 13.9 percent a year respectively, while the Lehman produced 10 percent. In *Stocks for the Long Run*, Jeremy Siegel documented that bonds consistently underperformed stocks in both low- and high-inflation periods.

In general, if stocks outperform bonds as experienced prior to the bubble burst, diversifying stock portfolios with bonds would bring portfolio returns to levels below those of equity-only portfolios, though with lower volatility. However, if equities produce only single-digit returns, diversification with bonds might not severely impact the returns of the resulting portfolios.

LONG-TERM INVESTING WITH LOW-CORRELATION ASSETS AND DOWNSIDE PROTECTION

As stocks outperformed bonds by wide margins during the bubble years, expectations of high returns among individual and institutional investors alike kept ratcheting up and allocations to equities reached extreme levels. Many corporate pension plans shifted 75 percent and more of their assets to stocks; some still maintain all-stock portfolios to this day. The virulent bear market and large losses suffered by investors with overly large exposures to equities have created an opportunity to heed some basic realities of investment.

First, diversification among high-correlation assets is not diversification to reduce risks. Simply adding higher-risk investments to a portfolio without regard to their correlation with the existing positions might increase the overall portfolio risk. It has been some 50 years since Harry Markowitz founded modern portfolio theory.[32] Beta, alpha, and other such Greek letters have become the second language of the investment industry. It is high time that the most basic aspect of Markowitz's theory is practiced with equal fervor.

As it turns out, hedge funds are truly unique in providing this lower-correlation characteristic while investing in the publicly traded stock and bond markets familiar to traditional investors. At the same time, as will be shown later, hedge funds have been documented to have the capability of producing returns higher than bonds and sometimes with bondlike low volatility. Many hedge funds actually have generated returns equal to or higher than those of traditional equities with much less volatility.

Second, the market does not go up forever, and certainly not in a straight line so that "investors could expect their wealth to grow steadily" as Raskob had suggested. Even in a period like 1962–1981 with volatility and return much in line with the S&P 500's historical averages and not unlike what is predicted for the upcoming years, there were years the market did post significant declines. In such years, unless the investors have other sources of income or funds, either spending would have to be cut or the shortfall would have to be made up from selling, instead of buying, into a declining market, which is contrary to the basic principle of long-term investing as recommended by Raskob and his followers. However, traditional long-only strategies have little protection in bear markets. Hedge funds, in contrast, are structured to guard against these risks. In fact, they always have short positions to offset their long exposures in varying degrees. They also seek to increase these short positions as the market goes lower. As a result, good hedge fund managers can in fact generate positive returns as the market declines, thus alleviating the need to confront the difficult choice of "to sell or not to sell" that long-only investors typically must face.

Hedge fund managers also are apt to reduce the funds they commit to the market, possibly on both the long and the short side as valuation becomes excessive. Thus, they sell their long positions into rising prices and take profit accordingly, with little concern for the chips still left on the table. Traditional long-only investors benefit little from the return above what they need for spending. To use the popular phrase, it's only paper profits, until they sell. However, traditional long-only managers typically not only stay fully invested, but usually increase their portfolios' risks in a never-ending quest to outperform the market for fear of the career risk of underperformance. When a talented manager like Jeff Vinik of Fidelity Investments shifted some of the Magellan Fund's assets into bonds toward the tail end of the 1990s bull market as overvaluation and the attendant risk of a collapse looked imminent, he was ridiculed in the press as Magellan's returns lagged, and eventually left the firm. If only Magellan's investors had known that the bubble would burst only a short while later! In volatile markets, hedge funds' readiness to take profits allows investors to capture the benefit of long-term investing with lesser risks of losses.

In the final analysis, this is what value-added long-term investing should be all about: capturing the long-term expected return with lesser risks. Hedge funds represent an investment strategy that exhibits lower correlation with long-only portfolios and provides downside protection not possible in long-only strategies, yet is capable of producing bondlike low volatility and long-term returns higher than those of bonds and, sometimes, equities. Hedge funds thus provide an attractive strategy to long-term investors with less exposure to the vagaries of the market and to the disastrous consequences of prolonged declines such as the 1929 Depression or the 2000 bubble burst.

But, not all hedge funds are alike. There are the good, the bad, and the mere mediocre. As the saying goes, buyer beware. The rest of this book focuses on shedding lights on the benefits and pitfalls of hedge funds in their roles of providing diversification and downside risk protection and how to evaluate and select the appropriate hedge funds for diversified portfolios.

CHAPTER 2

It's the Risk, Not the Return

Using Hedge Funds to Reduce Portfolio Risks

The diversification and downside risk protection benefits of hedge funds have long been recognized by sophisticated investors. But it took the 2000 bear market for hedge funds to gain acceptance by a wider audience.

Though by early 2003 the worst equity market decline in 70 years was coming to an end, this knowledge came only with the benefit of hindsight, for investors could not recognize the end of the bear market any more than the beginning of the burst of the bubble in 2000. Every day, strategists and money managers of all stripes continued to pound the table, predicting the worst was yet to come. To this day, although the tempo of the alarm has receded, the outlook has only changed from a state of depression to deep anxiety mixed with hopes and remembrances of the good old days.[1] In the meantime, by 2003 savvy investors had not failed to notice that many hedge funds produced positive returns, sometimes exceeding the 30 percent or more previously found only during the market bubble. In this atmosphere, hedge funds emerged as an attractive investment option. With losses piling up in the previous three years as the stock market continued to produce red ink with no end seemingly in sight, individuals and institutions alike were drawn to hedge funds in their search for a safe haven.

Sometimes wealthy individuals who had invested in hedge funds and were well connected with the industry led the charge in this foray. At times, their beliefs spilled over onto the institutions they were leading, and perhaps justifiably so. At one college endowment fund with assets approaching $2 billion, the chairman of the board of trustees convinced the investment committee to increase allocations to hedge funds to more than 40 percent, from virtually nothing. This occurred when the ink had barely dried on the staff's strategy report recommending that the endowment "stay the course," maintaining little involvement in hedge funds. To justify this abrupt change, the staff commissioned its consultants to produce a study extolling the virtues of hedge funds and how these investments could potentially enhance the risk-adjusted returns of the endowment's portfolio.

Empirically, in terms of the historical returns and volatility of returns recorded by hedge fund indexes this has been shown to be the case. The focus of hedge funds is very different from a typical long-only investment fund. They do not focus solely on returns versus some market benchmarks. Investors in hedge funds seek out investments that would be capable of producing consistent returns regardless of market direction. There is a trade-off between risk and return, and investors expect their hedge fund managers to produce a superior return adjusted for the risk taken by the managers. While there is no free lunch, there is such a thing as an attractive price; and the price for higher risk is higher return. As it turns out, hedge funds have been shown to be capable of producing returns similar to equities while doing so at lower volatility.

As the chief investment officer of a $1.1 billion college endowment said, "We expect hedge funds to protect our principal, bring down overall risk, and provide us with equity-like returns over the long run."[2]

NOT NECESSARILY HIGHER RETURNS

Indeed, hedge fund indexes have historically shown returns similar to the S&P 500 but with lower volatility of returns. In the past 10 years, the stock market went through periods of turmoil punctuated by the huge rise of interest rates in 1994, the Asian currency crisis of 1997, the collapse of Long-Term Capital Management in 1998, the spectacular rise of Internet stocks during the 1990s, three recent years of bear market declines, and of course, the subsequent recovery in 2003. Hedge funds did not escape unscathed from these upheavals. However, historical returns of hedge fund indexes have bolstered the case that hedge funds as a group have been able to cope with these event risks without completely sacrificing returns, at a significantly lower level of volatility than the stock market.

As shown in Table 2.1, in the 1994 to 2003 period the CSFB/Tremont Hedge Fund Index (which, along with its subindexes, is published by Credit Suisse First Boston and Tremont Capital Management) showed an annualized compound return of 11.12 percent, similar to the S&P's return of 11.07 percent. However, during the seven years that the S&P return was positive, 1999 was the only year in which the CSFB index return exceeded that of the S&P 500. Otherwise, in any year that the S&P 500 posted a positive return, this hedge fund index underperformed, and in one year,

TABLE 2.1 Hedge Fund Index Returns by Year

	S&P 500	CSFB/Tremont Hedge Fund Index	HFRI Composite Index
2003	28.69%	15.44%	19.55%
2002	−22.10	3.04	−1.45
2001	−11.89	4.42	4.62
2000	−9.10	4.85	4.98
1999	21.04	23.43	31.29
1998	28.58	−0.36	2.62
1997	33.36	25.94	16.79
1996	22.96	22.22	21.10
1995	37.58	21.69	21.50
1994	1.32	−4.36	4.10
1993	10.08	NA	30.88
1992	7.62	NA	21.22
1991	30.47	NA	32.19
1990	−3.10	NA	5.81
1994–2003			
Return	11.07%	11.12%	12.05%
Standard Deviation	15.84%	8.48%	7.47%
1990–2003			
Return	10.94%	NA	14.82%
Standard Deviation	15.05%	NA	7.08%

Sources: CSFB/Tremont, Standard & Poors, PerTrac.

1998, it recorded a loss whereas the S&P had a very strong 28.58 percent return. In the 2003 recovery, the S&P outdistanced the CSFB index by a wide margin.

Not all hedge fund indexes display the same results. Table 2.1 also shows the returns of the HFR Fund Weighted Composite Index. The HFR Composite Index and its component subindexes are published by Hedge Fund Research. The CSFB indexes differ from the HFR indexes and most others in one key aspect: The former are asset-weighted while the latter are equal-weighted. Thus, the performances of smaller funds have a lesser impact on the CSFB indexes' results than the larger funds. Other things being equal, returns on HFR and other equally weighted indexes should be higher than those of the CSFB indexes because the hedge fund industry is populated with smaller hedge funds, which tend to outperform larger funds, at least in their early years, and new funds are created every day.

For the same 1994–2003 period, the HFR Composite Hedge Fund Index posted an annualized compounded return of 12.05 percent, exceeding both the S&P and CSFB indexes by 1 percent per annum. Starting at the beginning of its history, the HFR Composite Index's annualized return also outperformed that of the S&P by almost 4 percent annually.

Looking at the different market environments since 1990, it is clear that the bear market of stocks between 2000 and 2002 allowed the hedge fund indexes to catch up with the S&P 500. As shown in Table 2.2, during the bull run of 1994–1999 both the CSFB and HFR indexes underperformed the S&P by a staggering 50 percent. The three-year bear market allowed the hedge fund indexes to record some modest returns while the S&P lost 14.55 percent annually.

During the 1990–1991 recession, the HFR Composite Index also showed higher returns than the S&P every year, even in 1991 when the

TABLE 2.2 Market Cycles and Hedge Fund Index Returns

	S&P 500	CSFB/Tremont Hedge Fund Index	HFRI Composite Index
Bull Market *1994–1999*			
Return	23.55%	11.94%	12.40%
Standard Deviation	13.64%	9.87%	7.65%
Recession *1990–1991*			
Return	12.44%	NA	18.26%
Standard Deviation	17.20%	NA	6.90%
Bear Market *2000–2002*			
Return	−14.55%	4.10%	2.68%
Standard Deviation	17.87%	6.27%	7.56%
Cycle I *1994–2003*			
Return	11.07%	11.11%	12.05%
Standard Deviation	15.84%	8.48%	7.47%
Cycle II *1990–2003*			
Return	10.94%	NA	14.82%
Standard Deviation	15.05%	NA	7.08%

Note: Annualized monthly return and standard deviation.
Sources: CSFB/Tremont, Standard & Poor's, PerTrac.

S&P posted a strong return of 30.47 percent. During these two years, the annualized return of the HFR Composite Index, at 18.26 percent, was close to 50 percent higher than that of the S&P. In the 2003 rally (see Table 2.1), by contrast, the HFR index lagged far behind the S&P, 19.55 percent versus 28.69 percent.

Notwithstanding differences in varying indexes' returns, there have been studies of individual hedge fund databases indicating that over the longer term, hedge funds have produced returns close to those of the S&P 500. Also, some studies have shown that over some prolonged as well as shorter-term periods, hedge funds have significantly underperformed the S&P 500.

The Quantitative Research team at Morgan Stanley Dean Witter conducted a study of a 10-year return history of hedge funds based on a database maintained by Financial Risk Management, Limited.[3] This database contained 1,748 hedge funds, which, for the purpose of the study, were then classified into four major strategies. The authors of the study observed that "the median returns of the four hedge fund strategy managers have been in the same ballpark as the median Lipper managers."[4] When compiled into an equally weighted index of an "All Hedge Funds" category, the hedge funds showed a compounded annual rate of return of 18.9 percent for the period between 1990 and June 2000. This compared favorably with the return of 17.2 percent by the S&P 500 and 16 percent by Lipper Large Cap Core managers, but was similar to the 18.7 percent return of the Lipper Large Cap Growth managers.

Bing Liang (2000)[5] found that during the equity bull market of the 1990s many hedge funds did not fare so well against the stock market. He looked at the period from 1990 to July 1999 in a study that included 1,921 hedge funds, both dead and alive, published by TASS Management Limited. He found that hedge funds had an annual return of 14.2 percent during this period, compared with 18.8 percent for the S&P 500 index. A $1 investment in hedge funds in January 1990 thus grew to $3.39 in July 1999, as opposed to $4.49 if invested in the S&P 500. The difference was an underperformance of 41 percent by hedge funds. Also, live funds outperformed dead funds by wide margins: The $1 investment would grow to $3.99 with live funds versus $1.84 with dead funds. However, my own calculations for the January 1990–July 1999 period showed the S&P 500's return at 17.76 percent. During the same period, the HFR Composite Hedge Fund Index had an annualized return of 17.39 percent, a virtual tie with the S&P.

In a study of the 1988 to 1995 period using data from Hedge Fund Research and Managed Account Reports (MAR), Ackermann et al. (1999)[6] found that hedge funds did not outperform the standard market indexes,

though they produced higher returns than mutual funds. For the period between 1994 and 1999, Gregoriou and Rouah (2002)[7] reviewed 204 hedge
funds and 72 funds of funds from the Zurich Hedge Fund Universe and the
Laporte Asset Allocation system, which included live offshore and onshore
funds. On the basis of the Sharpe ratio, they found that 22 percent of
hedge funds outperformed the S&P 500 and 41 percent beat the MSCI
World index. At the same time, only 11 percent of funds of funds exceeded
the S&P 500 and 17 percent surpassed the MSCI.

The point of all these statistics is that although in some periods hedge
funds have outperformed the stock market, investors should not expect this
outperformance to persist in the long term. In years that the stock market's
return is strong, hedge funds can be expected to lag. This happened in the
market recovery of 2003 when the S&P 500 rose by 28.69 percent, outdis-
tancing hedge fund indexes by wide margins. Sometimes hedge funds, on
average, can turn in losses amid a strong stock market rally. Over prolonged
periods, despite having positive results when the stock market posts losses,
hedge funds, on average, should not be expected to outperform the stock
market, certainly not by any significant margins. In fact, as indicated by the
uneven returns by live and defunct hedge funds cited earlier, it has been documented that hedge fund indexes have overstated hedge fund returns by 2
to 3 percent a year. This is due to data problems embedded in the indexes,
such as the survivorship bias. We return to this issue in Chapter 4.

CONSISTENCY OF RETURNS

If hedge funds do not produce greater returns than the stock market as
measured by the S&P 500, why invest in hedge funds? The answer is because hedge funds have lower risks, or more precisely, their returns have
exhibited lower volatility of returns. If risk is measured by standard deviation, studies of hedge fund returns have concluded that as a group, hedge
funds have had lower standard deviations of returns than stock market
benchmarks.

As shown in Table 2.1, the CSFB/Tremont Hedge Fund Index produced returns quite similar to those of the S&P 500, yet its volatility of returns was some 46 percent less; it outperformed the MSCI World Index
significantly on both counts. As shown in Table 2.3, the summary statistic
Sharpe ratio, which measures the risk-adjusted return, tells a dramatic
story. The CSFB Index's Sharpe ratio clocked in at 0.83, 3.3 times that of
the MSCI and 1.9 times that of the S&P 500.

In varying degrees, the individual CSFB subindexes outperformed both
the S&P and MSCI in terms of volatility, boosting their Sharpe ratios sig-

TABLE 2.3 Hedge Fund Indexes: Returns and Risks, January 1994–June 2004

Index	Annualized Total Return	Annualized Standard Deviation	Sharpe Ratio[a]
S&P 500	10.87%	15.50%	0.44
MSCI World Index	7.59	14.43	0.25
Lehman Aggregate Bond Index	7.59	3.97	0.90
CSFB/Tremont Hedge Fund Index	10.86%	8.31%	0.83
Convertible Arbitrage	10.02	4.74	1.27
Dedicated Short Bias	−3.06	17.67	−0.40
Emerging Markets	6.89	17.41	0.17
Equity Market Neutral	10.35	3.04	2.10
Event Driven (E.D.)	11.37	5.91	1.25
E.D. Distressed Securities	13.34	6.84	1.37
E.D. Multi-Strategy	10.27	6.23	1.01
E.D. Risk Arbitrage	8.23	4.37	0.97
Fixed Income Arbitrage	6.90	3.88	0.75
Global Macro	14.21	11.83	0.87
Long/Short Equity	11.84	10.78	0.73
Managed Futures	6.35	12.26	0.19
Multi-Strategy[b]	9.53	4.46	1.24

[a]Versus the S&P 500.
[b]Start April 1994.
Sources: CSFB/Tremont, Standard & Poor's, PerTrac.

nificantly higher than those of the long-only domestic and world stock indexes. Lowest volatility was recorded in Equity Market Neutral, Fixed Income Arbitrage (Arb), Risk Arbitrage, and Multi-Strategy. Their volatility was in the range of 3 to 4.5 percent, similar to the volatility of the fixed income market as represented by the Lehman Aggregate Bond Index during this 10-year period. The exceptions to this are the Dedicated Short Bias and Emerging Markets indexes. As will be seen in Chapter 5, these strategies are characterized by their predominant directionality, with Emerging Markets being mostly long and Dedicated Short Bias mostly short. Without hedges in the opposite direction, these strategies bear the brunt of the fluctuations of their market niches.

The S&P 500 showed higher volatility of returns than the CSFB and HFR indexes in the full cycle of bull and bear markets between 1990 and 2003. This is shown in Table 2.2. Both hedge fund indexes consistently exhibited a lower standard deviation than the S&P in bull as well as bear markets, and the differences were very significant. During the

1994–1999 episode when investors could not wait for market pullbacks to put more money into stocks, the S&P recorded a standard deviation of 13.64 percent, on the low end of its historical range. Still, the hedge fund indexes had lower volatility. Again in the three years of bear markets, both hedge fund indexes' volatilities were only about 40 percent of that of the S&P. In the up-down market of 1990–1991, the S&P's volatility was more than twice that of the HFR Composite Index.

In studies of individual hedge funds, as a group hedge funds were also shown to have lesser volatility than stock market indexes. In the Morgan Stanley study, the "All Hedge Funds" composite had a compounded annual return of 18.9 percent for the period between 1990 and June 2000.[8] Its standard deviation was 5.5 percent, which was even lower than that recorded for bonds, at 8.1 percent. For this period, the S&P 500 showed a standard deviation of 13.7 percent, and the MSCI Europe, Australasia, Far East (EAFE), 17.1 percent. The study also looked at four shorter periods during the 1990–2000 time frame. The results were essentially the same, showing hedge funds to have less volatility than the long-only stock indexes, although in shorter periods hedge funds' volatility tended to be higher than their longer-term volatility. Likewise, hedge funds were also shown to have less volatility than mutual funds, as represented by the Lipper indexes.[9]

Similar results were obtained in the study of 1,921 hedge funds by Bing Liang (2000)[10] cited earlier. Between 1990 and 1999, the stock market's volatility was recorded at 13.5 percent versus 5.8 percent by hedge funds. However, previously and with a smaller sample of hedge funds from the Hedge Fund Research database, Bing Liang (1999) found that hedge fund returns were more volatile than the S&P 500 during the years 1992 to 1996.[11] This finding came from a study of 385 hedge funds, both dead and live. During this five-year period, the annualized standard deviation of the sampled hedge funds was 14 percent while that of the S&P 500 was 11.7 percent. It should be noted, however, the S&P's volatility was rather low in this period, as its historical average ranged in the mid-teens in percentage. Also, 1994 was a period of turmoil for hedge funds, which were significantly affected by the rapid and substantial rise of interest rates as a result of aggressive tightening of the money supply by the Federal Reserve.

I calculated the standard deviation of the S&P 500 and the HFR Composite Index for the 1992 to 1996 period. The S&P had an annualized standard deviation of 8.66 percent while the HFR index's was 4.76 percent, lower by almost 4 percent.

In the Ackermann study,[12] the authors found that for the 1988 to 1995 period, hedge funds were more volatile than both mutual funds and market indexes, and hedge funds consistently outperformed mutual funds, but not standard market indexes.

In a more recent study that included two years of the bear market, Brooks and Kat (2002)[13] compared the mean returns and standard deviations of returns of the popular stock market benchmarks against those of the major hedge fund indexes, including CSFB, across investment strategies. The authors found that for the period 1990–2001, in aggregate, hedge funds, as measured by these indexes, had returns similar to the S&P 500, the Dow Jones Industrial Average, and NASDAQ. However, the hedge funds' volatility was much lower.

The studies of individual hedge funds by Bing Liang and others thus seem to show that hedge funds' returns have not been as high as reported by the indexes. Also, volatility of hedge funds, though varying in different periods, has consistently been shown to be lower than that of the S&P 500. This conclusion is affirmed in Table 2.2 showing standard deviations in different market conditions. Importantly, in periods of market declines, hedge funds have exhibited lower volatility, clearly because they have been positioned to take protective actions whereas long-only managers did not have or avail themselves of the same flexibility. This is a crucial point. Hedge funds are constantly on the lookout to protect themselves against market reversals. Sometimes such risk-protection moves have not paid off, resulting in underperformance vis-à-vis market indexes, which, however, is a lesser concern to hedge funds than to long-only managers. The latter's focus is to outperform market benchmarks, and they are apt to take risks in chasing after the market.

LOW CORRELATION WITH THE STOCK MARKET

Another way to look at the risks of hedge fund strategies is to examine their betas and correlations vis-à-vis a market index such as the S&P 500. This is shown in Table 2.4.

Whether measured by beta or correlations, the CSFB/Tremont hedge fund indexes have demonstrated very low correlation with the stock market. Even a predominantly long strategy like Emerging Markets had a beta of 0.54. The short-biased strategy Dedicated Short Bias had quite a large negative beta. As for Managed Futures, which can be either long or short, the market niche had a negative beta of −0.16. The Fixed Income Arb index registered virtually zero beta with the S&P. Convertible Arbitrage strategy, which hedges its bond holdings by shorting stocks of the same companies, registered a beta of only 0.04. Remarkably, Global Macro recorded a beta of only 0.19 during a period when the MSCI World index

TABLE 2.4   Hedge Fund Indexes: Risks and Correlations, January 1994–June 2004

Index	Annualized Standard Deviation	Correlation[a]	Beta[a]
S&P 500	15.50%	1.00	1.00
MSCI World Index	14.43%	0.94	0.86
CSFB/Tremont Hedge Fund Index	8.31%	0.47	0.26
Convertible Arbitrage	4.74	0.12	0.04
Dedicated Short Bias	17.67	−0.76	−0.86
Emerging Markets	17.41	0.48	0.54
Equity Market Neutral	3.04	0.40	0.07
Event Driven	5.91	0.55	0.21
E.D. Distressed Securities	6.84	0.54	0.23
E.D. Multi-Strategy	6.23	0.47	0.19
E.D. Risk Arbitrage	4.37	0.44	0.13
Fixed Income Arbitrage	3.88	0.03	0.01
Global Macro	11.83	0.23	0.19
Long/Short Equity	10.78	0.58	0.41
Managed Futures	12.26	−0.21	−0.16
Multi-Strategy	4.46	0.06	0.02

[a]Versus the S&P 500.
Sources: CSFB/Tremont, Standard & Poor's, PerTrac.

had a beta of almost 1 with the S&P. Clearly the flexibility Global Macro hedge funds used to navigate the three-year bear market in equities contributed to their lack of dependence on the world's equity markets.

Similarly, the other strategies recorded very low beta relationships with the stock market, although they invested in equity or equity-linked market segments in varying degrees. Thus, Equity Market Neutral's beta was almost zero while the Event Driven strategies recorded their betas of about 0.2. Only Long/Short Equity had a somewhat elevated beta, at 0.41.

PORTFOLIO EFFECTS OF HEDGE FUNDS

The combined effects of lower volatility of returns and low correlation to the stock market exert a powerful downward influence on portfolio risks when investors include hedge funds in portfolios of traditional stock and bond investments. Intuitively, when a low-risk investment is added to a high-risk investment—that is, by selling off part of the high-risk investment and investing the proceeds in the lower-risk alternative, or simply by investing newly available funds in the lower-risk investment—the overall risk of the resulting portfolio is reduced. This is true even if the two investments move in tandem.

The portfolio effect of correlation among risky assets is captured in a statistic called correlation coefficient, or correlation for short. In the language of portfolio theory, two investments that move in tandem have perfect correlation, or the correlation coefficient between them is equal to 1. Thus, if a portfolio is comprised of 25 percent CSFB/Tremont Hedge Fund Index and 75 percent S&P 500, the resulting portfolio would have an annualized return of 11.08 percent for the 1994 to 2003 period. This rate of return is due, of course, to the S&P 500 and the CSFB index producing virtually equal returns.

If these two investments move with perfect correlation, the resulting portfolio's volatility would be 13.7 percent. Thus, diversification with hedge funds as represented by the CSFB index results in a lower-risk portfolio, to the extent of 11.6 percent lower than the S&P 500's volatility. Since these two investments did not move in tandem in 1994–2003 and their correlation coefficient was only 0.47, the combined 25/75 portfolio of hedge funds and the S&P would record a volatility of 12.7 percent. This is a reduction in volatility by an additional 6.3 percent for a total reduction of 18 percent, as compared to the S&P 500's. This reduction of volatility results from a combination of lower standard deviation of the CSFB index and lower correlation of returns between it and the S&P.

In general, the lower the correlation of the investments, the lower the volatility of the portfolio combining them. If two investments have perfect negative correlation, that is, they move in opposite directions, it is possible to construct a portfolio of these investments with the resulting portfolio's volatility equal to zero. If the CSFB/Tremont Hedge Fund Index and the S&P 500 had had perfect negative correlation, the combined portfolio containing 65 percent CSFB index and 35 percent S&P 500 would have had zero volatility of returns. In other words, this portfolio would incredibly have had an annualized return of 11.1 percent without any volatility!

This is the powerful impact of risk reduction when a portfolio is constructed from investments with low correlation. The portfolio risk reduction effect is achievable even among investments of equal risks if their correlations are low enough. Table 2.5 shows the correlations of the different hedge fund strategies in the CSFB/Tremont Hedge Fund Index with the stock and bond markets, using the S&P 500 and the Lehman Aggregate Bond Index as proxies.

The correlations of the hedge fund strategies with the S&P 500 were lower than 0.5 with the exception of Long/Short Equity, Distressed Securities, and Event Driven strategies, which are highly equity oriented.

TABLE 2.5 Hedge Fund Indexes: Correlations with Stocks and Bonds

Index	Annualized Standard Deviation	Correlation with S&P 500	Correlation with Lehman Aggregate Bond Index
S&P 500	15.50%	1.00	0.04
Lehman Aggregate Bond Index	3.97%	0.04	1.00
CSFB/Tremont Hedge Fund Index	8.31%	0.47	0.21
Convertible Arbitrage	4.74	0.12	0.13
Dedicated Short Bias	17.67	−0.76	0.06
Emerging Markets	17.41	0.48	−0.06
Equity Market Neutral	3.04	0.40	0.13
Event Driven	5.91	0.55	0.01
E.D. Distressed Securities	6.84	0.54	0.06
E.D. Multi-Strategy	6.23	0.47	−0.03
E.D. Risk Arbitrage	4.37	0.44	−0.07
Fixed Income Arbitrage	3.88	0.03	0.20
Global Macro	11.83	0.23	0.30
Long/Short Equity	10.78	0.58	0.11
Managed Futures	12.26	−0.21	0.27
Multi-Strategy	4.46	0.06	0.04

Sources: CSFB/Tremont, Standard & Poor's, PerTrac.

Nevertheless, as compared with small-cap and international stocks, all hedge fund strategies exhibited highly attractive portfolio risk reduction benefits due to their low correlation with the equity market, as well as their intrinsic low volatility of returns. In fact, the traditional diversification strategies involving small-cap and international stocks would hardly provide any risk reduction benefits given their high correlation with the S&P 500, the standard equity market benchmark for this kind of asset allocation analysis. Of the 12 hedge fund strategies, two strategies, Fixed Income Arbitrage and Multi-Strategy, exhibited virtually zero correlation with the S&P. Two strategies, Dedicated Short Bias and Managed Futures, recorded negative correlation.

Among these four, Multi-Strategy stands out for its lack of correlation with the S&P, fairly low standard deviation, and return not much below that of the S&P 500 (Table 2.3). In lieu of the CSFB/Tremont Hedge Fund Index, further risk reduction can be achieved with a portfolio comprising 25 percent Multi-Strategy and 75 percent S&P 500. The resulting portfolio has a volatility of 11.4 percent.

To examine the effects of diversification with hedge funds on a portfolio of 60 percent in stocks and 40 percent in bonds, various asset allocations are plotted on Figure 2.1.

In Figure 2.1, various portions of the CSFB/Tremont Hedge Fund Index and its Multi-Strategy component are added to the 60/40 stock/bond portfolio. As the allocation to the CSFB index increases, the portfolio's return increases, and the standard deviation of returns also steadily declines. At the apex of the curve, the combination yields the optimal portfolio, which is to say that this is the least risky portfolio and there is no other possible combination of the CSFB index and the stock/bond portfolio that would produce the same return for lower risk or a higher return for the same amount of risk. The curve is the efficient frontier, à la modern portfolio theory, of the portfolios combining the CSFB/Tremont Hedge Fund Index and the 60/40 stock/bond portfolio.

The efficient frontier of the portfolios combining Multi-Strategy and the stock/bond portfolio shows the more dramatic impact of diversification with this strategy. Return increases as Multi-Strategy is added to the stock/bond portfolio while volatility declines until they reach the optimal levels with 90 percent in Multi-Strategy and 10 percent in stocks and bonds.

Thus, for traditional investors in diversified portfolios of stocks and bonds, diversification into hedge funds historically could improve not only returns but also the volatility of those returns. In contrast, returns of the portfolios combining stocks and hedge funds did not increase with additions in hedge funds. This is because historically and generally hedge funds have not outperformed the equity market over the longer term. Some

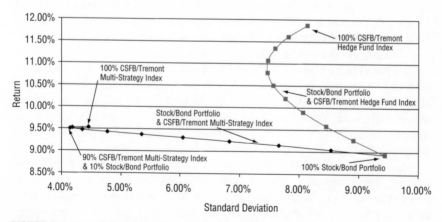

FIGURE 2.1 Stock/Bond Portfolios and Hedge Funds
Sources: CSFB/Tremont, Standard & Poor's, PerTrac.

strategies, such as Distressed Securities in the CSFB database, outperformed the S&P in the past 10 years, while others did not.

It follows that for traditional portfolios including both stocks and bonds, diversification into hedge funds could achieve both risk reduction as well as higher overall portfolio return.

One way to summarize the benefits of hedge funds in terms of both return and risk is the so-called Sharpe ratio. For any investment this ratio involves subtracting the risk-free rate (commonly the one-month Treasury bill rate is used as the proxy) from the investment's arithmetic or simple average rate of return and dividing the difference by its standard deviation. Higher—meaning more desirable—Sharpe ratios may result from either lower risk or higher return (or both). Thus, one way to think of the Sharpe ratio is in terms of the trade-off between return and risk.

In order to calculate the Sharpe ratios for different investments in different time periods, the values of the risk-free rates are required, for the Sharpe ratios equalize asset returns in different interest rate environments. However, to rank the risk/return trade-off of different investments in the same time periods, it would be more convenient to simply divide the return by the standard deviation. In investment literature, this ratio is called the reward-to-variability ratio or simply return-to-risk ratio. For the same time periods, investors can use this ratio to estimate the relative performances of different investments without doing research on the precise levels of interest rates.

We can also think of the return-to-risk ratio as the price of risk. For higher risks, we would want to extract higher prices; the higher the risk, the higher the price. Indeed, the price of risk in traditional stocks and bonds was historically much too low during 1994–2003 when compared to the price of risk in hedge fund strategies. Table 2.3 shows the Sharpe ratios of the CSFB hedge fund strategies and the stock and bond indexes.

The portfolio risk reduction benefits of hedge fund diversification have been extensively analyzed in many studies, using hedge fund indexes from different databases, for different periods. Invariably, the conclusions were that including hedge funds in traditional portfolios of stocks and bonds would reduce the volatility of the resulting portfolios. Investors could also extract higher prices for the risks they took and thereby enhance the Sharpe ratios.

In a study, Schneeweis and Georgiev (2002)[14] calculated the effects of adding the Evaluation Associates Capital Markets (EACM) 100 hedge fund index to a portfolio of stocks and bonds. Table 2.6 shows the return and risk properties of various investments.

By any measure of risk, during the period between January 1990 and December 2001 the EACM hedge fund index exhibited risk/return trade-

TABLE 2.6   Risk and Return: The EACM 100 Index and Stock and Bond Market Indexes

	EACM 100	S&P 500	Lehman Government/ Corporate Bond	MSCI World	Lehman Global Bond
Annualized Return	13.8%	12.9%	8.1%	6.5%	6.9%
Annualized Standard Deviation	4.3%	14.6%	4.2%	14.6%	4.9%
Sharpe Ratio	1.95	0.51	0.62	0.07	0.31
Price of Risk	3.21	0.88	1.92	0.45	1.41
Minimum Monthly Return	−4.5%	−14.5%	−2.5%	−13.4%	−3.0%
Correlation with EACM 100	1	0.39	0.17	0.39	0.06

Note: Implied interest rate = 5.45.
Source: Thomas Schneeweis and Georgi Georgiev, "The Benefits of Hedge Funds," Center for International Securities and Derivatives Markets (CISDM)/Isenberg School of Management, University of Massachusetts, June 19, 2002.

offs superior to those of stocks and bonds by wide margins. Importantly, the EACM index demonstrated such low correlation with stocks and bonds that adding it to traditional portfolios would reduce portfolio volatility beyond what its standard deviation would indicate. Table 2.7 shows the improvements in both risks and Sharpe ratios when 20 percent of the EACM index was added to either the 50/50 domestic stock and bond portfolio or the 50/50 global portfolio.

Using a more complicated technique, Amin and Kat (2002)[15] analyzed the effects of hedge funds on traditional stock and bond portfolios using the CSFB database between 1994 and 2001. This study, however, did not use the return and risk data of the hedge fund indexes. Instead, portfolios of 20 hedge funds were randomly selected. Due to the random procedure, some portfolios would have higher volatility than Multi-Strategy or the all-inclusive CSFB/Tremont Hedge Fund Index, such as those portfolios that did not include Equity Market Neutral or Fixed Income Arbitrage. Nevertheless, when such randomly selected hedge funds were added to traditional portfolios invested 50 percent in stocks and 50 percent in bonds, the resulting portfolios would have higher returns as well as lower volatility. The maximum diversification benefit would be derived from a 50 percent allocation to hedge funds; any greater additions to hedge funds

TABLE 2.7 Risk Reduction Benefits of Hedge Funds in the EACM Index, January 1990–December 2001

	Portfolio I: Traditional Portfolio	Portfolio II: Traditional Plus Hedge	Portfolio III: Traditional Global Portfolio	Portfolio IV: Traditional Global Plus Hedge
	50% S&P 500 + 50% Lehman Bond	20% EACM + 40% S&P + 40% Lehman Bond	50% MSCI + 50% Lehman Global Bond	20% EACM + 40% MSCI + 40% Lehman Global Bond
Annualized Return	10.71%	11.37%	6.98%	8.37%
Annualized Standard Deviation	8.12%	6.89%	8.40%	7.08%
Sharpe Ratio	0.65	0.86	0.18	0.41
Minimum Monthly Return	−6.25%	−5.89%	−5.63%	−5.39%

Source: Thomas Schneeweis and Georgi Georgiev, "The Benefits of Hedge Funds," Center for International Securities and Derivatives Markets (CISDM)/Isenberg School of Management, University of Massachusetts, June 19, 2002.

would result in increases in volatility. The implication of these findings is that if investors throw darts at a list of all hedge funds still in operation, picking out 20 to be added to traditional stock and bond portfolios, there would be a 50–50 chance that the investors would reap the benefits of higher return and lower volatility.

ALTERNATIVE INVESTMENTS IN UNCERTAIN MARKETS

While hedge funds represent an effective diversification strategy, in bear markets hedge funds stand out as viable strategies that produce attractive returns. A quick look at the CSFB/Tremont Hedge Fund Index's returns during the bear market of 2000–2002 indicates that, while the U.S. and global stock markets experienced the most prolonged and deepest bear markets since the crash of 1929, this index posted positive returns for each of the three years of the bear market.

Some of the individual hedge fund strategies have produced even better returns than the CSFB/Tremont Hedge Fund Index. As shown in Table 2.8, Global Macro had a cumulative compound return of 51 percent during 2000–2002. Equity Market Neutral, Fixed Income Arbitrage, and Convertible Arbitrage strategies also outperformed the composite index each and every year during these three years.

Interestingly enough, the average equity mutual fund, as measured by the Morningstar index, failed to avoid to any significant extent the losses suffered by the market as a whole. At the same time, as measured by the MSCI World Index, the world equity markets actually fared worse than the U.S. market. As such, international diversification did not help U.S. investors avoid the onslaught of the virulent market declines.

The positive returns produced by hedge funds were clearly beneficial to their investors during the bear market. As reported by HedgeWorld, a survey conducted by Commonfund for the fiscal year ending June 2003[16] found that endowments of colleges and other educational establishments that reported higher investment returns had greater allocations to alterna-

TABLE 2.8 Returns in the 2000–2002 Bear Market

Index	2000	2001	2002
CSFB/Tremont Hedge Fund Index	4.85%	4.42%	3.04%
HFR Composite Index	4.98	4.62	−1.45
NASDAQ	−39.29	−21.05	−31.53
S&P 500	−9.10	−11.90	−22.10
MSCI World Equity Index	−14.00	−17.80	−21.10
Morningstar Average Equity Mutual Fund	−5.10	−12.60	−20.30
CSFB/Tremont Indexes			
Convertible Arbitrage	25.64%	14.58%	4.05%
Dedicated Short Bias	15.76	−3.58	18.14
Emerging Markets	−5.52	5.84	7.36
Equity Market Neutral	14.99	9.31	7.42
Event Driven	7.26	11.50	0.16
E.D. Distressed Securities	1.95	20.01	−0.69
E.D. Multi-Strategy	11.84	6.79	1.22
E.D. Risk Arbitrage	14.69	5.68	−3.46
Fixed Income Arbitrage	6.29	8.04	5.75
Global Macro	11.67	18.38	14.66
Long/Short Equity	2.08	−3.65	−1.60
Managed Futures	4.24	1.90	18.33
Multi-Strategy	11.18	5.50	6.31

Sources: CSFB/Tremont, Standard & Poor's, PerTrac.

tive investments than lower-return institutions. It was suggested that because hedge funds made up nearly half of alternative investments, hedge
funds must have made a contribution to the performance of the higher-
return institutions.

In the same survey, which had 657 institutional respondents, the endowments ranked in the top decile and quartile in terms of investment returns used asset allocation strategies that were significantly different from
those of other institutions participating in the study. Their equity allocations were smaller whereas their commitments to alternative investments
were larger. At the same time, the percentages of hedge fund allocations in
these alternative investments were also smaller, with the larger portions going into private equity and energy and natural resources.

Overall, the average participating endowment had a return of a little
over 3 percent. Similarly, as reported by HedgeWorld,[17] the college endowments in the survey by the National Association of College and University
Business Officers had returns of 2.9 percent in the fiscal year ending June
2003, almost half of the reported withdrawal rate of 5.4 percent. During
this 12-month period, the S&P 500 lost –1.54 percent.

WEALTH PRESERVATION

Lower volatility of returns would have a direct impact on the growth of the
wealth of long-term investors. Recall in Table 1.1 we examined the patterns of available income and accumulated wealth of an investor who invested in the S&P 500 and each year set aside 5 percent to spend in the
following year. The amount set aside would reduce the capital available for
investing in the market at the beginning of each following year. In Table
2.9 similar calculations are made with the returns on the S&P 500 during
1994–2003.

As shown, the S&P's volatility of annual returns was much higher
than its annualized standard deviation of monthly returns. During this
period, the annualized monthly volatility was 15.84 percent, as shown in
Table 2.1; however, the volatility of annual returns was much higher, at
22.35 percent. The latter measure is directly applicable in the calculations, assuming that spending decisions are made on a yearly basis. The
high volatility of the S&P was transferred directly to the available income and wealth, which recorded the same amounts of fluctuations from
year to year.

Table 2.10 similarly shows the direct impact of annual volatility of returns on available income and wealth as recorded by the S&P 500, the
CSFB/Tremont Hedge Fund Index, and the HFR Composite Hedge Fund

TABLE 2.9 Impact of Volatility on Wealth and Income

	S&P 500 Returns	Available Income	Wealth
1994	1.32%	$ 5.07	$ 96.25
1995	37.58	6.62	125.81
1996	22.96	7.73	146.95
1997	33.36	9.80	186.18
1998	28.58	11.97	227.43
1999	21.04	13.76	261.52
2000	−9.10	11.89	225.82
2001	−11.89	9.95	189.02
2002	−22.10	7.36	139.89
2003	28.69	9.00	171.02
Volatility	22.35%	21.23%	21.23%

Source: Standard & Poor's.

Index. The lower volatility of hedge fund indexes means that instances and magnitudes of large depletions of wealth and reductions in available income were less severe with hedge funds than with the S&P 500. Although the S&P 500 and the CSFB/Tremont Hedge Fund Index had the same returns for the 1994–2003 period, available income and wealth derived from investing in the S&P suffered dramatic rises and falls pre- and post-2000. During the bear market, both indicators of prosperity based on the S&P

TABLE 2.10 Volatility of Wealth and Income

	Volatility of Returns	Volatility of Income and Wealth
1994–2003		
S&P 500	22.35%	21.23%
CSFB	10.36%	9.84%
HFR	11.06%	10.51%
1990–2003		
S&P 500	19.11%	18.36%
HFR	11.73%	11.27%

Sources: CSFB/Tremont, Standard & Poor's, PerTrac.

dropped a huge 46 percent. In contrast, the gains from hedge fund investing accumulated prior to 2000 remained largely intact during the same period. Overall, at the end of this 10-year period both indexes arrived at the
same level of wealth, $171.02 for the S&P 500 and $171.79 for the CSFB
index. However, were it not for the large recovery in 2003, wealth from the
S&P would have lagged behind.

Over a slightly longer duration, between 1990 and 2003, the HFR
Composite Index's returns exceeded those of the S&P 500. The combined
effect of higher return and lower volatility resulted in wealth derived from
the HFR index, calculated at $337.50, that was 61 percent higher than the
S&P 500–generated wealth, at $208.63. During the equity bear market,
the HFR index declined slightly, preserving most of the wealth generated in
prior years.

For most investors, the bear market posed a stark contrast between
hedge funds and investing in long-only strategies such as the S&P 500.
Hedge fund investors did not face a choice of "to sell or not to sell" at
such times because their investments did not produce large and unusual
losses. In contrast, for those who were exposed to the vagaries of the
market, facing accumulating losses and dropping income from investment returns while confronting uncertain future prospects as to whether
the market would recover, it may have been agonizingly difficult to hold
on to their investments. Even to this day, after the S&P rallied by 28 percent in 2003 but has since stalled, it is debatable whether the market
will continue to recover. Some prognosticators maintain that this has
been no more than a bounce in a secular bear market and the worst is
yet to come.

PROSPECTIVE LONG-TERM RETURNS AND RISKS OF STOCKS

In uncertain market environments, hedge funds offer unique opportunities
that would not be available with traditional long-only strategies. As the equity market recovers from the 2000 bubble burst, it remains uncertain that
the recovery will be sustained. Equity valuations have again returned to the
bubble levels, with the surviving Internet stocks gaining back their astro-
nomical price-earnings multiples. In the meantime, anticipation of rising
interest rates and inflation casts fear on both stocks and bonds. After gaining 28.69 percent in 2003, a rate of return matching the pre-bubble days,
the S&P 500 languished throughout the first half of 2004. This is only to
be expected, as the prospect of higher stock prices from gains in valuation
is not promising when interest rates are rising.

In the meantime, investors continue to harbor unrealistic expectations of equity returns. Many large corporations with defined benefit pension plans have not abandoned the highly optimistic assumed rates of returns for their investments.[18] Since these large institutional investors have not invested to any significant degree in hedge funds that are capable of generating excess returns from managers' specialized skills, these assumptions could only be extrapolations from the historically unsustainable returns of the late 1990s equity market.

Not only are equity returns expected to range in the mid to high single digits, volatility is bound to rise at least to the historical average levels. Experiences in other countries' stock markets also suggest possibilities of depressed equity prices for years to come, especially after the large returns in 2003.[19]

From a fundamental point of view, the coming years hardly resemble the onset of the 1980s when inflation came under control, interest rates were declining, and the advance of personal computer and Internet technologies brought excitement to the market's technology sectors. They do not resemble the early 1990s, either, when interest rates were falling again, the budget deficits turned into surpluses, and Internet stocks pushed valuations to unprecedented levels. The market environment going forward is now burdened with record trade and budget deficits, rising inflationary and interest rate expectations, a falling dollar, mature technology companies, and continuing threats of terrorist and geopolitical risks. Although it is difficult to predict how these forces will act out, they can hardly be expected to exert favorable influences on either the equity or the bond market.

In this environment, hedge funds can fill a role that traditional long-only strategies are ill-equipped to handle. That role is to devise and manage strategies that can produce positive and attractive returns regardless of the prospects of the equity and bond market conditions.

But hedge funds are neither a panacea nor suitable investments for every investor. In the preceding discussion, returns of hedge funds were characterized as those recorded by hedge fund indexes, in particular, those published by CSFB/Tremont and HFR. This qualification is important because not all hedge funds are alike; in fact, they are quite different from one another, even those that claim to follow similar strategies. More importantly, there are great disparities in returns among hedge funds. These disparities are not captured in the statistics of hedge fund indexes to the extent that traditional long-only indexes such as the S&P 500 may reflect the potential of the stock market. Sole reliance on hedge fund indexes may result in allocating too much or too little to hedge fund strategies. Importantly, volatility that reflects fluctuations of returns is not the only measure of risks or the only risk of hedge funds. Before its collapse, Long-Term Capital Management had produced stellar and steady returns for three consecutive years. This is a perfect example of the risk of total loss in hedge funds as well as the asymmetry of hedge fund returns: a string of stable and strong returns only to be followed by periods of large losses. Thus, we need to have a more detailed understanding of what hedge funds really are, as well as what really are their risks, before analyzing which funds can do what for investors. This is the subject of the next two chapters.

CHAPTER 3

Going for the Gold

Growth and Strategies of Hedge Funds

On the heels of the worst equity bear market in 70 years, the rush into hedge funds has continued unabated. Benefiting from a record year of asset inflows after a dismal year by comparison in 2002, when the industry raised only $16 billion, hedge funds received an inflow of $75 billion in 2003, as reported by Hedge Fund Research (HFR).[1] The prior record year was 2001 with $31 billion going into hedge funds. The InvestHedge Billion Dollar Club, which counts funds of hedge funds that have at least $1 billion of assets, grew from 61 members the prior year to 81 members in 2003, while assets managed by the group rose from $91.9 billion to $291.6 billion. Interestingly, underlying the Hedge Fund Research data, the asset gains were concentrated in macro funds, which saw increases of $73.95 billion. However, the gains of $61 billion recorded by arbitrage strategy funds in the convertible, fixed income, and relative value spaces were almost offset by the outflows of $42 billion seen in distressed securities, emerging markets, long/short equity, and sector funds.

SIZE OF THE HEDGE FUND INDUSTRY

The record inflows brought hedge funds' total assets under management to a new record, which Hedge Fund Research estimated at $817.5 billion at the end of 2003.[2] Though a large amount, it is still dwarfed by the $8 trillion mutual fund industry. Hedge Fund Research estimated that more than 38 percent of the assets went to funds of hedge funds. All of these funds would be by definition recycled back to individual hedge funds, resulting in double counting, which if subtracted from the $817.5 billion would result in actual total hedge fund assets under management of about $500 billion

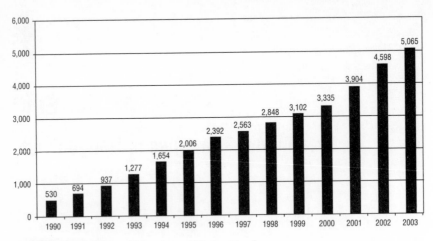

FIGURE 3.1 Estimated Number of Hedge Funds
Source: Hedge Fund Research.

at the end of 2003. Even so, this is a far cry from the estimated $9 billion of assets for the industry some 20 years ago.

Figure 3.1 shows the growth in the number of hedge funds (not including funds of hedge funds) since 1990, according to Hedge Fund Research. As money flowed in, hedge funds sprouted like mushrooms to meet the increasing demand. From a relatively small group of managers, according to TASS Research, 1,000 new hedge funds were launched in 2003, bringing the total number to approximately 6,700 hedge funds, of which 1,700 were funds of hedge funds. The number of fund closures declined by 4 percent.[3] For perspective, the Russell 3000 index, which captures 98 percent of the market values of all the public companies in the United States, contains only 3,000 names.

INVESTORS IN HEDGE FUNDS

As a departure from the past, institutions such as endowments and foundations are becoming key players in the hedge fund market. Although the assets these institutions invest in hedge funds remain a relatively small percentage of the total, their share has increased rapidly. It is now estimated that 20 percent of endowments and foundations invest in hedge funds.[4] However, pension plans have only about 1 percent of their assets invested with hedge funds. According to industry officials, allocations from institutional investors were the main reason for the substantial growth of assets in 2003. At the same time, 73 percent of high-net-worth individual investors invested in hedge funds as of early 2003. Obviously, as hedge funds are accepted as an asset class, participation by institutional investors can only increase going forward.[5]

In a survey by the Commonfund[6] of 657 educational endowments for the fiscal year ending June 30, 2003, 33 percent of these institutions' assets were indicated to have been invested in alternative strategies, 45 percent of which were hedge funds. The allocation to alternative investments has been rising, from 23 percent in 2000. One-third of the survey's respondents expected alternative investments to increase over the next year, while 20 percent of the responding endowments expected their institutions to reduce their allocations to fixed-income investments. Overall, U.S. equities accounted for 32 percent of the total assets of these investors and 14 percent of assets were in international equities, leaving only about 20 percent (and declining) in fixed income.

According to the National Association of College and University Business Officers,[7] college endowments' investments in hedge funds grew to 6.1 percent of the respondents' total assets in 2003, up from about 5 percent in 2002. Since first reported by the organization in 1993, the investments in hedge funds have increased every year from 0.7 percent. This increase has come largely from the big endowments, those with $1 billion or more of assets. These institutions have committed a new record amount of approximately 20 percent of their assets to hedge funds. The business officers organization also reported that allocations to private equity and venture capital had been falling, and now made up 1.3 percent and 0.8 percent, respectively, of its survey participants' assets. At the time of the survey, hedge funds were the largest segment among alternative investments. The survey of 723 participants, from Harvard University with $18.9 billion in assets to small colleges with less than $1 million, was conducted by the Teachers Insurance and Annuity Association–College Retirement Equities Fund (TIAA-CREF). TIAA-CREF reported a 19.9 percent hedge fund allocation by endowments with greater than $1 billion of assets. In contrast, endowments with assets of less than $25 million allocated only 1.6 percent to hedge funds.

The surging interest in hedge funds is not limited to institutional and very wealthy investors. Individuals who are merely affluent now have access to hedge funds that require relatively small amounts of minimum investments. Global Asset Management, Oppenheimer, and Deutsche Bank are offering a more affordable breed, a fund of hedge funds for minimum investments of $25,000 to $50,000. Even Charles Schwab, "home of the little guy," has rolled out a mutual fund version, the Schwab Hedged Equity Fund, with a minimum of $25,000.[8]

WHAT ARE HEDGE FUNDS?

Before we examine in detail whether in fact hedge funds do produce higher returns and lower risks than the stock market, it is necessary to examine what exactly hedge funds do. Generally understood, hedge funds are considered a subset of alternative investments, which include virtually any investments that do not restrict themselves to the traditional strategies of holding long-only positions in publicly traded stocks and bonds. Examples of alternative investments include private equity; inflation hedges such as timber and real estate; and, of course, hedge funds. A key difference between hedge funds and other alternative investments is that hedge funds mostly deal in publicly traded securities, although some that present themselves as hedge funds deal in private transactions such as private investments in public entities (PIPE). Still others engage in highly illiquid securities.

Structure

In terms of legal structures, hedge funds are largely unregulated private investment pools that are almost always organized as limited partnerships. The investors are limited partners, and the firms that manage the limited partnerships serve as the general partners.

Hedge funds also charge higher fees than traditional long-only managers. Typically, the fees consist of a management fee between 1 and 3 percent per annum and an incentive fee usually ranging from 10 percent to 25 percent. Some funds of hedge funds do not charge any incentive fee, or their incentive fees are subject to a hurdle rate. Single-strategy funds rarely limit their incentive fees to a hurdle rate and they typically charge a higher fixed annual management fee. However, incentive fees are always subject to a high-water mark, meaning that if a fund incurs losses, those losses must be recovered in subsequent periods before incentive fees can be charged on the profits. Thus, as an example, if after a year of producing a positive return of 15 percent bringing the initial capital of $100 million to $115 million, a fund loses 5 percent in the first quarter of year 2, then gains 5 percent in the second quarter, no incentive fee would be assessed on the second quarter's gain. Going forward, until the $115 million high water mark is exceeded, the manager does not earn any incentive fee. As a result, many hedge fund managers simply close up shop after large losses as expectations of recovery, and hence earning incentive fees, appear dim.

Hedge funds also impose certain liquidity restrictions that limit the ability of investors to exit. The first restriction is the lockup period during which investors must stay with the fund. Many funds require a lockup period of one year; a lockup period of three months would be considered short. Investors must also serve notice on a fund before redemptions can be made. This notice period mostly ranges between one and three months.

After notifying the fund of their intention to redeem, investors must then wait for the end of the month or the end of the quarter, depending on the fund's stipulations, to know the values of their investments—that is, how much they would receive. The actual payments, however, would be made sometime in the following month. There is also the provision that the fund managers may withhold such payments if they deem such payments may hurt the interests of other investors.

Furthermore, some funds impose the "liquidity gate" restriction of about 20 percent to 25 percent. During any month or quarter, if the total of all the redemption requests exceeds this liquidity gate, the excess amounts must wait until the next period. This would prevent a large investor from making a withdrawal greater than the liquidity gate limit, or any number of investors from exiting at the same time, driving down the fund's values.

Investment Objectives

Beyond these structural similarities, hedge fund investment strategies differ vastly, even among those that appear to use strategies of the same kind. These strategies can be as simple as hedging stock holdings by short selling certain index proxies such as Standard & Poor's Depositary Receipts (SPDRs), the S&P 500 exchange-traded fund known as Spiders. The mutual fund market-timing scandal[9] revealed that there were so-called hedge funds that colluded with mutual funds in using illegal practices of trading in and out of mutual funds after they had been closed for trading by other investors, or engaged in short-term trading of mutual funds in violation of these funds' prospectuses. However, most hedge funds employ complicated long and short trades, in stocks and bonds, using derivatives and structured products like those in mortgage-backed securities.

From the viewpoint of investors who have grown used to traditional long-only stocks and bonds, hedge funds are different from traditional investments in one key respect. That is, hedge funds do short sell stocks and bonds in addition to purchasing these securities. This was how Alfred Winslow Jones conceived of hedge funds back in 1949 when he used short selling as hedges against losses of values due to the decline in the stock market.

From this origin, hedge funds evolved to become an investment of choice for families who became wealthy and were more interested in preserving their fortunes as opposed to getting rich. As old money, these investors sought to avoid disasters such as the crash of 1929. Their focus was to achieve reasonable returns for their investments to maintain their lifestyles and such financial commitments as charities and foundations, with a minimum amount of risk to their capital. They did not focus on market benchmarks to compare with the returns on their investments. They did not care about the relative performances of such indexes as the S&P 500 or the NASDAQ. The most important yardstick for their investment returns was what they needed for their lifestyles and perhaps some growth for their capital. To get richer, they worked to expand their businesses, instead of taking risks with what they already had.

In fact, this sensible and pragmatic objective is still paramount among individual investors today, even those with only a few thousand dollars invested in mutual funds. That is why most individual investors are happy with their mutual fund managers even when these returns lag their market indexes, as long as these managers produce positive returns. They would be concerned only if their investments started to lose money. Thus, while the S&P 500 is a household name, most investors do not know what the Lehman Aggregate Bond Index is or how it is different from the Lehman Government/Corporate Bond Index, or that these are the indexes that institutional investors use to evaluate their bond managers. Indeed, individual fixed-income investors hardly care about these benchmarks at all.

The obsession with benchmark returns has its genesis from the sell side of the market. That is, as funds vie for attention from investors, they compare their returns with the S&P 500 index, or against their peers. They advertised heavily and proclaimed superior talent if their results exceeded the market benchmarks. Little, if anything, was mentioned about the risks they took to produce these results, such as how a stock like America Online (AOL) was suitable for a value portfolio during the Internet bubble. As a result, every money manager chases after market indexes. While the market keeps going up, prudence is no longer a virtue and falling behind the market is not a mark of wisdom or foresight.

Very large and presumably sophisticated investors also follow the same practice. On the advice of consultants armed with statistics on the potential returns of different strategies, from small-cap to large-cap stocks, to value versus growth investing, institutional investors compare their managers against market indexes and among the managers' peer groups. Indeed, managers who ranked below the average of their peer groups, even if they took lesser risks, usually ended up being shunned from consideration for additional investments from their existing clients— or worse, being fired.

A better manager is viewed as the one who outperforms the indexes and the peer group. If the market goes down, losing money is not bad performance, as long as the loss is less than that of the market.

However, individual investors, wealthy or otherwise, are less sanguine about losses. One cannot buy anything with losses, and certainly cannot become richer. This is where hedge funds come in.

Return Objective   The single most distinguishing characteristic of hedge funds from traditional long-only stock and bond investing is that hedge funds seek to deliver—and their investors demand—positive returns in all market conditions, up or down. The market in this context is the stock and bond markets, represented by such indexes as the S&P 500 and the like for stocks. With regard to bonds, the market pertains more to the direction of interest rates. Thus, fixed-income arbitrage hedge funds are supposed to produce positive returns whether interest rates rise or decline. The returns of such indexes as the Lehman Aggregate Bond index are irrelevant in judging such hedge funds.

Because of this objective of absolute returns regardless of market conditions, hedge funds are often called absolute return strategies, although not all funds seek this objective or are able to deliver absolute returns.

Beta and Alpha   To generate positive returns in all market conditions, hedge funds are designed to be independent of the market, for the market can generate both positive as well as negative returns. This is referred to as market neutral. Those hedge funds that are not entirely independent of the market are said to have low correlation with the market. As such, according to the jargon that has developed in the business, hedge funds generate alpha, as opposed to depending on beta (i.e., depending on the market to generate returns).

In a nutshell, beta is a measure of a fund's amount of dependence on the return of the market. The concept is rooted in portfolio theory pioneered by Harry Markowitz in the 1950s, which has evolved to express the relationship between risky assets, such as stocks, and the market.

Students of algebra would recognize the linear equation

$$Y = a + bX$$

where a and b are constants. Written with Greek letters, this equation becomes

$$Y = \alpha + \beta X \tag{3.1}$$

It is easy to see that

$$\alpha = Y - \beta X$$

In his capital asset pricing model (CAPM), William F. Sharpe (1964)[10] posits that the return of a portfolio can be explained by the sum of the risk-free rate of interest and the market portfolio multiplied by a factor. Similar to the linear equation (3.1), in its basic formulation, the expected return of a stock can be expressed as:

$$\bar{R}_i = r_f + \beta_i (\bar{R}_M - r_f) \tag{3.2}$$

The equation states simply that the expected return of a stock i or a portfolio i of different stocks, represented by $\bar{R}_i$, is the sum of the risk-free rate of interest, (r_f), and a portion, β_i or beta, of the excess return generated by the market, $\bar{R}_M$, over the risk-free rate.

Beta can have any value. When beta equals zero, the market's fluctuations are not supposed to have any impact on the portfolio. The higher the beta, the more the portfolio is dependent on the market for return. For hedge funds, beta is supposed to be low, often much less than one. Beta is also a measure of risk, in the sense that if the market goes up or down, the portfolio's return would rise or fall to the extent of the beta relationship, and therefore the portfolio is that much more or less risky than the market. Thus, a beta value exceeding one indicates the investment is riskier than the market.

If a portfolio's actual return is greater than that predicted by the $\bar{R}_i$, it is said that the portfolio has generated excess return or alpha. The term *alpha* originates from the Greek letter α, which is injected in equation (3.2) as follows:

$$\bar{R}_A = \alpha + r_f + \beta_i (\bar{R}_M - r_f) \tag{3.3}$$

where $\bar{R}_A$ is the actual return of the portfolio.

Compare the terms in equations (3.2) and (3.3):

$$\bar{R}_A - \bar{R}_i = \alpha$$

It is clear from the preceding expression that the smaller the value of beta, the more a portfolio is reliant on alpha for returns.

This is what hedge funds are supposed to do. They are supposed to be free from the market, free from its vagaries and fluctuations and risks. The values of their beta are supposed to be very low or near zero. For a fund manager to achieve such a feat, he or she must have exceptional skills or talent. That is why alpha is often claimed to be synonymous with a portfolio manager's talent or skills.

Traditional long-only portfolios rely mostly on beta and go up and

TABLE 3.1 Traditional versus Hedge Funds: Risk and Return Objectives

Traditional Investments	Hedge Fund Strategies
■ Objective: Outperform market benchmarks.	■ Objective: Achieve absolute returns in all market conditions.
■ Return: Beta dominates alpha.	■ Return: Alpha is generated by using specialized strategies.
■ Risk: (1) Relative to market; (2) implicit in taking the market's risk.	■ Risk: (1) Varies with strategy; (2) explicitly recognized in strategy and part of risk/return trade-offs.

down with the market. Sure, these managers are also expected to generate positive alpha by outperforming their benchmarks, such as the S&P 500. However, study after study as well as simple comparisons with benchmark returns have demonstrated that traditional managers have consistently failed to deliver benchmark returns while taking more risks. Table 3.1 is a summary of the key differences in the risk and return objectives of traditional long-only investments and hedge funds.

Risk Objective   If hedge funds do not rely on the market for returns, are their risks different from those of the markets? The answer is yes, their risks can be smaller or greater than the market's. Traditional long-only investments assume risks to be those of the market. To the extent that risks of the market are acceptable, the risks of such investments are also acceptable. However, hedge fund risks are dependent on the strategies that are employed. For Long-Term Capital Management, which blew up in 1998 and was the cause of an unprecedented intervention by the Federal Reserve for fear of a worldwide financial crisis, the risk was apparently much greater than expected by both its investors and its principals, including a couple of Nobel laureates. Not all hedge funds need to entail such catastrophic risks. In fact, if standard deviation of returns is used as the measure of risk, long/short equity funds as a group, according to CSFB/Tremont, have generated returns similar to those of the S&P 500 during the 1994–2003 period with about two-thirds of the S&P 500's risk. Similarly, distressed securities funds had less than half of the S&P 500's risk while generating 20 percent greater returns.

It is evident that not all hedge funds have the same risks and their risks vary with the strategies that they employ. It is therefore necessary to have an understanding of hedge fund strategies to know about their risks and return potential. We will return to this subject in Chapter 4, "The Skewed Statistics of Hedge Fund Returns."

HEDGE FUND STRATEGIES

Hedge funds are not as much a distinct asset class as a very different way of investing in stocks and bonds.[11] From the original hedge funds created by Alfred Winslow Jones, hedge funds have evolved and become virtually a catchall phraseology for any investment outside the traditional long-only stock and bond strategies as investors have known them. An example is one strategy that a fund of funds called "loan origination." It showed up as one of the underlying managers of this multibillion-dollar fund of hedge funds. Another fund of funds with $400 million under management invests 23 percent of its total capital in this strategy, and classified it under the fancy label "Private Credit Arbitrage." Hardly anything investors may conjure about hedge funds, this strategy actually involves short-term financing of inventory in transit to buyers. Because the borrowers have sub-prime credit ratings and are unable to obtain financing from traditional bank borrowings or capital market sources, the loans often carry interest charges far above prime rates, from the mid-teen percentages to the low twenties. They are also short-term, from 60 to 90 days. Furthermore, the buyers of the inventory that serves as collateral for the loans are often of prime credit. Questions can be asked about the so-called tail risks of these transactions or, as the head of a $600 million fund of funds that is part of one of the country's largest insurance companies pondered, "Where did this merchandise come from?" Importantly, are these investments legitimately hedge funds? In other words, do they generate alpha? Or are the seemingly excess returns in fact risk premiums for illiquidity and subprime credits?

Another group of funds more familiar to investors are Commodity Trading Advisors (CTAs), which have become an accepted hedge fund strategy. These managers do not hedge anything. In fact, regulators call them speculators. They make money by buying and selling commodities such as gold and silver, and financial instruments such as stock indexes like the S&P 500. But they do not own what they sell, nor do they take delivery of anything they buy. On their books are promises to buy or sell commodities at some future dates. However, they always cash in before the delivery dates to book the profits or accept the losses if these become unbearable. On both sides of the trades, they expect their long holdings to rise in prices, and their short positions to go down. In short, the strategy is a two-way bet on the financial and commodity markets. Since CTAs have historically produced returns that have low correlation to the stock and bond markets, they have nevertheless become part of the hedge fund landscape.

The changing landscape of the hedge fund industry is further accelerated by the flight of money managers from financial institutions, aided by their newfound wealth from the extraordinary bull run of the equity market in the 1990s. Among these new managers are proprietary traders from investment banks who made huge profits for their former employers with specialized trading strategies. Those with track records of consistently making money left their employers' proprietary trading desks, set up hedge funds, and applied the same trading strategies with investor assets. Though these strategies navigate the stock, bond, and currency markets, they trade frequently with high turnover rates and employ leverage to increase returns. Some strategies also stack layer upon layer of derivatives, carrying names like "swaptions," on top of ordinary stocks and bonds to manage risks code-named in Greek letters such as gamma or delta. Except for the Nobel laureates, the leaders of Long-Term Capital Management came from this proprietary trading background.

The proliferation of hedge funds underlies a hedge fund database publisher's characterization of them "as varied as the animals in the African jungle." As a result, no two individual hedge funds are alike, even if they purport to employ similar strategies. Given these variations, it is not easy to classify hedge funds into neat style boxes. Nevertheless, as a starting point, we can discuss hedge funds by using the classification scheme of the CSFB/Tremont Hedge Fund Index and subindexes. (See their web site at www.hedgeindex.com.) As the first asset-weighted hedge fund indexes, they are created from the TASS database of more than 3,000 hedge funds. Only more than 400 funds met the selection criteria of having at least $10 million under management and providing audited financial statements. They are requalified quarterly to assure compliance.

CSFB/Tremont Hedge Fund Indexes

The composite of all hedge fund styles is the CSFB/Tremont Hedge Fund Index, hereafter abbreviated as the CSFB Hedge Index. It contains 10 different styles as shown in Figure 3.2. One of these styles, Event Driven, is divided into three subindexes: Distressed Securities, Multi-Strategy, and Risk Arbitrage.

Only 8.1 percent of the assets of the hedge funds in the CSFB Hedge Index are dedicated to purely fixed income. All of the other strategies are substantially equity-oriented or involved in the global equity markets to some extent. The largest components are in equity strategies, which include Long/Short Equity, Equity Market Neutral, and Event Driven, although the last one can engage in fixed-income trades. These three strategies account for 51 percent of the CSFB Hedge Index.

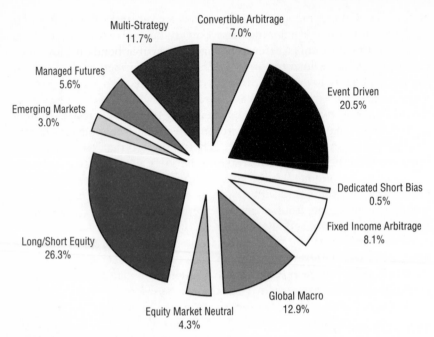

Multi-Strategy 11.7%

Convertible Arbitrage 7.0%

Managed Futures 5.6%

Emerging Markets 3.0%

Event Driven 20.5%

Dedicated Short Bias 0.5%

Fixed Income Arbitrage 8.1%

Long/Short Equity 26.3%

Global Macro 12.9%

Equity Market Neutral 4.3%

FIGURE 3.2 CSFB/Tremont Hedge Fund Indexes
Source: CSFB/Tremont.

Convertible Arbitrage

Convertible Arb hedge funds seek to exploit mispricings of any corporate securities that are convertible into stocks, including convertible bonds, convertible preferred, and warrants. Convertible bonds are fixed-income securities with an equity component. If the underlying stock increases in value, the convertible bond's price also appreciates because the bondholder can convert the bond into the rising stock. Conversely, if the stock declines in value, the price of the convertible bond also goes down, to a level at which the bond behaves like a straight bond. If the stock does well, the convertible bond behaves like a stock; if the stock does poorly, the convertible bond behaves like distressed debt.

The strategy involves buying convertible securities, then selling the underlying stocks to hedge against the risk caused by movements in the stock prices. The hedge ratio may be substantially less than 100 percent, thus leaving the positions exposed to the equity risks. Usually, managers also employ leverage, often to several times the amounts of the base capital, thus further magnifying the equity risks of the underlying securities. Like all fixed-income securities, convertible bonds are subject to the fluctuations of the general levels of interest rates. They are also exposed to the credit risks of the issuing corporations. Though convertible bonds mostly carry credit ratings below investment grade, the default risks of Convertible Arb funds are actually lower than the bond ratings to the extent of the equity short hedges. This is because in case of bankruptcy, the values of the stocks would go down to zero while the bonds usually retain some residual value.

There are two principal ways to generate alpha from convertible arb. One is from superior credit analysis, thereby detecting the underpricings of the convertible bonds. The other is from the mispricings of the conversion values of the underlying stocks. In periods of volatility in the capital markets, volatility traders exploit these short-term mispricings in otherwise directionless market environments, especially when credits are fairly priced. However, in generally bullish equity markets, Convertible Arb funds that are less than 100 percent hedged would ride on the back of the rising stock market to generate returns. Of course, such funds would fall harder when the stock market declines. Convertible bonds would also do well when interest rates decline because convertibles are long-duration bonds.

Dedicated Short Bias

Short sellers profit from the declines in the prices of securities they sold but did not own. They sell securities that they borrow from third parties, and hope to buy these securities back in the open market at lower prices. Then they return the borrowed securities to the third parties, pocketing profits in the meantime. Of course, the purchase prices may be higher than the sale prices, resulting in losses to the short sellers.

To accomplish short selling, traders must post margin in cash or securities with their brokers, and must add to this margin if the underlying securities rise in price. As such, when the general market condition improves and stock prices go up, requiring the posting of larger margins by short sellers, the pressure on them to liquidate their short positions can mount to unbearable levels. Such was the situation facing short sellers during the long bull run in the equity market. As a result, nowadays it is rare that short-selling hedge funds are 100 percent short. They are now short biased, meaning they hold both long and short positions and the short side exceeds the long.

Emerging Markets

Emerging Markets hedge funds invest in stocks and bonds of countries in Latin America, Africa, parts of Asia, Eastern Europe, and the former

Soviet Union. The credits of the issuers from these regions, including government entities, often carry ratings at par with U.S. high-yield or junk bonds. Aside from the usual risks stemming from markets, company fundamentals, credits, and interest rates, these securities are also subject to risks that are inherent in the unstable government policies prevalent in these less-developed capital markets. A recurrent theme in Latin American countries has been sudden currency devaluations. Defaults on government debts to foreign investors have happened in Russia in 1998 and all too often been a real threat in Venezuela, Brazil, and other countries. Exchange controls that were rampant during the 1997 Asian crisis are often urged by the International Monetary Fund upon foreign governments in times of debt crisis. Furthermore, many emerging markets countries do not have viable derivatives and futures markets, either regulated or over-the-counter among banks and brokers. Short selling is also not allowed. As a result, Emerging Markets hedge funds employ mostly long-only strategies.

Long/Short Equity

The Long/Short Equity strategy includes hedge funds specializing in holding long and short positions in U.S. stocks. Long/Short Equity managers go long the stocks they expect to rise and sell short those stocks they believe will either decline or appreciate less than their long holdings. Conversely, the long positions may decline in price while the shorts decline to an even greater extent, producing a net profit for the portfolio.

Long/Short Equity funds seek to reduce the overall market exposures of the hedge fund portfolios. However, returns can be generated from both the long and the short sides. This is because, given superior stock selection, long positions may appreciate while at the same time short positions may decline. These two-directional bets can occur if the long and short stocks belong to different sectors; have different fundamentals, such as earnings growth; or respond differently to market forces, including interest rates and economic growth or lack thereof. Thus, it may very well occur that the shorts actually rise in value while the long positions decline. Consequently, poor stock selection may lead to the risk of a long/short equity portfolio being greater than that of a long-only fund.

However, superior stock selection and effective risk management allow a long/short fund to hedge away the systematic risk of the market while potentially benefiting from the appreciation of the long positions to a greater extent than any losses on the short side. To reduce the risks of two-directional bets, certain hedge funds employ pairings and other strategies to match up the characteristics of the long and short stocks. Thus, long positions would be matched up against shorts of companies in the same sectors, thereby reducing risks from sector as well as market factors.

Long positions in Long/Short Equity are usually larger than the short positions. Typically these funds are not net short; that is, the short amounts are smaller than the longs. If they are net short, though, they behave like short sellers. Nor would they hold equal dollar amounts on both the long and short sides. If such a posture is maintained, the strategy is called Equity Market Neutral.

Equity Market Neutral

Equity Market Neutral hedge funds seek to generate returns from the differentiated performances of their long and short stock holdings while neutralizing the systematic risk of the market.

Typically, these funds maintain a permanent posture of equal dollar amounts on both the long and short sides. This is the dollar neutral strategy. A zero-beta strategy seeks a total offset of the beta of the long side by an equal amount of beta on the short side. If coupled with pairings (the practice of matching longs with shorts of the same industry sectors), zero-beta equity market neutral funds would minimize the systematic market risk as well as factor risks including interest rates that may affect various sectors differently.

Fixed Income Arbitrage

In general, Fixed Income Arbitrage is a strategy that seeks to profit from mispricings among similar fixed income securities. Like their equity counterparts, Fixed Income Arb hedge funds may employ relative value or market neutral strategies. Market neutrality seeks to eliminate risks from interest-rate fluctuations. Such neutrality is measured by interest-rate duration, which by itself can be mathematically calculated in significantly different ways. Relative value funds, by contrast, aim at diversified risk profiles without systematically targeting duration neutrality.

Fixed Income Arb is a generic description of a wide range of strategies in different sectors of the fixed income market. Common strategies include yield curve arbitrage, corporate versus Treasury spreads, cash versus futures, and U.S. versus non-U.S. government bonds. Other varieties are interest rate swap arbitrage, forward yield curve arbitrage, and mortgage-backed securities (MBS) arbitrage.

Mortgage-backed arb funds seek pricing inefficiencies in the primarily U.S.-based mortgage-backed securities markets. These pricing anomalies can be substantial. Most funds focus on AAA-rated bonds, but others exploit the illiquid niches of nonrated MBSs. Mortgage-backed issues include government agency, government-sponsored enterprise, private-label fixed-rate or adjustable-rate mortgage pass-through securities, fixed-rate or adjustable-rate collateralized mortgage obligations (CMOs), real estate mortgage investment conduits (REMICs), and stripped mortgage-backed securities (SMBSs).

Event Driven

As the name implies, the Event Driven strategy seeks to capture profits generated from price movements of securities of companies experiencing significant corporate events. Common events are mergers, combinations, or acquisitions. Other transactional events include bankruptcies, corporate restructurings, share buybacks, and spin-offs. The securities in these Event Driven transactions include common and preferred stocks as well as debt securities and options.

Leverage may be used by some funds. Managers may hedge against market risk by purchasing S&P put options or put option spreads. Like Long/Short Equity or Equity Market Neutral hedge funds, Event Driven funds structure long and short positions depending on their evaluation of the relative performances of the individual securities, and their success depends on their ability to assess the probability of failure or success of these corporate events. Event Driven funds may use derivatives such as options as lower-risk alternatives to outright purchases or sales of securities. There are several subcategories of Event Driven strategies: risk (merger) arbitrage, distressed/high-yield securities, Regulation D, and multistrategy.

Risk or Merger Arbitrage   Risk Arb funds simultaneously go long and go short in the companies involved in a merger or acquisition.

Typically the trades are long in the stock of the company being acquired and short in the stock of the acquirer. The objective is to capture the price spread between the current market price of the targeted company and the price offered by the acquiring firm. By shorting the stock of the acquirer, the market risk is hedged out, and the trade's exposure is limited to the outcome of the announced deal. The principal risk is deal risk: Should the deal fail to close, the trade would lose. For this reason, Risk Arb funds that are skeptical of the deal may go long the would-be acquirer and go short the target. As in the General Electric and Honeywell proposed acquisition in 2002, which was rejected by the European Commission, some hedge funds shorted Honeywell and went long GE, booking profits when the deal fell through. Risk Arb funds also invest in equity restructurings such as spin-offs, leveraged buyouts, and hostile takeovers.

Distressed Securities As a specialized Event Driven strategy, these hedge funds invest in securities of companies in some form of financial distress such as reorganizations, bankruptcies, distressed sales, and other corporate restructurings. They may go long or short these securities, which range from publicly traded corporate bonds to bank debts, trade claims, common stock, preferred stock, and warrants. The strategy may be subcategorized as high-yield or orphan equities. Leverage may be used, and some funds put on market hedges using options on the S&P or financial futures.

Companies in financial distress typically need legal action or restructurings to restore financial viability. Their securities trade at substantial discounts to par value because of difficulties in calculating their fair values, lack of street analysts' coverage, or an inability by traditional investors to manage their legal interests during restructuring proceedings. As a result, these distressed securities present opportunities for substantial profits if hedge fund managers with specialized skills in law, corporate finance, and investment banking can discover the underlying values and steer the turnarounds in their favor. A typical strategy consists of buying the distressed securities, holding them through the whole restructuring process, and selling them after they have recovered to a point closer to fair values. Managers may also take arbitrage positions within a company's capital structure, typically by purchasing a senior debt and short selling its common stock, in the hope of realizing returns from shifts in the spread between the two securities.

Regulation D or Reg. D The Reg. D subset, which includes private investments in public entities (PIPEs), refers to investments in micro and small capitalization public companies that are raising money in private capital markets. These investments usually take the form of a convertible security with an exercise price that floats or is subject to a look-back provision that insulates the investor from a decline in the price of the underlying stock. This means that the exercise or conversion price is reset as the stock price declines, granting more stock to the PIPE investor.

As such, Reg. D investors profit from arbitrage between the purchase price of a company's stock, which is issued at a discount by the company, and the sale price from short selling. However, some Reg. D players have been accused of stock manipulation by using this feature to engage in massive short selling of the stocks of small companies in dire financial need, driving their stocks further down. In a complaint against Rhino Advisors, the Securities and Exchange Commission gave an illuminating description of how Rhino allegedly drove down its target company's stock price from $1.43 a share and obtained a conversion price of as low as $0.64398.[12]

Event Driven Multistrategy   As implied by its name, these hedge funds navigate across the different strategies in the Event Driven category, from Risk Arb to Distressed Securities, and sometimes are involved in Reg. D transactions.

Global Macro

The world is indeed their oyster. Global Macro hedge funds face no limits on their strategies as they go long and short in stocks, bonds, currencies, and derivatives, including options and futures. They traverse national boundaries, investing among developed countries as well as emerging markets. They use leverage at will as the opportunities arise to increase returns. The best-known of them all is the Quantum Fund of the financier George Soros.

Unlike most other types of hedge funds, Global Macro managers rely on the top-down global approach to a worldview. They make forecasts on such developments as the world's economies, currency devaluations, government changes, political fortunes, or global imbalances in the supply and demand for key commodities. To effect these trades, Global Macro funds often use exchange-traded funds such as Spiders and over-the-counter derivatives such as forward foreign exchange contracts, rather than individual stocks and bonds.

Managed Futures

These funds are required by regulatory authorities including the Commodity Futures Exchange Commission to register as Commodity Trading Advisors (CTAs), and sometimes as Commodity Pool Operators (CPOs). They trade mostly on regulated exchanges in financial and commodity futures, but also in over-the-counter markets of banks and brokers.

They employ leverage by the use of margin or derivatives. They are referred to as systematic traders if they use computer-generated signals that are derived from technical analyses of price movements. Discretionary managers rely on judgment to put on positions or liquidate them, though they also depend on technical analysis. In either case, they are mostly momentum players, riding on trends in the financial and commodity markets. They get stopped out—that is, they take losses or profits prematurely— when the anticipated trends fail to materialize and possibly reverse. They trade frequently and observe strict rules in profit taking or liquidating positions, especially if certain limits of losses have been hit or surpassed. Some CTAs specialize in very short-term trades, being content with small amounts of profit from small price movements while attempting to limit losses from individual trades.

Multi-Strategy

This is a catchall category for hedge funds that employ a multitude of the other strategies. These funds employ portfolio managers who are specialists in any of the aforementioned disciplines. Their success therefore depends not only on the performances of their individual portfolio managers, but also on their ability to allocate capital to these managers. Thus, Multi-Strategy funds share certain similarities with another category of hedge funds: funds of hedge funds. Funds of funds also allocate investor capital to third-party hedge funds, and charge an additional layer of fees on top of those levied by the third-party managers. Like Multi-Strategy funds, funds of funds depend on a stable of hedge funds of different strategies to generate performances. We will return to the subject of funds of funds in Chapter 10.

Figure 3.3 shows the percentages of assets under management by dif-

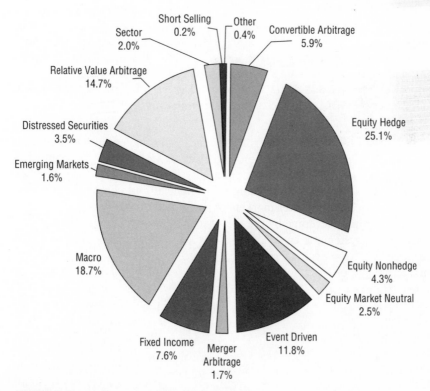

FIGURE 3.3 Hedge Fund Research Indexes
Source: "Macro Hedge Funds Return to Favour," *Financial Times*, February 9, 2004.

ferent strategies as of the end of 2003, as estimated by Hedge Fund Research. HFR figures also include predominantly long-only fixed income and equity hedge funds. Nevertheless, similar to the CSFB Hedge Index, HFR data shows the dominance of equity strategies and the relative small asset base of fixed-income hedge funds. Including even mostly long mortgage-backed and high-yield securities, fixed-income funds accounted for only 7.6 percent in the HFR. The HFR figures include the assets in relative value arbitrage hedge funds that classify themselves as such. These usually are hedge funds that engage in paired trades, options arbitrage, and yield-curve trading across markets in equities, debts, options, and futures. As such, they seek price anomalies not only among securities but also in groups of securities or in the overall market.

PERFORMANCE OF HEDGE FUNDS

In the previous chapter, hedge funds as a group were shown to generate returns not dissimilar from the S&P 500 over the full market cycle of rising markets in the 1990s and the 2000–2002 bear market. However, hedge funds' performances vary vastly across different strategies, time periods, and managers. Most notably, as shown in Table 3.2, during the three years of bear market of 2000–2002, in different degrees, all of the CSFB/Tremont indexes outperformed the U.S. and world equity markets.

Bear Market Returns

Remarkably, when any of these indexes suffered negative returns, the losses were relatively small compared to the declines in the equity markets. This is shown in Table 3.2.

Several strategies stood out even more: Equity Market Neutral and those engaged in multiple strategies that could diversify across different market sectors and strategies. Global Macro, which navigates in markets around the world, generated strong positive returns and even outperformed the historically bear market safe haven, the Lehman Aggregate Bond Index. The Multi-Strategy index also posted respectable results vis-à-vis the bond index while outperforming the S&P 500 by wide margins. Fixed Income Arb and Convertible Arb, both of which are fixed income oriented, also generated very strong returns during the long market decline. Remarkably, Equity Market Neutral produced consistently positive results and was quite competitive with the Lehman index even in a declining stock market.

Long/Short Equity and Event Driven, as well as the Event Driven substrategies, did not perform consistently during the bear market, as they were mostly equity oriented—although, as previously noted, they performed far

TABLE 3.2 Hedge Fund Returns in Equity Bear Markets

Index	Rate of Return		
	2002	2001	2000
CSFB/Tremont Hedge Fund Index	3.04%	4.42%	4.85%
Convertible Arbitrage	4.05	14.58	25.64
Dedicated Short Bias	18.14	−3.58	15.76
Emerging Markets	7.36	5.84	−5.52
Equity Market Neutral	7.42	9.31	14.99
Event Driven (E.D.)	0.16	11.50	7.26
E.D. Distressed Securities	−0.69	20.01	1.95
E.D. Multi-Strategy	1.22	6.79	11.84
E.D. Risk Arbitrage	−3.46	5.68	14.69
Fixed Income Arbitrage	5.75	8.04	6.29
Global Macro	14.66	18.38	11.67
Long/Short Equity	−1.60	−3.65	2.08
Managed Futures	18.33	1.90	4.24
Multi-Strategy	6.31	5.50	11.18
S&P 500	−22.10%	−11.89%	−9.10%
MSCI World Index	−19.54	−16.52	−12.92
Lehman Aggregate Bond Index	10.27	8.42	11.63

Sources: SCFB/Tremont, Standard & Poor's, PerTrac.

better than the S&P and MSCI indexes. Emerging Markets likewise did not record notable performances, although that strategy's access to wide-ranging markets sometimes allowed it to produce interesting returns.

The Dedicated Short Bias strategy also was capable of producing positive returns in stock market declines, although its record during the three-year bear market was not consistent. In rising stock markets this strategy, as its name suggests, produced mostly losses, sometimes catastrophic as in 2003. (See Table 3.3.) In contrast, there was no pattern in the performance record of Managed Futures, hence its historical virtually zero correlation with the S&P 500. However, this strategy produced good results only sporadically—in bear markets for stocks, as shown in Table 3.2, as well as in rising stock markets, shown in Table 3.3. No wonder this strategy and Dedicated Short Bias were the worst performers among the CSFB/Tremont indexes in their 10-year history.

Bull Markets

The best-performing hedge funds in rising equity markets were consistently those engaged in equity investing, such as Long/Short Equity and Event

TABLE 3.3 Hedge Fund Returns in Equity Bull Markets

Index	Rate of Return				
	2003	1999	1997	1996	1995
CSFB/Tremont Hedge Fund Index	15.44%	23.43%	25.94%	22.22%	21.69%
Convertible Arbitrage	12.90	16.04	14.48	17.87	16.57
Dedicated Short Bias	−32.59	−14.22	0.42	−5.48	−7.35
Emerging Markets	28.75	44.82	26.59	34.50	−16.90
Equity Market Neutral	7.07	15.33	14.83	16.60	11.04
Event Driven	20.02	22.26	19.96	23.06	18.34
E.D. Distressed Securities	25.12	22.18	20.73	25.55	26.21
E.D. Multi-Strategy	17.19	23.00	20.53	22.71	12.91
E.D. Risk Arbitrage	8.98	13.23	9.84	13.81	11.90
Fixed Income Arbitrage	7.97	12.11	9.34	15.93	12.50
Global Macro	17.99	5.81	37.11	25.58	30.67
Long/Short Equity	17.27	47.23	21.46	17.12	23.03
Managed Futures	14.13	−4.69	3.12	11.97	−7.10
Multi-Strategy	15.04	9.38	18.28	14.06	11.87
S&P 500	28.68%	21.04%	33.36%	22.96%	37.58%
MSCI World Index	33.76	25.34	16.23	14.00	21.32
Lehman Aggregate Bond Index	4.11	−0.83	9.68	3.61	18.48

Sources: CSFB/Tremont, Standard & Poor's, PerTrac.

Driven. (See Table 3.4.) Those that had access to world markets were capable of producing very large gains, as did Global Macro in 1997 and Emerging Markets in 1996 and 1999.

Multi-Strategy and Equity Market Neutral were not far behind. The consistent records of these two strategies in both rising and declining markets have made them the mainstay of diversified hedge fund portfolios such as funds of hedge funds. Convertible Arb with its equity exposure likewise posted respectable returns during 1995–1999 as well as 2003. Funds of funds also like Convertible Arb for its ability to act like a fixed income hedge strategy or alternatively as an equity player in varying market conditions. The Fixed Income Arbitrage strategy also posted good results in years of rising stock markets, although its returns lagged those with equity market exposures.

Thus, except for Managed Futures and short selling strategies, hedge funds have demonstrated a track record of strong positive returns in bullish equity market environments, although they generally fell behind long-only equity strategies as represented by such indexes as the S&P 500.

Times of Crisis

The bear market for hedge funds comes about in times of crisis in the capital markets. In recent history 1998 was a good example. Briefly, the Asian crisis prompted the Federal Reserve to cut interest rates sharply, in an effort to pump liquidity into the financial system. Though beneficial to the capital markets, the sudden and large declines of interest rates led to the widening in the yield differentials between Treasuries and securities of lesser quality such as corporate bonds. Since hedge funds rely on these yield differentials to be stable or narrowing to generate profits, the spread widening caused problems for hedge funds, especially those engaged in fixed income arbitrage. The collapse of Long-Term Capital Management was the headline example in this crisis environment. The threat to the stability of the global financial markets also wreaked havoc on the equity markets worldwide.

Table 3.4 shows the returns of hedge funds in the third quarter of 1998. August 1998 was clearly not a good month for most hedge fund strategies. Nor was it a good period for the U.S. and foreign stock markets, as evidenced

TABLE 3.4 Hedge Fund Returns in a Market Crisis—I

Index	1998				
	July	Aug.	Sept.	Oct.	Year
CSFB/Tremont Hedge Fund Index	0.90%	−7.55%	−2.31%	−4.57%	−0.36%
Convertible Arbitrage	0.52	−4.64	−3.23	−4.68	−4.41
Dedicated Short Bias	2.72	22.71	−4.98	−8.69	−6.00
Emerging Markets	0.08	−23.03	−7.40	1.68	−37.66
Equity Market Neutral	−0.10	−0.85	0.95	2.38	13.31
Event Driven	0.04	−11.77	−2.96	0.66	−4.87
E.D. Distressed Securities	0.39	−12.45	−1.43	0.89	−1.68
E.D. Multi-Strategy	−0.27	−11.52	−4.74	0.26	−8.98
E.D. Risk Arbitrage	−0.37	−6.15	−0.65	2.41	5.58
Fixed Income Arbitrage	0.48	−1.46	−3.74	−6.96	−8.16
Global Macro	1.80	−4.84	−5.12	11.55	−3.64
Long/Short Equity	0.61	−11.43	3.47	1.74	17.18
Managed Futures	−1.12	9.95	6.87	−4.76	20.64
Multi-Strategy	0.70	1.15	0.57	1.21	7.68
S&P 500	−1.06%	−14.46%	6.41%	8.03%	28.58%
MSCI World Index ex-U.S.	0.65	−12.77	−2.86	10.41	24.80
Lehman Aggregate Bond Index	0.21	1.63	2.34	−0.53	8.67

Sources: CSFB/Tremont, Standard & Poor's, PerTrac.

by the losses recorded by the S&P 500 and the MSCI World Index ex-U.S. As a consequence, hardest hit were those engaged in equity trading. Even Fixed Income Arbitrage suffered from the lingering effects of the crisis despite the lower interest rate environment. Only such predominantly directional strategies as Dedicated Short Bias and Managed Futures were able to take advantage of the declines in the prices of stock and non-Treasury securities.

The year 1994 was another year best forgotten for hedge funds. The sudden and sharp increase of interest rates begun by the Federal Reserve in February 1994 sent interest rates rocketing higher and the stock and bond markets worldwide into a tailspin. This is shown in Table 3.5.

For hedge funds, though the bulk of the impact was felt in the year's early months, they never quite recovered from the shock. As a result, the CSFB/Tremont Hedge Fund Index posted a loss of 4.36 percent for the year. Worst-performing strategies were Long/Short Equity, Convertible Arbitrage, and Global Macro. Fixed Income Arb stood out as it recorded a small gain despite losses early in the year. The strategies performing best in that year were Dedicated Short Bias, Emerging Markets, and Managed Futures.

TABLE 3.5   Hedge Fund Returns in a Market Crisis—II

| | 1994 | | | |
Index	Feb.	March	April	Year
CSFB/Tremont Hedge Fund Index	−4.09%	−3.57%	−1.74%	−4.36%
Convertible Arbitrage	0.15	−0.97	−2.52	−8.07
Dedicated Short Bias	2.00	7.19	1.28	14.91
Emerging Markets	−1.14	−4.61	−8.36	12.51
Equity Market Neutral	0.24	−0.24	0.25	−2.00
Event Driven	−0.15	−1.29	−0.66	0.75
E.D. Distressed Securities	−0.34	−1.83	−0.71	0.67
E.D. Multi-Strategy	0.11	−0.83	−0.57	0.62
E.D. Risk Arbitrage	−0.44	1.86	−0.96	5.25
Fixed Income Arbitrage	−2.00	−1.68	−0.20	0.31
Global Macro	−5.65	−4.27	−1.59	−5.72
Long/Short Equity	−2.47	−3.90	−1.56	−8.10
Managed Futures	1.20	2.60	0.86	11.95
Multi-Strategy	0.23	1.86	1.70	NA
S&P 500	−3.00%	−4.57%	1.15%	1.32%
MSCI World Index ex-U.S.	−0.45	−4.30	4.05	5.58
Lehman Aggregate Bond Index	−1.74	−2.47	−0.80	−2.92

Sources: SCFB/Tremont, Standard & Poors, PerTrac.

Low and High Volatility

The 2000–2002 equity bear market gave rise to greater investor interest in hedge funds. In response to this demand, a crop of funds of funds was launched, investing primarily in hedge funds that employ strategies with low volatility while producing good returns. Table 3.6 classifies hedge fund strategies in accordance with their volatilities.

Clearly the high-volatility strategies tend to engage in directional bets, whether in emerging markets or in long/short equity trading. The low-volatility strategies are mostly in fixed income and their historical volatilities are either lower or not much higher than the Lehman Aggregate Bond Index. The one standout is Equity Market Neutral with the

TABLE 3.6   Low- and High-Volatility Hedge Funds

	Standard Deviation 1994–2003	Annualized Return 2000–2002
CSFB/Tremont Hedge Fund Index		
High Volatility		
Global Macro	11.83%	14.87%
Long/Short Equity	10.78	–1.08
Managed Futures	12.26	7.92
Dedicated Short Bias	17.67	9.66
Emerging Markets	17.41	2.39
Low Volatility		
Equity Market Neutral	3.04%	10.53%
Fixed Income Arbitrage	3.88	6.69
Multi-Strategy	4.46	7.63
Convertible Arbitrage	4.74	14.42
Intermediate Volatility		
Event Driven	5.91%	6.20%
E.D. Distressed	6.84	6.71
E.D. Multi-Strategy	6.23	6.53
E.D. Risk Arbitrage	4.37	5.38
CSFB/Tremont Hedge Fund Index	8.31%	4.10%
Lehman Aggregate Bond Index	3.97	10.10
S&P 500	15.50	–14.55
MSCI World Index	14.43	–16.37

Sources: CSFB/Tremont, Standard & Poors, Pertrac.

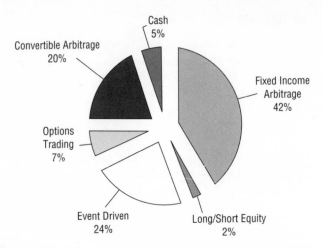

FIGURE 3.4   Allocations of a Low-Volatility Fund of Funds, July 2003

lowest volatility among all strategies. Those strategies in the Event Driven category experience volatilities in the intermediate range, although they, too, seek to arbitrage away the market's systematic risk.

Unsurprisingly, the funds of funds that seek low volatility concentrate their investments in low-volatility strategies. Equally notable is that they prefer Fixed Income Arbitrage and Convertible Arbitrage strategies, as many of them allocate few assets to Equity Market Neutral, which is structured to neutralize and hedge away the systematic risk of market fluctuations. Not unlike the behavior of traditional long-only investors who shy away from stocks and seek safety in bonds in an uncertain equity environment, these funds of funds avoid anything related to the equity market. Thus they avoid Long/Short Equity and similar high-volatility strategies. For illustration, Figure 3.4 shows the actual hedge fund strategy allocations of a low-volatility fund of funds in July 2003.

This chapter has provided an overview of the hedge fund industry and its investors. We also have described the structure of hedge funds and the different strategies in some detail, as well as their performances in various market conditions. We now turn to a review of the analytical methodologies that help evaluate them and assess their return and risk characteristics, for the simple reason that the conventional methods traditionally used for long-only strategies are less applicable to hedge funds. This will be discussed in Chapter 4.

TWO

Evaluating and Selecting Hedge Funds

In Part One we discussed the misconceptions about long-term investing and diversification in asset allocation and how hedge funds can fill the void left open by traditional long-only investments to achieve long-term investment objectives with lower volatility. But hedge funds are not for everyone, and much needs to be investigated beneath the surface of impressive claims and statistics expressed in Greek letters. Though hedge fund managers will likely not agree that "[m]aybe hedge funds aren't so different from the market after all,"[1] the risk and return characteristics of hedge funds are not well understood, sometimes even by those who manage or sell them to investors. This is partly because return and risk data on hedge fund indexes are rife with flaws and questions. The analytical tools that have often been used to assess hedge fund risks are also not adequate to fairly estimate their potential risks. For hedge funds to be properly and effectively evaluated, it is therefore essential to seek a better understanding of the risk characteristics and the limits of the return potential of hedge funds. These issues will be the subjects of Chapter 4. Chapter 5 deals with evaluating hedge fund strategies. In Chapter 6, the focus is on the analysis, evaluation, and selection of individual hedge funds. The selected hedge funds then need to be assembled so as to produce the targeted returns and risks. This will be discussed in Chapter 7.

To achieve the desired benefits, hedge funds need to be assembled into diversified portfolios. This involves three distinct phases. First, the investors need to identify the fund managers and evaluate their strategies. The better a hedge fund's strategy is understood and evaluated, the better grasp investors would have of the potential return and risk of the fund. This is the manager research and evaluation phase. Once a number of hedge funds have been selected, next is the task of allocating the investment capital to these managers. This is the portfolio construction phase. After the portfolio of hedge funds is in place, the performances and risks of the funds in the portfolio need to be measured, evaluated, assessed, and monitored on an ongoing basis. This is the performance evaluation and risk management part of the cycle. The diagram illustrates the interlocking nature of these three phases.

As the cycle evolves, information and knowledge gained in each phase will be brought to bear on the evaluation and decisions that take place throughout the entire process. Thus, as the performances and risks of the strategies of the managers in the portfolio are evaluated in the context of

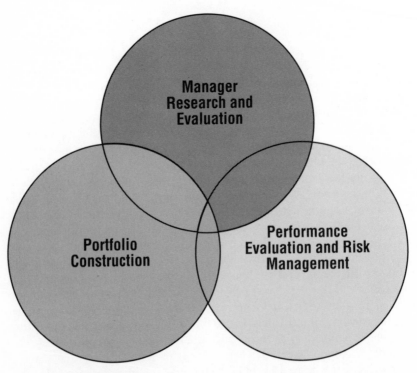

The Cycle of Hedge Fund Investing

real-life portfolios, changes in the composition of the portfolios would occur, new managers may be added and existing managers may be replaced, or new money may be allocated to them.

Part Two of the book is devoted to the issues concerning manager research and evaluation and portfolio construction. The issues of performance evaluation and risk management are discussed in Part Three.

CHAPTER 4

The Skewed Statistics
of Hedge Fund Returns

Past Results Are Not Necessarily Indicative
of Future Performances

Attracted by hedge funds' strong returns during the three-year equity bear market, investors flocked to hedge funds in 2003. Looking over the longer term, they were impressed by studies and analyses showing that hedge funds have produced better risk-adjusted returns than stocks and bonds. Armed with the teachings of modern portfolio theory and statistics such as standard deviation and Sharpe ratio, analysts pored over the records of hedge fund indexes provided by CSFB/Tremont, Hedge Fund Research, TASS, and others. The conclusions were seemingly inescapable. Over time, hedge funds, so said the indexes, have produced returns similar to—and sometimes higher than—those of the major stock market indexes such as the S&P 500, while exhibiting lower volatility of returns. Outperformances of hedge funds would have been higher if transaction costs and management fees had been deducted from the S&P index's returns because hedge fund returns were net of all expenses and fees. Furthermore, hedge funds exhibited low correlation with the stock market, meaning they were capable of producing positive returns even when the stock market declined.

The combination of similar returns and lower risk (therefore higher risk-adjusted returns), coupled with low correlation, acts as a powerful rationale for investing in hedge funds. Why would anyone not prefer lower risks for similar and often higher returns? Adding hedge funds to existing traditional stock and bond portfolios would accordingly increase returns and at the same time reduce the volatility of portfolio returns. Alas, as it turns out, this was only part of the story.

The media has circulated headlines such as "Hedge Funds May Give Colleges Painful Lessons."[1] Certainly, the story of the collapse of Long-Term Capital Management with its Nobel Prize winners has been etched into the collective memory of the investing public. In the past few years, researchers in academia as well as industry practitioners have scrutinized the historical data on hedge fund returns and have found increasing evidence that the potential for such disastrous losses is real and ever present. Looking beyond the standard deviation, they use obscure statistics such as "negative skew," "high kurtosis," and "fat tails" to prove that in fact the risks of hedge funds are prospectively higher than the standard deviations of hedge fund indexes are purported to show, and that investors may be tempted to overallocate to hedge funds if their decisions are based on only risks measured by standard deviations.

Additionally, researchers have estimated that hedge fund returns as reported in the indexes supplied by CSFB/Tremont, Hedge Fund Research, and other database providers were overstated. This was not as much the fault of these vendors, for these return figures were supplied to them by hedge fund managers, as the problem was that these numbers were voluntarily reported and there was a lack of standard disclosures required of hedge fund managers.

If in fact hedge funds are riskier and their returns are lower than reported, is the case for diversification into hedge funds undermined? A short answer is that evidence continues to show the advantages of diversification into hedge funds. However, the overall benefits are not as much or as straightforward as analyses with hedge fund indexes and the mean-variance framework, which used standard deviation as the measure of risk, would indicate.

In this chapter we examine these issues and attempt to shed light on the kinds of risks that should concern investors.

PERCEPTION OF RISKS: NUMBERS AND REALITY

The claim that, overall, hedge funds have lower risks than equities, using the S&P 500 as proxy, rests solely on one statistical measure called standard deviation. An offshoot of this measure is the Sharpe ratio. These statistics have been used to support the thesis that hedge funds provide superior risk-adjusted performance. So favorable to the case for hedge funds are they that they have become buzzwords in hedge fund shop talk. It is therefore useful to review exactly what they mean, and whether they do measure what they are said to measure.

Standard Deviation Is Not Adequate

Standard deviation is a statistical measure familiar to anyone taking first-year statistics. Used as a measure of the risk of investing in risky assets, it is a pillar of an analytical approach called modern portfolio theory (MPT) that was developed half a century ago by Harry Markowitz,[2] a professor of economics at the University of Chicago who later won a Nobel Prize for his work. Although the tenets of MPT and the related principles have been part of the investment landscape for quite some time, never before have their Greek letters been used with such flourish.

MPT assumes that the returns of a security or portfolio can be described graphically in the form of a symmetrical bell-shaped curve called normal distribution, as illustrated in Figure 4.1.

Any normal distribution can be mathematically defined by two measures: the arithmetic or simple average and the standard deviation. A key characteristic of a normal distribution is that there are equal chances for a return to be greater or smaller than the average by the same amounts. For example, if the average return is 10 percent and standard deviation is 17 percent, there is a 68.3 percent chance that an actual return will be no more than 27 percent (average of 10 percent plus one standard deviation of 17 percent) and no less than a loss of 7 percent (average of 10 percent minus one standard deviation of 17 percent). Alternatively, there is a 31.7 percent chance that either the loss will be more than 7 percent or the return will be greater than 27 percent. In academia, the common way to express this probabilistic statement is to say that there is a 68.3 percent chance that the return will be between –7 and +27 percent. Likewise, there is a 95.4 percent chance that the returns will fall within two standard deviations from the average, or between a loss of 14 percent and a gain of 34 percent.

The average return of a stock over 5 years is simply derived by adding the 5 annual returns and dividing the sum by 5. Subtracting this average

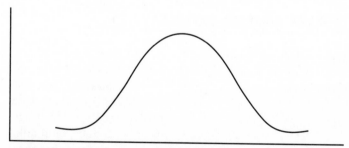

FIGURE 4.1   Shape of a Normal Distribution

from the 5 individual yearly returns, squaring the differences, adding them up, and dividing the sum by 5 would result in the value of the variance. The square root of the variance is the standard deviation. Thus the standard deviation measures the deviations from the simple, not compounded or geometric, average of a time series of investment returns. A fund producing a gain of 10 percent in one year and a loss of 10 percent in the next has an annualized average return of zero percent in the two-year period but a compound negative rate of return or a loss of 0.5 percent. It does not matter whether the deviations are positive or negative. Squared into positive numbers, "good" or better-than-average deviations are undifferentiated from "bad" or worse-than-average deviations.

Why Not Mean-Variance?

The problem is that the assumption of normal distribution in MPT has been found to be absent in the returns of hedge funds.

Negative Skew   If an asset's or fund's return distribution is nonnormal, the chances of actual returns to be above the average or below the average are unequal. If the chances for below-average returns are greater than the chances for above-average returns, the distribution is said to have negative skew, or it is negatively skewed. A nonnormal distribution with negative skew has higher probability of below-average returns than a normal distribution that has zero skew with the same standard deviation. The lower the skew (or the more the skew is negative), the greater the probability of below-average or negative returns, and vice versa. Figure 4.2 shows a nonnormal distribution with negative skew.

Research has shown that hedge fund returns are nonnormal and nega-

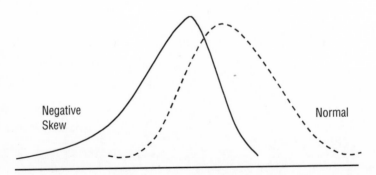

FIGURE 4.2   Distribution with Negative Skew

tively skewed. In other words, the standard deviation as a measure of risk understates the risk of losses of a hedge fund.

Excess Kurtosis   Furthermore, the average of a hedge fund's returns may be pushed higher by the presence of a few large returns. By themselves, these unusual high returns are not undesirable. It is another matter if the hedge fund's stream of past returns would consist of a few good years and mostly mediocrity and losses in other years. But the presence of a few good years, which are unlikely to be seen again, raises the average of a fund's past returns. In such a situation, the hedge fund return distribution is said to have high or excess kurtosis. The kurtosis of a normal distribution is 3; a value greater than 3 is excess kurtosis. As kurtosis of a nonnormal distribution is shown net of 3, excess kurtosis is represented by a value different than zero. Generally, a fund with negative skew and excess kurtosis would be riskier than a fund with the same standard deviation but smaller negative skew (or higher skew) and lower or neutral kurtosis. Thus, when a hedge fund is shown to have lower standard deviation than the S&P 500, it does not necessarily mean that it is less risky. Figure 4.3 illustrates a distribution with negative and excess kurtosis.

Negative Skew Suggests Higher Risks   A fund that has a track record of significantly negative skew is one that has instances of significant losses or gains that are significantly below the average. These instances of below-average returns or losses indicate the asymmetric nature of the fund's market niche. Or they signify that there are flaws in the fund's

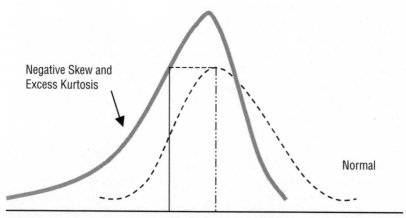

FIGURE 4.3   Negative Skew Plus High Excess Kurtosis

risk management or mistakes in trading, or the fund has taken excessive or above-normal risks.

A significantly positive skew is a signal that the fund's strategy and its execution have in a few instances worked to the advantage of the fund. In those instances, the fund's managers may have taken above-normal risks and the bets have paid off. Or some big moves occurred in the market and the managers, with exquisite timing, were able to take advantage of them and scored big profits. However, those nonnormal bets could have gone the other way and could have produced losses instead of gains.

Whether negative or positive, nonzero skew suggests that nonnormal risks have been taken by the managers. Negative skew is an *ex post* or after-the-fact proof that the bets have gone wrong. Positive skew would be used by the managers as a proof of their talent, without mentioning the nonnormal risks that they may have taken.

A Dangerous Combination   A fund can claim a perfectly respectable track record if it has above-average returns and a standard deviation within some acceptable range. Yet it can be very risky and dangerous to the financial health of unsuspecting investors if the fund's average has been boosted by a few instances of very large gains. Intuitively, it is easy to recognize that the few instances of very large gains would boost the average return of the fund and such large gains are not likely to occur again under normal circumstances. The instances of abnormal losses would show up in the negative skew, that is, in the form of a longer left-hand side of the distribution, as compared to the right-hand side. Because of the longer tail, negative skew is also referred to as the "left tail" risk.

The HFRI Fixed Income Mortgage-Backed Securities Arbitrage Index had a compounded annualized return of 10.8 percent during the January 1993 to June 2004 period, and a standard deviation of 4.2 percent. This would be a perfectly good track record, as its return was comparable with equities over the same period but with less than half of the volatility. However, the strategy had an exceptionally negative skew, at –4.2. The excess kurtosis was recorded at a very high 23.3 compared to zero for a normal distribution. To visualize the substantial "left tail" risk inherent in these numbers, consider the distribution of the monthly returns of this HFRI index shown in Figure 4.4.

Most of the time, the index produced good stable performance, punctuated by sudden and significant drawdowns. In half of its 138 months of history its monthly return exceeded 1 percent, and gains averaging 1.15 percent were recorded in 123 months. Yet losses in the other 15 months were large enough to bring the monthly average down to 0.8

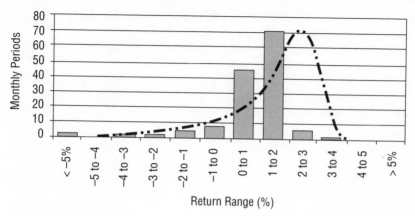

FIGURE 4.4 HFRI Mortgage-Backed Securities Arbitrage: Negative Skew and Excess Kurtosis
Sources: Hedge Fund Research, PerTrac.

percent. The largest consecutive losses totaled 13.48 percent for the 7 months between March and October 1998. In October alone, it lost 9.24 percent.

Similar, albeit smaller, deviations from normality were found in other hedge fund index databases. In a study covering the period between January 1995 and April 2001, Brooks and Kat (2002)[3] examined the returns and risk characteristics of hedge fund indexes published by Hedge Fund Research, Zurich Capital Markets (www.marhedge.com), CSFB/Tremont (www.hedgeindex.com), Hennessee Group (www.hennesseegroup.com), Van Hedge Fund Advisors (www.vanhedge.com), Altvest (www.altvest.com), and HedgeFund.net (www.hedgefund.net). The authors found that "all except the macro and emerging markets indices combine a relatively high mean with a relatively low standard deviation."[4] The authors observed, "This would be clear proof of market inefficiency were it not that compared to stocks and bonds many hedge-fund indices also exhibit relatively low skewness and high kurtosis. Especially convertible arbitrage, risk arbitrage, distressed securities, and emerging markets exhibit not only high negative skewness but also large excess kurtosis. This means that for these indices, large negative returns are much more likely than would be the case under normal distribution."[5]

Table 4.1 examines the monthly returns, standard deviations, skew, and kurtosis of the CSFB indexes, the S&P 500, and the Lehman

TABLE 4.1   Return and Risk: CSFB Hedge Fund Indexes, Stocks, and Bonds, January 1994–June 2004

Index	Mean	Standard Deviation	Skewness	Kurtosis	Annualized Standard Deviation
CSFB/Tremont Hedge Fund Index	0.89%	2.40%	0.10	1.90	8.31%
Convertible Arbitrage	0.81	1.37	−1.49	3.79	4.74
Dedicated Short Bias	−0.13	5.10	0.93	2.30	17.67
Emerging Markets	0.68	5.03	−0.58	3.91	17.41
Equity Market Neutral	0.83	0.88	0.25	0.27	3.04
Event Driven (E.D.)	0.92	1.71	−3.50	23.82	5.91
E.D. Distressed	1.07	1.97	−2.78	16.84	6.84
E.D. Multi-Strategy	0.83	1.80	−2.71	17.56	6.23
E.D. Risk Arbitrage	0.67	1.26	−1.32	6.49	4.37
Fixed Income Arbitrage	0.56	1.12	−3.28	17.07	3.88
Global Macro	1.17	3.42	−0.02	2.20	11.83
Long/Short Equity	0.98	3.11	0.24	3.57	10.78
Managed Futures	0.58	3.54	0.04	0.48	12.26
Multi-Strategy	0.77	1.29	−1.32	3.60	4.46
Lehman Aggregate Bond Index	0.54%	1.16%	−0.48	0.89	4.02%
S&P 500	0.81%	4.47%	−0.59	0.41	15.48%

Sources: CSFB/Tremont, PerTrac.

Aggregate Bond Index during the period between January 1994 and June 2004.

Event Driven and Fixed Income Arb strategies stand out as having the lowest negative skew and highest kurtosis. What this means is that although they exhibited similar or only slightly higher standard deviations than the Lehman Aggregate Bond Index, they were in fact far riskier.

The only strategy that was less volatile than the S&P and Lehman indexes yet with zero skew and kurtosis is Equity Market Neutral.[6] At the same time, it produced average returns very similar to the S&P, at 0.83 percent a month. Two other strategies have exhibited desirable risk characteristics: Global Macro and Long/Short Equity. They both have approximately zero skew and slightly elevated kurtosis, which are positive characteristics, while recording lower standard deviations than the S&P 500. Multi-Strategy and Convertible Arb have slightly negative skew, but their statistical risk profiles are improved by excess kurtosis and standard deviation comparable to that of the Lehman index.

Managed Futures showed no skew or kurtosis, suggesting its standard deviation fairly depicts its riskiness. The two mainly directional strategies in this hedge fund index series are Dedicated Short Bias and Emerging Markets. Unsurprisingly, they exhibited higher volatility, with some skew and excess kurtosis.

In summary, the data from the CSFB/Tremont hedge fund subindexes indicate that individual hedge fund strategies have recorded lower standard deviations than stocks. However, two broad groups of strategies, Event Driven and Fixed Income Arbitrage, have significantly negative skew combined with substantial excess kurtosis, indicating much higher risks than commonly expected. At the same time, the riskiness of Equity Market Neutral, Global Macro, Long/Short Equity, Multi-Strategy, and Convertible Arb, in that order, appeared to be fairly represented by their standard deviations.

Maximum Losses   Negative skew signifies nonnormal tail risks. However, it does not indicate the full extent of potential losses. For this, practitioners resort to a statistic called "maximum drawdown," which measures the maximum loss from the prior peak return. As shown in Table 4.2, during the January 1994–June 2004 period, the maximum drawdown experienced by the S&P 500 was 46.28 percent lasting for 25 months (as of June 2004 it had not recovered from this decline). The S&P's second largest drawdown was 15.57 percent during July–August 1998, and it took the index three months to recover to the prior peak.

In terms of risks of large drawdowns, the three worst strategies in Table 4.2 are the S&P 500, Dedicated Short Bias, and Emerging Markets. They have experienced the largest drawdowns, in addition to the highest standard deviations. The Event Driven strategy and its subcategories, though experiencing negative skew and high kurtosis, have not suffered drawdowns to the same extent. Fixed Income Arb has been riskier than indicated by its standard deviation, showing negative skew, high kurtosis, and much larger drawdowns than the Lehman Aggregate Bond Index. The only hedge fund strategy that exhibits lowest risk by any measure is Equity Market Neutral with insignificant drawdowns, virtually zero skew and kurtosis, as well as standard deviation lower than the Lehman Aggregate Bond Index and the S&P.

TABLE 4.2 Maximum Drawdowns: CSFB Hedge Fund Indexes, Stocks, and Bonds, 1994–2003

Index	Largest Drawdown	Length in Months	Time to Recover in Months	Second Largest Drawdown	Length in Months	Time to Recover in Months
CSFB/Tremont Hedge Fund Index	−13.81%	3	13	−9.13%	3	15
Convertible Arbitrage	−12.03	3	10	−9.10	11	7
Dedicated Short Bias	−44.37	67	NA	−23.33	45	5
Emerging Markets	−45.14	18	55	−28.60	6	21
Equity Market Neutral	−3.54	5	4	−1.15	1	1
Event Driven	−16.05	5	10	−6.04	5	4
E.D. Distressed	−14.33	5	8	−8.53	5	4
E.D. Multi-Strategy	−18.54	5	14	−4.95	2	6
E.D. Risk Arbitrage	−7.61	4	7	−5.93	19	5
Fixed Income Arbitrage	−12.48	7	13	−3.89	3	4
Global Macro	−26.79	14	18	−11.12	3	15
Long/Short Equity	−15.04	29	17	−11.43	1	4
Managed Futures	−17.74	8	15	−14.23	21	6
Multi-Strategy	−7.11	5	5	−4.76	1	4
Lehman Aggregate Bond Index	−5.15%	5	8	−3.17%	4	5
S&P 500	−46.28%	25	0	−15.57%	2	3

Sources: CSFB/Tremont, PerTrac.

GAMING THE SHARPE RATIO

William F. Sharpe has become the preeminent name in the investment business as the progenitor of the capital asset pricing model (CAPM).[7] His reputation has reached far and wide and the so-called Sharpe ratio has become the standard measure of the risk-adjusted performance of a portfolio of stocks.

The mathematics of this ratio is fairly straightforward and so is the logic. To arrive at this ratio, one would subtract the interest rate of short-term Treasury bills (which are considered equivalent to a risk-free investment) from the return of the portfolio. This is the excess return. Dividing excess return by the standard deviation results in the Sharpe ratio. One can think of this ratio as the reward generated by the portfolio per each unit of risk that it undertakes, just as the price of a dozen apples divided by 12 would give the price of each apple. Thus, the higher the reward per unit of risk, the better performing the portfolio is after factoring in the risk. If two investments have identical excess returns, the investment with the higher Sharpe ratio is considered the better performer.

The reason why the risk-free rate is subtracted from the denominator is because interest rates do change from period to period. For the same average return and standard deviation, the Sharpe ratio would be higher when interest rates are lower. Thus, the Sharpe ratios of a portfolio would change over time depending on what Treasury bill rate one uses, the period under consideration, as well as the length of the period. Without subtracting the Treasury bill rate from the denominator, the ratio is called the reward-to-variability or return-to-risk ratio.

Standard deviation again figures prominently in the Sharpe ratio or the return-to-risk ratio calculations. To the extent that standard deviation is an accurate measure of risk, the Sharpe ratio would give a fair representation of the relative performances of different portfolios having different returns and standard deviations. However, like standard deviation, the Sharpe ratio does not discriminate upside from downside risks or above-average versus below-average returns. It penalizes both types equally.

Importantly, as seen earlier, hedge fund returns are nonnormal distributions and some strategies such as Event Driven and Fixed Income Arb have substantial deviations from normality. The high excess kurtosis and negative skew exhibited by these individual strategies render calculations of their risk-adjusted performance based on standard deviations almost meaningless. The Sharpe ratio suffers from this weakness. Also, remember that hedge fund indexes as well as individual hedge funds, even those within the same strategies, have different skew and kurtosis values. Their

Sharpe ratios can be misleading when used as a basis for comparing their risk-adjusted returns even on an *ex post* basis.

Furthermore, the Sharpe ratio can be artificially inflated by taking on asymmetrical risks. One strategy is to sell a combination of deep out-of-the-money naked call and put options. Covered call option writing involves selling a call option against the long position in a similar security. In naked call option writing, the underlying long position is nonexistent. This naked call and put option writing strategy has been used by one hedge fund that collected close to $100 million from investors. Its basic strategy is to hold short and intermediate-term Treasury securities, which have little volatility. To generate so-called alpha, the hedge fund manager has sold put and call options on the S&P 500 exchange-traded fund Spiders. Over a period of a little more than two years ending in early 2004, this fund, sold under the label Fixed Income Arbitrage, was reported to average close to 11 percent annual returns. Evidently, this fund did not hedge anything. Worse, it took on substantial left tail risks. This is because the short puts lengthen the left tail of the return distribution, raising the probability of abnormal losses. The short call positions similarly expose this fund to left tail risk. Together and individually, the short put and call option positions increase the negativity of the skew (lower the skew) of the fund's returns.

Characterized as "an artifice employed by unscrupulous hedge fund managers,"[8] this strategy does not require the manager to have any skill or alpha, while charging high fees (1 percent management fee and 20 percent sharing of any profit). And it "can often survive for several years without being hit. For example, writing a 10 percent out-of-the-money put on a portfolio indexed to the S&P 500 each month would generate 2 to 2.5 percent in annual premiums. Based on the empirical distribution of monthly returns, this strategy has a two-thirds chance of surviving three years without paying off once, and a 50 percent chance of surviving five years."[9] In the meantime, "if the manager is lucky, this strategy will show a significantly higher Sharpe ratio, as the premiums [on the written call and put options] flow directly to the bottom line with no apparent increase in volatility."[10]

The Sharpe ratio also overestimates the value of covered call writing. Though considered a legitimate strategy, "call writing truncates the right-hand side of a distribution and results in negative skewness (undesirable), while put buying truncates the left-hand side of a distribution and results in positive skewness (desirable). . . . As the Sharpe ratio ignores the asymmetric reduction of the variance, its application to optioned portfolios effectively overstates the performance of call writing and understates the performance of put buying."[11]

Generally, reliance on the Sharpe ratio would reward stable returns but it does not recognize the asymmetric risks of sudden abnormal losses. Besides option writing, there are other strategies that can generate steady returns and consequently high Sharpe ratios. However, when losses occur, they are extreme. Some of these strategies include taking on default risk, illiquidity risk, or other such catastrophic risks. Readers will recall the discussion in Chapter 3 of Private Credit Arbitrage, Structured Notes, or such fancy names for subprime inventory financing. This strategy assumes not only default risk, but also illiquidity risk. Its Sharpe ratio would be high, but when losses occur, they would be total.

All of these techniques help a manager smooth out a fund's return stream, hence high Sharpe ratio, without changing the long-term expected return profile. In the case of the short put/call trades, the additional consequence is that the fund would be exposed to abnormal losses that would not otherwise occur.

ALPHA: HOLY GRAIL OR WIZARD OF OZ?

Recall the formulation of the pricing of asset returns as posited in Chapter 3 in the form of a linear equation:

$$\overline{R}_i = r_f + \beta_i(\overline{R}_M - r_f)$$

Stripped of the Greek, this equation simply states that the average return of a portfolio is equal to the risk-free rate (usually the Treasury bill rate) plus the average return of the market portfolio minus the risk-free rate, adjusted by a factor called beta. Beta is a measure of how much a stock is sensitive to movements of the market.

The alpha of this portfolio is

$$\alpha_i = (\overline{R}_i - r_f) - \beta(\overline{R}_M - r_f)$$

Underlying this formulation is the theory that the return on a portfolio of stocks is simply a function of the level of interest rates and the return produced by the market. To the extent that a portfolio's return exceeds this "given," that is, if alpha is positive, the portfolio manager can be said to have skill, to be able to produce excess return above and beyond what is "given" by the market.

Two immediate questions come to mind. First, what is the market? Second, is this formulation the correct description of the return-generating process of risky assets?

The short answer to the first question is no one knows for sure. As a proxy for the market, the convention is the S&P 500. Or maybe it should be the Russell 3000, or the MSCI. What if a hedge fund strategy uses futures trading (as managed futures managers do) or fixed income arbitrage? Then shouldn't the market proxy be something other than a stock market index of any kind? Thus, the alpha of a fixed income arbitrage fund with the S&P 500 as the market proxy and an arbitrary number as the risk-free rate gives little insight as to the skill or excess return generated by the hedge fund manager.

As to the second question, since its creation in the 1960s, the research community has not been able to prove or disprove the thesis conclusively. This is partly because no one knows what the true market portfolio is.

Acknowledging these shortcomings of CAPM as a general description of the return-generating process and the sources of security return, it is empirically true that the return of a portfolio of stocks is to a significant extent dependent on the stock market. Whereas the S&P 500 may not fully explain the return of a small-cap portfolio, it is difficult to deny that there is manager skill if a portfolio containing only S&P 500 stocks actually outperforms the S&P 500 over some meaningful time frame.

Just as apples should be compared with apples, this simple observation highlights the essential point: Alpha can be a valuable tool to evaluate the excess return generated by manager skill if the portfolio being evaluated is a subset of the market factor. It makes little sense to assess the returns of distressed securities, global macro, or managed futures strategies against the S&P 500 and to conclude that there is alpha or that manager skill is positive. These strategies travel in universes that have little to do with the S&P 500.

And there is no market index that would capture the dynamics of all these strategies as they respond to a myriad of factors, such as:

- The stock market, including small-cap, mid-cap, initial public offerings (IPOs), etc.
- Interest rates (short- and long-term) and yield curve shifts.
- Credit spreads between corporate bonds and Treasuries, and between conforming and nonconforming mortgage-backed securities.
- Volatility in stocks and bonds, and between them.
- Market exposure undertaken by the individual portfolios.
- Amounts of leverage.
- Liquidity or lack thereof.

On the issue of liquidity risk, readers may ponder the alpha of subprime inventory financing labeled as private credit arbitrage or structured notes, as well as other hedge funds that take on illiquidity, receive premiums for it, and sell the illiquidity premiums as alpha.

It should also be noted that to calculate alpha, some practitioners have omitted one or two key items in the CAPM equation. One version of these variations is using the risk-free rate or Treasury bill rate as the benchmark for performance evaluation. In this case, the value of alpha is

$$\alpha = \overline{R}_i - R_f$$

This is based on the notion that any return on a market neutral portfolio in excess of the Treasury bill rate represents alpha or manager skill. There are several objections to this assumption.

A portfolio's market neutrality is not risk free simply by being long and short by the same amount. One reason is that the portfolio's weighted average beta, which is the weighted average of the betas of the underlying securities, is unlikely to be zero. With the weighted average beta being a nonzero number, the systematic risk of the portfolio is still present. Second, even if the weighted average beta is zero, unless it is a well-diversified portfolio, the securities' specific risks are still present in the portfolio. Third, there is no true market portfolio, therefore beta cannot be zero for all market neutral portfolios.

In other words, because a residual risk in equity market neutral funds is ever present, their returns are certainly not comparable with the risk-free rate. In some very restrictive conditions, one may construct a market neutral portfolio with respect to, say, the S&P 500, by being long and short only S&P 500 stocks in such a way that the resulting beta with respect to this market index is equal to zero. Even so, there still may be a residual risk from the specific risks of the underlying securities. To neutralize these security-specific risks, the portfolio would need to be well diversified, in effect replicating the S&P 500. However, few would expect such a market neutral portfolio to generate any excess return.

RETURNS OF HEDGE FUNDS REVISITED

Hedge fund index publishers compile the index return data supplied by hedge fund managers. There are some 7,000 hedge funds in operation. These funds vary in size, from small funds with a few hundred thousand dollars of assets under management to behemoths managing billions of dollars. Some have long track records of 10 years or more; others were recently established. The funds' strategies, as we have seen, vastly differ, even among those that operate in similar spaces, such as long/short equity, because of their different emphases on market cap, sectors, the amounts of net long, leverages, and so on.

Which Index?

No data publisher has all these hedge funds in its database. Any of them would have only a few hundred funds in their individual indexes. CSFB/Tremont, reported to have more than 3,000 funds in its database, nevertheless compiled its March 2004 CSFB/Tremont Hedge Fund Index's data based on "more than" 400 funds, "across ten style-based sectors." Barclay/Global HedgeSource had 1,840 funds included in its March 2004 Barclay/GHS Hedge Fund Index results.

From this limited number of managers who have chosen to report their funds' returns to these particular publishers, the database providers divide the hedge funds into subindexes. Some publishers, such as CSFB, choose to report the index returns with the individual managers' returns weighted by their assets under management. Others, like Barclay/Global, simply use the equally weighted average, thus giving the same consideration to the performances of small managers as to their much larger rivals.

It is apparent from the preceding discussion that reported returns would differ among different publishers. In fact, for 2003, Barclay reported a return of 18.01 percent for its composite index; for the first quarter 2004, the return was 3.64 percent. The HFR Composite Index produced 19.55 percent while the first quarter's return was 3.70 percent. CSFB showed a return of 15.44 percent in 2003 for its hedge fund index, and 3.42 percent for the first quarter.

Since return and risk figures vary across different database providers, analyses based on them would give different results. Instances have also been noted suggesting that the quality of the databases' published information is not uniform or homogeneous. For example, when comparing reported returns with the percentage changes in net asset values, the U.S. Offshore Fund Directory's figures showed a discrepancy of 29 basis points per year on average.[12]

Furthermore, as the hedge fund industry has experienced exponential growth, the managers whose returns were included in the indexes in the early years have been vastly outnumbered by new managers. It was also reported that half of the managers disappeared after an average of 30 months and only 4 percent of managers have been in business for 10 years.[13] Bing Liang (2001)[14] found that from 1990 to 1999, the average attrition rate was 8.5 percent; that is, on average 8.5 percent of hedge funds disappeared every year. In difficult years, attrition was much higher; for example, in 1998, the attrition rate was 13 percent.

Yet, index returns have been treated as if hedge fund managers constituted a uniform universe whereby the returns of many years past were being produced today by the same or a similar number of managers, using basically the same strategies, facing no limits as to the amount of assets that could be managed. Inasmuch as hedge fund returns are supposed to be generated by the talents and skills of managers, the majority of thousands of managers cannot be expected to have the skills necessary to exploit the windows of opportunity that rapidly narrow as assets under management and fierce competition increase. Along with the crowding out of the playing field, the entry of new managers and the turnover of manager ranks suggest judiciousness in projecting the records of the few to the many.

Reporting Biases

There are even more problems. Returns data collected by hedge fund publishers are subject to reporting biases that tend to overstate the results.

Survivorship Bias   One flaw in the data on returns of hedge fund indexes is the so-called survivorship bias. This refers to the fact that the indexes contain only the information from funds that are still in operation, the survivors. The funds that went out of business do not report anymore. Obviously successful firms with good performance stay in business and continue to report, whereas funds that do not have good performance numbers cease to exist or simply stop reporting. Therefore, indexes containing only surviving funds would have higher returns than those that also include defunct funds. In other words, the survivorship bias leads to an upward bias in the reported returns of hedge fund indexes. Researchers estimated this bias to range from 1.5 to 2.5 percent.[15]

For these reasons, adjusting index returns for the survivorship bias and backfill bias (discussed next) would reduce estimates of hedge fund returns. In a survey of the TASS database of 2,016 hedge funds for the 1990 to 1999 period, Bing Liang (2000)[16] found 1,407 surviving funds and 609 defunct funds. The 1,407 surviving funds indeed outperformed the 2,016-fund group as a whole by an average of 0.14 percent a month or 1.69 percent a year; this is the amount estimated for the impact of the survivorship bias. And the surviving funds outperformed the dead funds by 0.67 percent a month or 8.04 percent a year.

Backfill Bias   Another flaw in the data is the backfill bias. This is the result of funds that have been in business for some time but choose to report only at a later date. Upon these funds' entry into the databases, the publishers backfill or add their performance figures into the earlier dates. What would be the impact of the entry of these funds into the databases? Their entry would tend to raise the return figures of the indexes for prior periods. This occurs because failing funds with poor performance would not enter the databases. The late entrants would want to make sure their performance numbers were strong before making their entry, most likely because of marketing motives. Their entries therefore create an upward bias on the indexes' return series. It has been estimated that this backfill bias is about 1.4 percent per annum.[17]

A corollary of this bias is the selection bias. This refers to the fact that only successful funds would choose to report their returns to databases, presumably resulting in higher index returns than if all funds were included in the indexes. However, researchers have concluded that this bias is negligible.

The reality is that investors would be able to examine only funds that are still in operation; defunct funds simply would not be around. Also, it would make sense that investors are interested in funds that have become successful and therefore decide to register with hedge fund databases. Of course, at any point in time investors would not know which funds would become defunct. Therefore, the return differences between surviving funds and indexes that include dead funds represent the risk of choosing wrong funds that later experience bad performance and go out of business.

BENEFITS OF HEDGE FUNDS REVISITED

Adjusting for the data biases and nonnormal risks, the benefits of hedge funds as stand-alone investments or diversification alternatives become less straightforward than analyses using indexes' unadjusted average returns and standard deviation would show; the returns of hedge fund indexes may be overstated by several percentage points. In Table 4.3, the returns and Sharpe ratios of the CSFB hedge indexes were recalculated assuming that their returns were 2 percentage points lower than reported to account for the reporting biases.[18]

The results were that hedge fund indexes' returns were indeed less competitive with those of the S&P 500, at least during 1994–2003. In this respect, one should remember that if it were not for the three-year equity bear market, the S&P 500 would have handily outperformed the hedge fund indexes.

In terms of risk-adjusted returns, the Sharpe ratios of the hedge fund indexes would be reduced sharply if their returns were cut by 2 percent due to the various biases in hedge fund reporting. As shown in Table 4.3, the Sharpe ratio of the composite CSFB Hedge Index retains only a slight edge

TABLE 4.3 Hedge Fund Returns and Sharpe Ratios, 1994–2003, Adjusted for Reporting Biases

Index	Annualized Total Return	Adjusted Return	Sharpe Ratio	Adjusted Sharpe Ratio	Increase/ Decrease of Sharpe Ratio
S&P 500	10.87%	10.87%	0.44	0.44	0%
MSCI World Index	7.59%	7.59%	0.25	0.25	0%
CSFB/Tremont Hedge Fund Index	10.86%	8.86%	0.83	0.58	–30%
Convertible Arbitrage	10.02	8.02	1.27	0.85	–33
Dedicated Short Bias	–3.06	–5.06	–0.40	–0.51	–28
Emerging Markets	6.89	4.89	0.17	0.05	–70
Equity Market Neutral	10.35	8.35	2.10	1.43	–32
Event Driven	11.37	9.37	1.25	0.91	–27
E.D. Distressed	13.34	11.34	1.37	1.07	–22
E.D. Multi-Strategy	10.27	8.27	1.01	0.69	–32
E.D. Risk Arbitrage	8.23	6.23	0.97	0.51	–47
Fixed Income Arbitrage	6.90	4.90	0.75	0.23	–69
Global Macro	14.21	12.21	0.87	0.69	–20
Long/Short Equity	11.84	9.84	0.73	0.54	–26
Managed Futures	6.35	4.35	0.19	0.03	–85
Multi-Strategy	9.53	7.53	1.24	0.79	–36

Source: CSFB/Tremont.

over the S&P. Several other strategies would have lost their advantages. In particular, Fixed Income Arbitrage's Sharpe ratio would have fallen below that of the S&P. Convertible Arb, Long/Short Equity, Global Macro, and Multi-Strategy still retain their edges, but these are significantly less than before. A standout exception is Equity Market Neutral which retains an attractive Sharpe ratio of about three times that of the S&P. Event Driven and two of its subcategories still show significantly higher Sharpe ratios. However, their negative skew and high kurtosis, which underlie their tendencies to have abnormal losses and occasionally abnormally high returns, undermine the reliability of their Sharpe ratios.

Thus, if analyses are conducted with raw data on returns of hedge fund indexes, which were most likely overstated, hedge funds could be overallocated. The overallocation could be more severe if the asset allocation analysis is conducted within the mean-variance framework, because of hedge funds' negative skew and high kurtosis. Negative skew and excess kurtosis imply greater risks for the same returns. Figure 4.5 shows how

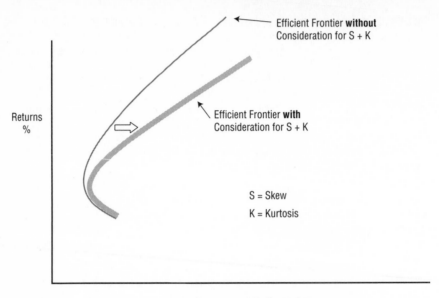

Efficient Frontier **without** Consideration for S + K

Efficient Frontier **with** Consideration for S + K

Returns %

S = Skew

K = Kurtosis

Normal and Modified Value at Risk %

FIGURE 4.5   Effects of Negative Skew and High Kurtosis on Optimal Asset Allocation
Source: Laurent Favre and Andrew Singer, "The Difficulties of Measuring the Benefits of Hedge Funds," *Journal of Alternative Investments*, Summer 2002.

consideration of skew and kurtosis could shift the efficient frontier rightward. The extent of the rightward shift depends on the magnitudes of the skew and kurtosis.[19]

From the perspective of risks, Kat and Amin (2002)[20] demonstrated that adding hedge funds to traditional stocks and bonds would lead to the combined portfolio having lower (worse) skew and higher kurtosis. In other words, portfolios diversified with hedge funds would have greater risks than their standard deviations would suggest. For investors who may wish to replace bonds in their portfolios with hedge funds, the eventual risks that they take on may be greater than they expect. From their study of 1,195 live and 526 defunct hedge funds for the period of 1994 to 2001, Kat and Amin concluded that "the net effect of the inclusion of hedge funds consists of (1) a higher probability of a very large loss, (2) a lower probability of a smaller loss, (3) a higher probability of a low positive return, and (4) a lower probability of a high positive return."[21] It follows that "skewness drops with the drop being most striking for those cases where the mean or standard deviation improves most. This emphasized that the improvement in mean and/or standard deviation is simply bought by accepting a higher probability of a relatively large loss. . . . Kurtosis rises with the highest rise occurring when the hedge fund allocation is highest."[22] This conclusion should not be surprising. The reason is that since lower skew and higher kurtosis are the hidden risks of hedge funds, the greater the allocations to hedge funds, the greater the risks.

These findings suggest that hedge fund strategies with no skew and no excess kurtosis, most notably equity market neutral, increase portfolio risk-adjusted return and lower standard deviation when they are added to traditional portfolios of stocks and bonds. This conclusion is reached whether the analysis is done within the confines of the mean-variance modern portfolio theory framework or when skew and kurtosis are explicitly taken into account. In fact, as demonstrated by Agarwal and Naik (2000),[23] "the results suggest that when deviations from normality are small, mean-variance framework provides a good approximation to the more robust and general gain-loss analysis. But when the deviations from non-normality are extremely severe as may be the case for individual hedge funds, it warrants the need for gain-loss analysis."

As previously shown, the event driven and fixed-income arbitrage strategies stand out as having exhibited significantly negative skew and extremely high kurtosis. Though their standard deviations are similar or only slightly higher than the Lehman Aggregate Bond Index, their risks are actually substantially greater. This effect is further evidenced by the large drawdowns that these strategies have experienced. Traditional analyses with mean and variance would underestimate the risks as well as overestimate the contribution to the risk-adjusted return of portfolios diversified with hedge funds using these strategies.

In contrast, the composite CSFB Hedge Index with no skew and insignificant excess kurtosis deviated little from a normal distribution. Equity Market Neutral is an exceptional case, as it has exhibited zero skew and excess kurtosis. Long/Short Equity also has no skew with a slight elevation in kurtosis. Deducing from Agarwal and Naik, this small deviation should have negligible effect on its mean-variance contribution to reducing portfolio volatility while enhancing risk-adjusted return. Likewise, Convertible Arb, Global Macro, and Multi-Strategy, with only small deviations from normality, would demonstrate diversification benefits of increasing risk-adjusted return even in the context of mean-variance analysis.

In conclusion, significant positive diversification effects of hedge funds still exist even after data biases in hedge-fund indexes and nonnormal characteristics of hedge fund returns are taken into consideration. However, actual historical returns of hedge fund indexes are probably lower than reported. Also, the risks of some strategies, notably event driven and fixed income arbitrage, are actually much higher than their standard deviations indicate. Traditional analyses with mean and variance would underestimate these strategies' risks and overestimate their risk-adjusted returns.

On the other hand, Equity Market Neutral, Long/Short Equity, Convertible Arbitrage, Global Macro, and Multi-Strategy are the hedge fund strategies in the CSFB database that exhibited very desirable risk and return characteristics, including lower standard deviation than that of the S&P 500 and little deviation from normality.

CONCLUSION

In this chapter we have reviewed and examined the properties of the statistics measuring hedge funds' risks. We have shown that hedge fund returns have nonnormal distributions. As a result, the standard deviation statistic that is commonly used to describe the risks of a hedge fund is inadequate. When the returns of a hedge fund exhibit negative skew and excess kurtosis, standard deviation underestimates its risks. The Sharpe ratio may also overestimate the risk-adjusted return of a hedge fund. Furthermore, returns of hedge funds as represented by hedge fund indexes suffer from overestimation due to survivorship and backfill biases. Nevertheless, significant diversification benefits of hedge funds still exist after adjusting for the biases in hedge fund indexes and the nonnormality of hedge fund returns. In the next chapter, we delve further into the return/risk characteristics of these hedge fund strategies in order to assess their potential roles and added values in diversified portfolios of hedge funds.

CHAPTER 5

Evaluating Hedge Fund Strategies

We now know that not all hedge funds are alike. They are a diverse group with vastly different investment strategies even within individual styles. Unlike traditional long-only strategies, which are dependent on the market or beta, hedge fund returns are purported to have low or zero correlation with the stock and bond markets, as they seek to generate positive returns even in market declines. As a result, hedge fund returns are said to be generated by manager skills and talents, or alpha.

The reality, however, is actually mixed. Hedge funds do not emphasize tracking the popular market benchmarks to generate returns. However, their strategies have been shown to be driven by certain market factors, including returns of the stock and bond markets, to a greater extent than indicated by correlation analysis. In this chapter we discuss the factors affecting returns of hedge fund strategies and their potential risks over and beyond the information obtained from correlation analysis and such measures as standard deviations of returns. This understanding will hopefully shed more light on the types of strategies that investors should or should not invest in.

WHICH STRATEGIES?

Hedge funds provide diversification benefits because of their reported low volatility of returns and low correlations with the traditional stock and bond markets, while producing Sharpe ratios superior to traditional bonds and equities. However, the benefits vary with strategies. Some strategies have historically produced returns lower than equities but with very low volatility of returns and low correlation with traditional markets. Such strategies would serve well to reduce portfolio volatility when they are added to long-only portfolios. They will be referred to as "Risk Reducers."[1]

Risk Reducers

Fixed income arbitrage is a risk-reducing strategy due to its low standard deviation and little correlation with the equity market as well as the direction of interest rates. For these characteristics, funds of funds that seek low volatility of returns allocate significant amounts of their assets to fixed income arb funds. Investors of these funds would not be disappointed in 1994 when the CSFB Fixed Income Arbitrage index was among the best performers of the CSFB indexes. It held on to a minuscule gain while the sharp hikes in interest rates by the Federal Reserve caused volatility in both stocks and bonds, with U.S. bonds posting their largest annual losses in memory. During the equity bear market of 2000 to 2002, fixed income arb funds also held up quite well, with the CSFB Fixed Income index averaging 6.7 percent annually, versus huge losses in the S&P and lackluster performance in Long/Short Equity.

However, a more in-depth analysis would reveal that fixed income arb funds have exhibited significant negative skew. That is, they are susceptible to potential dislocations in the capital markets, as in 1998. In that year, due to the Asian crisis and Long-Term Capital Management (LTCM), the CSFB Fixed Income Arbitrage index ranked dead last and had a loss of –8.16 percent. During August–October of that year, the index lost –11.75 percent. Losses of this magnitude are possible because of the practice of using huge amounts of leverage to capture small spreads between fixed income securities. LTCM was notorious for its exploitation of these small spreads and suffered disaster as a result. Nevertheless, the practice continues to this day. One fixed income arb manager boasted that he continued to make money in the volatile market of April 2004 though the spreads were as low as six basis points, by leveraging up to the limits. It is therefore understandable why some investors show a disdain for fixed income arbitrage. The head of a multibillion-dollar public retirement plan described the strategy as "grabbing pennies on the railroad track" while oblivious of the oncoming freight train.

Convertible arbitrage can also be considered a Risk Reducer because of its low volatility and low correlation with stocks. In fact, it was a favorite during the equity bear market years, as this strategy hedged the underlying long convertible bonds with short positions in stocks, capturing the declines in stock prices while preserving the bond gains. Multistrategy is another Risk Reducer. Multistrategy funds employ portfolio managers managing different hedge fund strategies. These funds distribute assets and can change allocations quickly among their employees/portfolio managers. This organizational setup allows multistrategy funds to take advantage of the best strategies in any given market conditions.

Among the CSFB/Tremont strategies, Equity Market Neutral uniquely stands out as a Risk Reducer. In addition to low volatility and correlation, this strategy has exhibited zero skew and kurtosis, and little in the way of drawdowns in its recorded history. Both Equity Market Neutral and Multi-Strategy have shared an important characteristic in their 10-year recorded history: Their returns have been comparable with those of the S&P 500 and the Long/Short Equity strategy. The CSFB/Tremont Multi-Strategy index showed an annualized return of 10.96 percent during 1995 to 2003. Its standard deviation of 4.54 percent was in the same range as Fixed Income Arbitrage and Convertible Arb. In 2003, the index had a return of 15.04 percent.

The CSFB Equity Market Neutral index produced a return not significantly less than Long/Short Equity with less than one-third of the volatility. Equity Market Neutral hedge funds were more structurally ready to take protective measures in market downturns, hence their ability to preserve capital in market declines. Thus, in 2001 and 2002 they had respectable positive rates of return, generating an annualized average of 8.36 percent gain, whereas Long/Short Equity had losses. Both Multi-Strategy and Equity Market Neutral also experienced relatively low maximum drawdowns historically.

Core Diversifiers

The records of Multi-Strategy and Equity Market Neutral to perform consistently in diverse market conditions (also shown in their virtually zero betas) suggest that they can be added to long-only portfolios for volatility reduction without undue unexpected surprises or much sacrifice in returns. Thus, they could serve well as core positions in diversified portfolios of hedge funds, or as Core Diversifiers.

Return Enhancers

At the other end of the return-risk payoff spectrum are higher-volatility strategies that have high correlations with the equity market and large drawdown risks but with higher return potential. These can be referred to as Return Enhancers, as they are suitable for portfolios seeking enhanced returns. Among the CSFB indexes, these strategies include Long/Short Equity, Global Macro, Event Driven, and Emerging Markets. The last strategy, Emerging Markets, has experienced grievous drawdowns, though at times, such as in 1996 and 1999, it has produced particularly strong returns. And it has been as volatile as one might expect, registering a standard deviation of 17 percent, higher than that of the

S&P 500. It lost 37 percent in 1998, only to gain 44 percent the next year. Its correlation with the S&P and other market indexes, however, has been low. This is the result of the different economic cycles in emerging markets. Typically when interest rates rise moderately in the United States, this would be because of economic growth and moderate inflation. Stronger economic growth and modest inflation are beneficial to emerging markets for they usually are exporters of commodities, which would rise in value with global demand and higher prices. However, if U.S. and world interest rates rise sharply, driving down stock prices and consumer demand, emerging markets would experience disproportionately larger declines. This asymmetric response gives rise to the low correlation. Thus, emerging markets funds would enhance returns in times of strong economic growth in the United States even if the U.S. financial markets experience lackluster returns. But the negative impact on these emerging markets would be magnified if the U.S. markets experience large and prolonged declines.

Event Driven has exhibited significant negative skew and high kurtosis, as well as large drawdowns. As such, its reported low volatility underestimates its potential risk. Nevertheless, it has at times produced top-performing returns, especially during the years of strong equity results.

Long/Short Equity was among the best performers during the 1990s, but ranked dead last during the equity bear market. Overall, this strategy follows the stock market, being the best performer in 1998 and 1999 and the worst in 2001 and 2002. During 1994–2003, it produced slightly higher returns than the S&P 500 with some 25 percent less volatility. It tracked the S&P fairly closely, with a correlation of 0.58 against the S&P and 0.76 versus the NASDAQ. In fact, in periods of sharply rising stock markets, Long/Short Equity has been among the top performers. No wonder that several big fund of funds firms with assets in the billions of dollars have launched funds of funds dedicated to long/short equity strategies. Global Macro has proven to be a strong return producer even during the 2000 to 2002 bear market. In fact, it managed to be among the three top-performing indexes in seven out of ten years.

Risk Diversifiers

The other two strategies, Short Bias and Managed Futures, in their best light, can be characterized as Risk Diversifiers. They have high volatility, mediocre or negative return, and unattractive Sharpe ratios. Nevertheless, they have historically acted countercyclically to the equity market. In fact, they both registered negative correlation to the S&P 500. Managed Futures funds or Commodity Trading Advisors (CTAs) trade in the noncash futures markets regulated by the Commodity Futures Trading Commission. At the most basic level, these funds are not hedge funds. In fact, regulators classify them as speculators versus hedgers. Unlike equity and fixed income hedge funds, they do not hedge. Managed futures funds engage in two-directional bets in a variety of markets, from stocks and bonds to precious metals and currencies, using the regulated futures markets. They bet that what they are long will go up and what they are short will go down. As might be expected, the reverse may happen. Since these funds tend to be highly leveraged, when losses occur, they often are disastrous.

Presumably short-biased funds provide an effective vehicle to neutralize the market risk of a long-biased fund, except with greater alpha. This is because supposedly short-selling managers are more proficient at picking stocks that are expected to decline in both rising and declining markets; simply selling short the market index is profitable only when the market declines.

Short-biased funds have shown negative correlation with the equity market. Their correlation with the S&P 500 is a negative –0.76, thereby fulfilling one condition for effective diversification. That is, combining two negatively correlated assets should result in a reduction of volatility of returns. This was in fact the case. One naive way to look at the contribution of short-biased funds as a hedge against market declines is to combine the CSFB Dedicated Short Bias index with the S&P 500 to construct a minimum-risk portfolio. Using the data of the 10-year period from 1994 to 2003, this combination would consist of 53.65 percent in the S&P 500 and the rest in Short Bias. This minimum-risk portfolio yielded a return of 4.47 percent annually and standard deviation of 5.83 percent, for a return-to-risk ratio of 0.765. The much lower standard deviation was achieved on the combination despite the high standard deviations in both the Short Bias funds and the S&P 500, at 18.02 percent and 15.84 percent respectively, because of their negative correlation. In comparison, the annual return of the Long/Short Equity index was 12.16 percent with a standard deviation of 11 percent, giving a return-to-risk ratio of 1.11. The return on the Equity Market Neutral index was 10.65 percent with a standard deviation of 3.07. A traditional investor in the Lehman Aggregate Bond Index in the same 1994–2003 period would have achieved an annualized return of 6.95 percent with a volatility of 3.96 percent. Thus, historically traditional equity investors who wish to have protection against market declines would have been better off with long/short equity or equity market neutral than diversifying with Short Bias hedge funds.

Furthermore, one should note that between 1994 and 2003, cumulatively the CSFB Dedicated Short Bias index lost 37.5 percent for an annual compound loss of 3.17 percent. In 2001, this index lost 3.58 percent as the S&P 500 declined by 11.89 percent. And the index got hit hard in 2003 by the market rally, losing 32.59 percent. Thus, as stand-alone investments, short sellers have not proved profitable. In a sense, short selling is a far riskier strategy than long-only. The maximum loss in a long-only portfolio is total loss of capital. Short sellers, in contrast, face the potential of infinite losses because theoretically there is no limit to how high a security's price can climb.

Summary

Table 5.1 summarizes the values added by different hedge fund strategies.

Core Diversifier strategies can be held as core positions in diversified portfolios of hedge funds, or as additions to traditional long-only portfolios. The Risk Reducers can help to reduce portfolio volatility at the price of lower return, significantly so in the case of Fixed Income Arbitrage. In either case, they are subject to the potential of sudden losses, sometimes total losses in individual cases such as Long-Term Capital Management or Beacon Hill Asset Management (see Chapter 9). The Return Enhancers present attractive return opportunities in some years, but mediocre returns or losses in some others. This is because they are more influenced by the up and down moves in the equity and bond markets. The Risk Diversifiers act countercyclically to stock and bond movements. They are poor stand-alone investments but they can dampen the impacts of volatility from the Return Enhancer strategies.

TABLE 5.1 Diversification Benefits: Risk Reduction versus Return Enhancement

CSFB/Tremont Hedge Fund Index	Risk/Return	Value Added to Diversified Portfolios
Fixed Income Arbitrage	Risk Reducer	Lower volatility; risk of large losses
Convertible Arbitrage	Risk Reducer	Lower volatility; risk of large losses
Equity Market Neutral	Core Diversifier	Core holding
Multi-Strategy	Core Diversifier	Core holding
Long/Short Equity	Return Enhancer	Opportunistic returns
Global Macro	Return Enhancer	Opportunistic returns
Event Driven	Return Enhancer	Opportunistic returns
Emerging Markets	Return Enhancer	Opportunistic returns
Managed Futures	Risk Diversifier	Countercyclical
Dedicated Short Bias	Risk Diversifier	Countercyclical

IS IT UNCORRELATED, REALLY?

The fund of funds manager wrote to his clients that the fund "has suffered a severe drawdown in April 2004, a loss of 8.96 percent," after a loss of 1.26 percent in March. He continued, "The performance of our CTA positions, in particular, was an unpleasant surprise. In past times of turmoil, uncertainty, and dislocation, CTAs have typically provided an 'insurance policy'—given the uncorrelated nature of their historic returns to the rest of the alternative 'universe.' . . . Equities and bonds declined in tandem, with most commodities following suit. CTAs—far from providing hoped-for 'insurance' in such conditions—could not turn the corner fast enough."

Although this fund of funds was leveraged, the reported leverage of 1.47:1 could not account for the loss, for the leverage was within the limits of such funds. Neither was the lack of diversification; it invested in a very large number of managers. Through February, it claimed a standard deviation of 7.55 percent, far below that of the S&P 500. It also boasted a Sharpe ratio of 4 (based on a Treasury bill rate of 1 percent).

Though its loss was more pronounced, this fund was not alone in seeing its uncorrelated hedge fund investments move in tandem with the decline in stocks and bonds. Barclay/Global Fund of Funds subindex recorded a loss of –0.71 percent in April and 11 out of its 17 subindexes were negative in April. The HFRI Fund of Funds Composite Index lost 0.93 percent. Even subindexes with diversified strategies such as multistrategy and global macro recorded negative returns. The Barclay/Global Macro index showed a loss of –2.12 percent, almost as much as during the LTCM debacle in August 1998; HFRI Macro lost 2.79 percent. Both HFRI Equity Hedge and Barclay Long-Biased Equity indexes lost more than 2 percent. The S&P 500's loss of 1.68 percent appeared tame by comparison.

Like the more widely publicized summer of 1998, the losses in April 2004 were a manifestation of a phenomenon called "phase-locking" behavior whereby seemingly uncorrelated events suddenly occur all at once and become synchronized.[2] This is not supposed to happen with uncorrelated hedge funds! However, as the surging strength of the economy brought anew to the forefront concerns of the Federal Reserve raising interest rates, stocks and bonds pulled back, the dollar surged against the Japanese yen and the euro, while commodities and gold eased back from their peak levels. Many hedge funds, with the presumed manager talents and skills that should allow them to successfully navigate the markets in times of turmoil, got caught up in the whirlwind. Barclay/Global reported that the worst hedge fund return in April was a loss of 39.13 percent, while the highest was a gain of 18.14 percent. Losses, however, predominated as the median return was a negative 1.95 percent and the average return was a minus 2.96 percent. Apparently, smaller funds fared worse in this period than larger funds. While the Barclay/Global index returns were equal-weighted, the CSFB/Tremont Hedge Fund Index was asset-weighted in favor of larger funds. This methodology difference partly explains why the CSFB Hedge Index had a loss of 0.58 percent versus Barclay/Global's loss of 1.22 percent. Also, out of CSFB Hedge Index's 13 subindexes, 5 were negative, whereas 11 out of Barclay/Global's 17 subindexes had losses.

At the same time, the losses suffered by hedge funds amid declines in stocks and bonds, to which they are supposed to be uncorrelated or have low correlation, should not come as great surprises. The not-so-hidden secret is that hedge funds have common exposures to the directions of stocks, interest rates, currencies, commodities, and market factors such as market volatility to a greater extent than historical correlation statistics may show.

In most market conditions, market factors such as these do not move in tandem and therefore do not create the phase-locking behavior among different hedge fund strategies. Even in summer 2003, interest rates spiked more sharply than in April 2004, leading to big losses in mortgage-backed securities arbitrage funds; Beacon Hill was the notorious case. The currency market also reversed course and the dollar sharply rallied after months of losses. The stock market, however, continued its recovery. As a result, investors with diversified portfolios of hedge funds, such as funds of funds or multistrategy funds, did not suffer losses on average. Similarly, in the textbook case of systemic crisis of summer 1998 with the Russian debt default and Long-Term Capital Management's collapse, managed futures funds recorded some of their best gains ever. Even long/short equity and equity market neutral funds recovered strongly with the equity market after a setback in August. Amid the atmosphere of crisis in the financial markets, the Fed cut interest rates aggressively and pumped liquidity into the banking system to aid LTCM. Normally Fed easing would help fixed income investments. Yet the worst-hit sector was fixed income arbitrage. This created the false impression that the demise of LTCM led to havoc in the entire spectrum of hedge fund strategies when in fact sustained losses were mostly contained in fixed income arb funds.

Nevertheless, hedge fund strategies are subject to systemic risks. Like traditional long-only portfolios, though in different fashions, they are impacted by movements in the markets of stocks, bonds, currencies, and commodities. A case in point is the fixed income arbitrage strategy. Unlike long-only bond portfolios, which would lose value if interest rates rise, fixed income arb funds have recorded big losses in both rising and declining interest rate environments. This is because they bet on the direction of the so-called interest rate spreads, although not on the direction of interest rates. Thus, interest rates may rise or fall, but as long as spreads stay stable or contract, fixed income arb funds are profitable. When spreads widen, especially as a result of market dislocations as in 1998 or sudden turns in the market as in summer 2003, fixed income arb funds suffer.

Not only do seemingly uncorrelated strategies move in tandem in times of stress, but hedge funds are highly correlated among themselves. As in herding behavior, most hedge funds follow the same strategies. They pile onto profitable trades at the same moment, and exit them at the same time. Except for the best hedge fund managers, those who follow them in these trades stand to lose money, as opposed to generating alpha. In a study in 2003, Bridgewater Associates "grabbed data for over 1,600 hedge funds and looked as best we could at the typical correlation of managers within different hedge fund 'strategies.'"[3] The results are shown in Table 5.2.

The authors commented, "These high correlations within strategies are rough evidence that many hedge fund managers are making money by employing similar 'strategies' to take in risk premiums, rather than actually creating alpha by outsmarting other market participants. In many cases, these betas are not hard to strip out. . . . The most popular strategy over the last twelve months has been fixed income arbitrage, attracting over $6 billion in new money. This is a classic beta strategy. . . . These funds are buying illiquid, risky securities and shorting more liquid, less risky securi-

TABLE 5.2 Correlation among Managers of Same Strategies

Hedge Fund Groups by Strategy	Average Correlation of Return above Cash for Funds within Group
Convertible Arbitrage	60%
Dedicated Short Bias	51
Emerging Markets	59
Equity Market Neutral	42
Event Driven	66
Fixed Income Arbitrage	52
Global Macro	47
Long/Short Equity	63
Managed Futures	57
Multi-Strategy	53

Source: Greg Jensen and Jason Rosenberg, "Hedge Funds Selling Beta as Alpha," Bridgewater Associates Daily Observations, June 17, 2003.

ties. Some funds probably can sort the good securities from the bad ones, but in aggregate, fixed income arb funds have simply returned the beta of buying illiquid, fixed income instruments."[4] Another example is the strategy of subprime lending. In spring 2004, as the influx of funds continued and hedge fund capacity was strained, many funds of funds began to invest in this strategy, which can only be characterized as illiquid and subject to high risks of default. Investing in it, these hedge funds can charge alpha fees while taking on beta risks of illiquidity and default. In fact, several funds of funds in my sample that marketed themselves as low-volatility funds liked this strategy because of the steady returns they could record each month.

HOW NEUTRAL IS MARKET NEUTRALITY?

Traditional portfolios are always long in the stock and bond markets they invest in. Hedge funds typically do have short positions. If the short positions are smaller than the long side, such funds are said to be long-biased. If they are larger, the funds are short-biased. Equity market neutral funds may have equal dollar amounts on both the long and the short side. An alternative approach is to construct a zero-beta portfolio. Fixed income arb funds achieve neutrality by having zero duration.

However, available evidence has indicated that fixed income arb funds are not immune to interest rate movements, and equity funds have greater exposures to the stock market than expected.

Market Neutrality in Fixed Income Arbitrage Funds

Fixed income arb funds use leverage extensively to enhance return. And hedges include futures, short sales, options, derivatives, and structured notes. A market neutral fixed income portfolio is one where the portfolio's duration is equal to zero. This is easy to achieve in a fund that invests in bonds that have fixed maturity dates, such as corporate bonds or Treasuries. To achieve neutrality, the portfolio manager could sell short securities of sufficient amounts so that the short side has the same duration as the long securities. As such, interest rate movements presumably would have no impact on the portfolio.

Basic Trades Fixed income arb funds typically hold on the long side bonds that carry higher yields than those on the short side. Accordingly, their portfolios earn positive interest rate spreads being equal to the differences between the yields on the long securities and those on the short bonds. If the market stays flat as interest rates are stable, the portfolios would earn a positive rate of return. Because this positive interest rate is usually small, from a few basis points to a few percentage points in most market conditions, fixed income arb funds must use leverage to achieve double-digit rates of return. Hedge fund managers would not systematically short higher-yielding securities against lower-yielding bonds because of the negative interest carries that would result. For such a portfolio to generate positive return, prices of the low-yielding bonds must rise to a greater extent than the higher-yielding bonds, sufficiently to more than offset the negative carries. Before this happens, the portfolio would have negative return. But sometimes this does happen. In times of recession, low-yielding Treasury securities appreciate in price more and faster than higher-yielding corporate bonds and mortgage-backed securities. Invariably this condition would create havoc to fixed income arb funds.

A yield curve arbitrage trader might buy 10- or 30-year Treasury bonds and sell shorter-term, say, 2- or 5-year Treasury notes. Though the amounts of the long position and the short position are not equal, they are adjusted so that the duration of the combined positions would be zero. Other arbitrage trades may be long mortgage-backed securities (MBSs) or corporate bonds and short Treasuries. Derivatives such as options of different kinds and structures are usually added on top of the long and short bonds. Structured products such as principal only (PO) and Interest Only (IO) securities are staples of arbitrage funds specialized in the mortgage sector as their prices move in opposite directions.

Convertible arbitrage funds seek delta neutrality to achieve market neutrality. Convertible bonds tend to be underpriced because of market segmentation (i.e., investors discount securities that are likely to change types). Hedge fund managers buy these securities and then hedge part or all of the associated risks by shorting the stock. Delta neutrality is often targeted. Delta measures the relationship between the price moves of a convertible bond given a change in the price of the underlying stock. However, overhedging may be engaged when there is concern about default as the excess short position may partially hedge against a reduction in credit quality. As a matter of fact, an ever-growing number of convertible arbitrage managers have turned to arbitrage credit risks rather than implicit volatility.

Returns Returns of fixed income arb funds consist of the positive interest carry plus any gains in principals or prices of the bonds if the interest rate spreads narrow—that is, if the higher-yielding securities appreciate in price more than the lower-yielding securities on the short side, multiplied by the amounts of leverage. This condition can occur with interest rates generally rising or falling. In calm market conditions, fixed income arb funds can generate handsome returns with very low volatility or standard deviation because interest rate spreads have much less volatility than bond prices or interest rates in general.

Market Factor and Interest Rate Risk   Although a fixed income arb portfolio has zero duration, it is in practice not risk free. Just as a trader in the Treasury market would know, news that the economy may be stronger than expected, perhaps leading to higher interest rates, would drive prices of three-month Treasury bills lower, even though these securities are supposedly risk free. Conversely, Treasury bills' prices may rise in anticipation of cuts in interest rates. Yet, in academic research as well as in industry practice, Treasury bill rates are used as proxies for the risk-free rate of interest.

A neutral duration fixed income portfolio derives its profits and losses from factors different from a long-only portfolio. When interest rates decline, the bonds in a long-only portfolio would rise. The extent of the bonds' price increases varies with the individual bonds. A Treasury bond of 30-year maturity would usually have larger increases than a Treasury bond of shorter maturity, say, a 5- or 10-year note. However, a corporate bond would in all likelihood experience a smaller increase in price, sometimes even a decline. This is because usually interest declines are associated with an economic recession or slowdown. In such an environment, corporations typically suffer slower business, lower revenue, and even reduced profits. In reaction, credit rating agencies may cut the creditworthiness of corporate bonds. Such anticipation would lead to reduced demand for the affected bonds, even short selling. These market forces eventually discount the positive effects of interest rate cuts that would otherwise accrue to the bonds.

Mortgage-backed securities also would experience smaller price increases. The reason is that as interest rates decline, homeowners are motivated to prepay in order to refinance their mortgages at lower rates, driving the prepayment rate higher. Thus, a 30-year mortgage now becomes a bond with a shorter maturity, which would have a smaller price increase than a longer-maturity bond. The uncertainty over the prepayment is the single largest risk in MBSs, because it determines the maturity, hence the price, of a mortgage bond.

When spreads widen, being long in higher-yielding securities, which appreciate more slowly and less than the bonds on the short side, would cause fixed income arb funds to lose money. Thus, though duration neutral, fixed income arb funds are subject to the risk of interest rate movements. This interest rate risk would be most acute in times of sudden and large moves in interest rates. First, such moves lead to sharp changes in yield spreads, which are differences between short- and long-term rates. This was documented by Fung and Hsieh (1996)[5] for the 1977 to 1994 period in the United States and the 1990–1994 period in non-U.S. markets, when there were extreme changes in the short-term interest rates and in the spreads between six- and three-month Treasury rates. This means that in such times, duration neutral portfolios, which many fixed income arb funds are supposed to be, are subject to the risk of rising and falling interest rates.

Second, Hsieh and Fung (2002)[6] demonstrated that when credit spreads (between Treasury and corporate bonds) widen, other fixed income spreads, namely, convertible, high yield, and mortgage versus Treasury, also widen. They noted that volatility in credit spreads during the 1990s was rather subdued compared to the period between 1925 and the mid-1980s, when large increases of credit spreads occurred several times. If credit spread volatility experiences historical norms, fixed income arb funds would see larger losses than recorded during the relatively short history of hedge funds.

What are the potential losses? Between June and October 1998, credit spreads increased by 110 basis points, implying a loss of 4.94 percent by a typical fixed income arb fund.[7] The HFR Fixed Income Arbitrage index recorded an actual loss of 11.8 percent[8] while the CSFB Fixed Income Arb index lost 12.3 percent. By comparison, the Lehman Aggregate Bond Index recorded a single monthly loss of 0.53 percent during the same period. Looking back in history, the spread increase in 1998 was relatively modest compared to the widening that occurred in April 1932, which was 187 basis points. If a spread increase of this magnitude were to occur today, losses by fixed income arb funds would be far larger than seen in any period during the 1990s.

Another phenomenon is that fixed income arb funds may register losses when traditional bonds perform well, and vice versa. This is reflected in the low correlation between the Lehman Aggregate Bond Index and HFR Fixed Income Arb (–0.07), and Lehman versus CSFB Fixed Income Arb (+0.18). Thus, one of the worst losing periods recorded by the Lehman index was a 5.15 percent drop during the five months between February and June 1994. In the same period, the HFRI Fixed Income index reported a gain of 5.7 percent whereas the CSFB Fixed Income index showed a loss of 3.5 percent. During June to October 1998, the Lehman index had a gain of 4.5 percent while the two hedge fund indexes recorded double-digit losses. This only served as fodder for the financial press to highlight the risks of hedge funds.

Lack of Liquidity   The basic strategy of fixed income arb funds is to be long higher-yielding bonds and short lower-yielding securities. High-yield securities are less liquid, and the higher the yields, the less liquid they are. Illiquid securities are often difficult to value and trade for the reason that they do not have actively traded secondary markets. In periods of heightened market volatility due to sharp changes in interest rates, stock prices, and currency movements, liquidity for high-yield securities and their derivatives often dries up quickly. Invariably, in such periods, fixed income arb funds would suffer losses from credit spread widening while their brethren in the traditional world might benefit from the Fed lowering interest rates.

Fixed Income Arbitrage Is Not Market Neutral   In conclusion, it is true that fixed income arb funds are not influenced by the rise and fall of interest rates in the same fashion as long-only strategies, and their portfolio structure is designed to be insulated from such interest rate movements. Nevertheless, these funds are subject to interest rate movements just the same, sometimes more drastically and at times when traditional bonds may perform well. The market factor or beta that fixed income arb funds depend on for generating returns is credit spreads, just as long-only managers derive returns largely from the stock market and long-only bond funds lose value when interest rates rise. When credit spreads widen, fixed income hedge funds suffer. Furthermore, they are subject to systemic risks in times of sharp volatility in interest rates and unusual widening of credit spreads that often occur when the global financial markets experience stress. The Russian debt default in 1998 was an example. Fixed income arb funds, despite zero duration exposure, are far from market neutral!

Equity Market Neutral Funds

Equity market neutral funds usually seek market neutrality by being long certain stocks and selling short other stocks by the same amounts.

Dollar-Neutral Portfolios   In a simplest example, a fund may buy $1 million of Lowe's Companies (LOW) stock and simultaneously sell short by the same amount the stock of Home Depot (HD); and similar transactions are repeated throughout the portfolio. Since both LOW and HD are in the home improvement business, they are affected by the market virtually the same way. In fact, in 2003, except for dividends, both stocks had virtually the same rate of return, 47.5 percent. This type of strategy of matching is called pairing. It is the most risk-minimizing form of long/short equity trades.

Sometimes pairing yields very handsome results. Let's say LOW was bought on September 21, 2001, and HD was sold on the same day when the stock market and both of these stocks were at their lows after the September 11 attacks. If these positions were held through the end of 2002, the paired trade of these two stocks would yield a total return of about 67 percent, with 39.7 percent from the long trade and 27.2 percent from the short side as HD continued to decline. During this period, the S&P 500 lost 8.9 percent, not counting dividends. The same trade in 2003 would net a fractional loss while the S&P 500 went up by more than 26 percent.

Consider matching a pair such as Microsoft (MSFT) against People-Soft (PSFT) in 2003. This trade would produce a loss of 18.6 percent if MSFT was bought and PSFT was sold. The short side bet incurred a loss of 24.5 percent because PSFT rallied instead of declining whereas MSFT rose but by only a modest amount of 5.9 percent. Of course, if both paired trades were structured the opposite way, the HD/LOW coupling would produce a loss of 67 percent and the PSFT/MSFT pair would have a gain of 18.6 percent.

In both cases, the systematic or market risk as well as the sector or industry risk are said to have been neutralized and there remains only the specific or unsystematic risks of the individual securities. In traditional long-only portfolios, if they are well diversified, the market risk would be retained and the company-specific risks are neutralized by reason of diversification. Now, consider a trade to go long HD and short MSFT during the period between September 21, 2001, and December 31, 2002. It would have been a foolish trade as it turned out. But there are plenty of times when a fund would buy one stock and short another that has nothing in common with the first one. The point of the HD/MSFT example is that these two stocks are in two different sectors of the economy and more likely than not they respond to movements in the stock market and developments in the economy in different ways. As it turned out, the HD/MSFT pairing would have resulted in a loss of 31.5 percent. (Incidentally, the MSFT/PSFT trade would have produced a profit of 13.6 percent during the same period.) In this case, sector risks are retained and the market risk is neutralized by virtue of being long and short by the same amount.

A dollar-neutral equity market neutral fund would have all of the aforementioned trades on its portfolio such that the total dollar amounts in long positions would approximately equal the short amounts. Additionally, in lieu of individual stocks, the short side may be in market indexes in the form of exchange-traded funds (ETFs) such as the S&P 500 Spiders (ticker: SPY) or the Russell 2000 index (ticker: IWM).

Conventionally, such a portfolio is said to be market neutral. However, intuitively, one would think that the HD/MSFT combination (or inversely, long MSFT and short HD) is inherently riskier than the other two paired trades. This is because a dollar-neutral portfolio is rarely market neutral in the context of modern portfolio theory.

Zero-Beta Portfolios   Similar to equation (3.2) in Chapter 3, the pricing of asset returns can be recast in terms of excess return, which is the return over the risk-free rate:

$$\bar{R}_i = \alpha_i + \beta_i \bar{R}_M$$

where $\bar{R}_i$ and $\bar{R}_M$ are the excess return of the investment and the market, respectively.

When two stocks are combined in equal amounts to form a dollar-neutral long/short portfolio with stock 1 on the long side and stock 2 being short, the return of the portfolio can be expressed as:

$$\bar{R}_p = (\beta_1 - \beta_2)\bar{R}_M$$

To be a zero-beta market neutral portfolio, the fund would have its weighted average beta, which is the weighted average of the individual securities' betas, equal to zero. A portfolio with equal long and short positions would not necessarily be zero-beta, even when the stocks belong to the same sector. LOW's beta was 1.08 while HD's beta was 1.41. Assuming these figures are their true betas, a dollar-neutral portfolio of these two stocks would leave a weighted average beta of negative 0.16. Such a negative-beta portfolio would subject the portfolio to losses when the market bounced. Similarly, a dollar-neutral portfolio of MSFT (beta = 1.585) and PSFT (beta = 2.526) would have a negative beta of −0.47.

The appropriate amounts of longs and shorts to form a zero-beta portfolio are given in the following formulas. The amount of the long portfolio:

$$X_L = \frac{-\beta_S}{\beta_L - \beta_S}$$

The amount of the short portfolio:

$$X_S = \frac{-\beta_L}{\beta_L - \beta_S}$$

Applying these formulas to the LOW/HD, MSFT/PSFT, and HD/MSFT trades, we have the following results.[9]

	LOW/HD	MSFT/PSFT	HD/MSFT
Long Amount	56.63%	61.44%	52.92%
Short Amount	43.37	38.55	47.08
Net Long	13.26	22.89	5.84

To achieve zero beta neutrality, each of the three trades would need to be net long in dollars in the indicated amounts. Conversely, if the trades are set in opposite directions, they would have to be net short to achieve zero beta.

It is clear that buying and selling stocks by the same amounts would not generate a zero-beta portfolio. In the preceding paired trades, dollar-neutral positions would result in overhedging. Theoretically, a zero-beta portfolio is risk free in the sense that it is not sensitive to the movements of the market. This makes sense if the return of a stock, and by extension, the return of a portfolio of risky assets, is a function of the risk-free rate and the market factor. Since estimates of future betas for individual securities are not true betas, the portfolio's beta of the combined long and short positions is never truly equal to zero.

Table 5.3 shows the changes in the beta and market exposures in dollar terms of a long/short equity fund over the course of 2004.

This fund does not use any options, futures, or derivatives, and it does not engage in high-frequency trading. Note the significant discrepancies between the net long amounts versus weighted average betas in each month. In dollar terms, this fund has a very significantly long bias. However, measured in beta, it is virtually a zero-beta portfolio. In fact, the CSFB/Tremont Equity Market Neutral index has a beta versus the S&P 500 of 0.07 and its Long/Short Equity index's beta is 0.42. When the portfolio's returns are regressed against the S&P 500, its beta is 0.16. Interestingly enough, the portfolio had a modest return of 0.74 percent with a beta of 0.28, and was net long 70 percent in February when the S&P was up 1.22 percent. In June, the portfolio was still net long though beta was close to neutrality and it generated a 2.57 percent return (implying a gross return well in excess of 3 percent) in a market where the S&P took a big hit and the NASDAQ simply crashed, losing 7.8 percent. These patterns were repeated throughout the portfolio's 12-month history. It is clear that to this hedge fund, beta was a key barometer of market risks and that this portfolio's return was generated from stock picking prowess with modest beta exposure variations adding value in market upside and risk reduction in times of stress.

TABLE 5.3 Beta Exposure of a Long/Short Equity Hedge Fund

2004	Weighted Average Beta	Net Long Percent
January	0.14	56%
February	0.28	70
March	0.13	18
April	−0.14	10
May	0.03	40
June	0.12	52
July	0.15	41
August	0.17	37
September	0.08	27
October	0.19	11
November	0.38	41
December	0.25	26
YTD '04	0.15	36

MARKET RISKS OF HEDGE FUND STRATEGIES

Fixed income arb funds not only are affected by interest rate movements, but they are also exposed to turmoil in the equity market. This equity risk exposure in fixed income arb funds has not been detected from the analysis of these funds' historical data.

For fixed income funds, as shown in Table 2.4 in Chapter 2, the correlation between the stock and CSFB Fixed Income Arb indexes was a negligible 0.03. However, when Fung and Hsieh (2002)[10] performed regression analyses of credit spreads and the S&P 500, they detected a far greater impact of the S&P on fixed income arb funds if the stock index had monthly losses of 5 percent or greater. They found that fixed income arb funds could lose 1.5 percent if the S&P 500 were to fall by 10 percent. This stands to reason. If such a large loss occurs in the stock market, historically the Fed might cut interest rates to curb systemic risks, helping long-only bond funds to rally. Such sudden moves in the Treasury rates, however, would likely cause credit spreads to widen, prompting losses to fixed income arb funds.

The equity risk exposure is probably embedded in all hedge fund strategies, not just equity-oriented funds. In a study of the CSFB/Tremont indexes, Asness, Krail, and Liew (2001)[11] found significant correlation between these hedge fund indexes' returns and the S&P 500. The same conclusions were confirmed with HFR indexes. These results are also shown in Table 5.4, column 1, taken from the authors' analysis of the 1994 to 2000 period.

As shown previously in Table 2.4, the CSFB/Tremont indexes exhibited quite low correlations with the S&P. In the case of Fixed Income Arb and Convertible Arb, there was virtually no correlation at all.

However, when the lagged effect of the S&P 500—that is, the effects from the stock index's returns from prior periods (column 3)—are accounted for, the CSFB/Tremont Hedge Fund Index's "beta more than doubles from 0.37 (column labeled 1) in the simple monthly regressions to

TABLE 5.4 Summary of Monthly Regressions of Hedge Fund Returns on S&P 500 Returns, January 1994 to September 2000

	(1)	(2)	(3)	(4)	(4) – (1)
		Betas from Lagged S&P 500 Regressions			
Portfolio	Simple Monthly Regression Beta	Contemporaneous Beta (β_0)	Sum of Lagged Betas $(\beta_1 + \beta_2 + \beta_3)$	Total Summed Beta $(\beta_0 + \beta_1 + \beta_2 + \beta_3)$	Difference in Beta
Aggregate Hedge Fund Index	0.37	0.40	0.44	0.84	0.47
Convertible Arbitrage	0.04	0.08	0.35	0.43	0.38
Event Driven	0.28	0.31	0.30	0.61	0.33
Equity Market Neutral	0.12	0.13	0.08	0.20	0.09
Fixed Income Arbitrage	0.02	0.05	0.31	0.36	0.33
Long/Short Equity	0.55	0.57	0.42	0.99	0.45
Emerging Markets	0.74	0.79	0.46	1.25	0.51
Global Macro	0.37	0.41	0.57	0.98	0.61
Managed Futures	0.01	−0.01	−0.17	−0.19	−0.20
Dedicated Short Bias	−0.99	−1.01	−0.25	−1.27	−0.28

Source: Clifford Asness, Robert Krail, and John Liew, "Do Hedge Funds Hedge?," *Journal of Portfolio Management*, Fall 2001.

0.84 (column labeled 4) when we account for lagged relations. Perhaps most surprising, Convertible Arbitrage betas increase dramatically from 0.04 to 0.43. Other large increases include Event Driven, which increases from 0.28 to 0.61, and Fixed Income Arbitrage, which increases from 0.02 to 0.36. In fact, in every category save managed futures, the betas are magnified. The styles with positive betas produce even larger positive betas and the styles with negative betas produce even more negative betas."[12] If the S&P 500's lagged effects are neutralized, the equity risk exposure is still present in all strategies except Equity Market Neutral, Emerging Markets, Managed Futures, and Dedicated Short Bias. Most notable was the large presence of the equity risk exposure in Event Driven, Convertible Arb, and Fixed Income Arb. Also, surprisingly, Long/Short Equity experienced a very large jump in its beta vis-à-vis the S&P, to 0.99. Although the authors posited that this figure could have been on the high side, they believed the lagged effects of the S&P were still present and significant. The lagged effects on hedge funds from the equity market could have been due to the stale prices that were used to mark to market illiquid securities that were traded over-the-counter, thinly traded, or otherwise valued at nonmarket prices. Alternatively, the lagged effects "might be due to hedge fund [managers] actually reacting to moves in the market at a lag (not a lag in marking [of securities' prices to market])."[13] However, whether hedge funds change strategies based on old information or use stale prices to mark to market their holdings, "it does not matter which explanation is correct as both explanations imply more market risk for the hedge fund buyer."[14]

LEVERAGE AND HEDGE FUND RETURNS

By definition, hedge funds depend on leverage to generate returns. In some strategies such as fixed income arbitrage, without leverage their returns would not match those available in traditional stocks and bonds.

Leverage can be achieved in different ways. The most common is borrowing (and selling) securities on margin with the expectation that the borrowed securities can be bought back in the future at lower prices for profits. However, sometimes it is difficult to detect and measure the extent of the leveraging. It is easy enough to create derivative structures to achieve the leveraging effects of multiple times of the face value of a security. One method is using an unregistered 144A security structured to respond to certain movements in interest rates or currencies; the resulting gains (and losses) are calculated to be as if the actual capital is in multiple amounts of the face value of the security. Without transparency at the position level, this type of leveraged holdings would not be apparent to investors. Other ways to create leverage include options and futures, which require only small amounts of margin to control trades worth 20 to 30 times more than the margin amounts.

There are different ways to calculate leverage. One simple method is to add up the notional amounts of all holdings and divide the sum by the investor capital. Thus, the face value of a call option, not the option premium, would be counted toward calculating the leverage. This method surely would overstate the amount of leveraging, for it is well understood that the value of an option would not respond to the price changes of the underlying security on a one-to-one basis. The sensitivity of such changes, or delta, is less than 1. Likewise, the duration or exposure to interest rate risks of mortgage-backed securities is calculated on an option-adjusted basis to incorporate the uncertainty of the prepayment rate. To account for these factors, true leverage needs to reflect the delta of the sum of the long and short positions over the investor equity capital. This adjustment would result in a leverage amount significantly smaller than if the notional amounts of all holdings are used.

At the same time, all of these fine points, though technically correct, are not apparent to investors, especially given the opaqueness of hedge funds' disclosure. Furthermore, delta or price change sensitivity varies with a host of factors, including strike prices, maturity, interest rate levels, and not least, liquidity. In times of liquidity crisis, volatility and delta rise sharply, increasing the effects of leveraging. Thus, a seemingly small delta-adjusted leverage may increase dramatically and result in unexpectedly high exposures. This was the experience of Long-Term Capital Management in 1998 as it bore the full brunt of its 120-to-1 leveraged portfolio when the Russian debt default occurred.

Another aspect of leveraging is that a leveraged portfolio of liquid securities may be less risky than another portfolio with less leveraging but owning illiquid investments. The reason is simple. The former portfolio can be rid of its holdings in times of need and these securities can likely be sold at prices reasonably close to fair values. Selling illiquid securities when demand for them dries up not only is difficult, but always is done at prices below fair values. For example, during the Russian debt crisis in 1998, some dealers did not pick up telephones to answer calls from clients. As a result, fund managers would likely sell their most liquid holdings when they need to raise cash and reduce leverage. But the resulting portfolios, though at reduced leverage, may be riskier than the original portfolios because of the greater share of the illiquid securities.

For these reasons, investors need to be aware of the extent of leveraging in hedge fund portfolios that have high leverage in terms of notional amounts, without adjustments for volatility and such factors. Among hedge fund strategies, fixed income arbitrage is perennially most highly leveraged. According to prime brokers' reports, delta-adjusted leverages employed by main strategies range as indicated in Table 5.5, and are ranked as follows:

Lowest Leverage

- Equity market neutral
- Merger arb
- Distressed securities
- Long/short equity

Moderate Leverage

- Multistrategy
- Relative value
- Event driven
- Global macro

Highest Leverage

- Fixed income arb
- Convertible arb

Considering the effects of leverage, negative skew and kurtosis, and drawdown history, it is no wonder that hedge fund blowups that have caught media attention have been in fixed income arbitrage—most recently

TABLE 5.5   Leverage Amounts in Hedge Fund Strategies

Strategy	Leverage
Fixed Income Arbitrage	20 to 30 times
Convertible Arbitrage	2 to 10 times
Risk Arbitrage	2 to 5 times
Equity Market Neutral	1 to 5 times
Long/Short Equity	1 to 2 times
Distressed Securities	1 to 2 times

Source: Pascal Lambert and Pete Rose, "Risk Management for Hedge Funds—A Prime Broker's Perspective," Bear Stearns International Limited, citing report by HBV Alternative Investments—Corporate Markets, June 2002 (www.eubfn.com/arts/760_bearstearns.htm).

Beacon Hill. It also reinforces the perception that fixed income arb is far riskier than its historical standard deviation has indicated.

LOW CORRELATIONS: THE GOOD AND THE POOR

A prime motivation for investing in hedge funds is diversification from traditional investments. Low correlations with the volatile stock market underlie this important benefit. However, these low correlations also mask the different reactions of hedge fund strategies to the stock market when it is up and when it is down.

In an examination of the performance of hedge funds as represented by the Evaluation Associates Capital Markets (EACM) indexes, researchers at the Center for International Securities and Derivatives Markets (CISDM), University of Massachusetts, found that many strategies did not perform as hoped.[15] During the 1990 to 2002 period, most strategies showed high correlations with the S&P 500 during months that the stock index performed the worst. In contrast, these hedge fund strategies showed little or negative correlation with the S&P in months of best performance by the stock market. A summary of the analysis is shown in Table 5.6.

TABLE 5.6   Hedge Fund Strategies: Correlations with Up and Down Stock Markets

Strategy	All S&P Months	Worst 48 S&P Months	Best 48 S&P Months
Relative Value	0.12	0.59	−0.12
Event Driven	0.49	0.62	−0.21
Equity Hedge	0.62	0.54	0.00
Global Asset Allocators	0.07	−0.01	0.09

Notes:
Relative Value includes Equity Market Neutral, Convertible Hedge, Bond Hedge, Rotational.
Event Driven includes Arbitrage, Bankruptcy, Multi-Strategy.
Equity Hedge includes Domestic Long, Long/Short, Global/International.
Global Asset Allocators includes Discretionary and Systematic.
Source: Alper Daglioglu and Bhaswar Gupta, "The Benefits of Hedge Funds," Center for International Securities and Derivatives Markets (CISDM), Isenberg School of Management, University of Massachusetts, March 2003.

These data mean that these hedge fund strategies followed the stock market down when it performed the worst. Yet, they trailed the stock market when the latter was particularly strong. Though probably incurring lesser losses than long-only stock portfolios, these hedge fund strategies were likely to produce negative returns in poor equity environments. They were also unlikely to perform as well as equities when the latter had particularly bullish runs. In other words, the probability of the impact of poor equity performance on hedge funds was stronger than the likely effects of positive equity results. Thus, the influence of equities was asymmetric, stronger when the stock market performed poorly and weaker when market performance was strong.

TABLE 5.7 Hedge Fund Strategies: Correlations with Stock and Bond Markets

EACM Strategy	All S&P Months 1/1990–4/2000	Bottom 40	Top 40	Difference	Correlation
Relative Value					
Equity Market Neutral	–0.06	–0.04	0.16	0.20	Consistent
Convertible Arb	0.08	0.24	–0.13	–0.37	Poor
Bond Hedge/Fixed Income Arb	0.02	0.40	–0.19	–0.58	Poor
Rotational	0.00	0.37	–0.08	–0.45	Poor
Arbitrage					
Merger Arb	0.45	0.61	–0.04	–0.65	Poor
Bankruptcy/ Distressed	0.29	0.51	–0.18	–0.69	Poor
Multi-Strategy	0.40	0.55	–0.14	–0.69	Poor
Equity					
Long-Biased	0.60	0.55	–0.06	–0.61	Poor
Hedge/Long-Short	0.17	0.28	–0.20	–0.49	Poor
Global/Int'l	0.56	0.53	0.19	–0.34	Poor
Short-Biased	–0.68	–0.60	–0.41	0.19	Consistent
Global Allocators					
Discretionary	0.28	0.27	0.01	–0.26	Consistent
Systematic	0.02	–0.20	0.41	0.62	Good

Source: Thomas Schneeweis and Richard Spurgin, "Hedge Funds: Portfolio Risk Diversifiers, Return Enhancers or Both?" Center for International Securities and Derivatives Markets (CISDM), Isenberg School of Management, University of Massachusetts, July 2000.

An earlier study at CISDM looked at how hedge fund strategies were correlated with 50/50 portfolios combining the S&P and the Lehman Government/Corporate Bond Index.[16] Using the same EACM indexes for the period between January 1990 and April 2000, the authors found similar effects of the stock and bond markets: Hedge fund strategies were more correlated with stocks and bonds when these markets experienced losses than when they were gaining. This is shown in Table 5.7.

Funds that had positive correlation with the stock/bond portfolios when the latter were rising (or negative correlation when portfolios were declining) were classified in the study as "good correlation." "Poor correlation" strategies behaved in the opposite way: positive correlation when stocks/bonds went down, and vice versa.

Most hedge fund strategies offered "poor correlation" benefits. A notable exception was the equity market neutral strategy, which had little correlation with stocks and bonds. Short-biased funds lost money when stocks and bonds went up. Global allocators include managed futures or CTAs who seek to capture trends in the stock and bond markets, going long when they think the markets will go up and short when the market is in a downtrend. Table 2.3 in Chapter 2 showed that the CSFB Managed Futures strategy produced 6.35 percent annual returns with annualized standard deviation of 12.26 percent during 1994–2004. Its indicated Sharpe ratio was one of the worst among hedge fund strategies. Nevertheless, as trend followers, the strategy showed consistent or good correlation with stocks and bonds, though not significantly high.

CONCLUSION

In this chapter we have evaluated hedge fund strategies in terms of how they react to changes in the capital markets of stocks and bonds, how they perform in varying market environments, and the roles they can play in diversified portfolios of hedge funds. To highlight the return and risk profiles that can be expected from the different strategies, we classified them as Risk Reducers, Core Diversifiers, Return Enhancers, and Risk Diversifiers. We also found that hedge fund strategies are correlated among themselves to a high degree; that market neutral funds, whether fixed income or equity oriented, have residual risks and are thus far from being risk free; and that hedge fund strategies are significantly subject to the risks of the stock and bond markets, and are consequently dependent on them to generate returns to a greater extent than correlation analyses suggest. In times of stress, the effects of these market factors on leveraged funds can increase substantially, even if they are purportedly market neutral, due to spikes in volatility and reduced liquidity. Furthermore, although hedge funds are generally less correlated to stocks and bonds than long-only strategies, their low correlations are not necessarily in the desirable direction: Their returns have followed the stock market when there was a decline, but fell behind in rallies.

In the next chapter, we continue with evaluating hedge funds by focusing on the individual hedge funds.

CHAPTER 6

Picking the Winners

There are some 7,000 hedge funds in operation as of latest estimates, more than the number of companies listed on the New York Stock Exchange and the NASDAQ combined. And new ones are being formed every day. This sheer size of the hedge fund population dwarfs even the most resourceful and largest of investors. So, how do investors learn about managers? How do they evaluate them and pick out the winners? The answer to the first question is it's done the old-fashioned way: from someone they know. To answer the second question, they get to know the managers.

SOURCING HEDGE FUNDS

It used to be that the population of hedge funds was much smaller, and the information about them as well as access to them were limited. So, wealthy investors relied on their contacts to source hedge fund managers.

Today, funds of hedge funds still claim that they have a competitive edge because of their vast network of contacts in Wall Street. This is not an empty boast. Funds of funds and other institutional investors experienced in hedge fund investing have accumulated databases of hedge funds over time, containing details about individual funds' strategies, track records, and portfolio managers, and hosts of other information, much of which is not available in commercial databases. They also maintain a smaller "buy" list of funds that have met their investment criteria whose track records they follow closely on a regular basis and whose lead portfolio managers they have become acquainted with.

This practice is akin to traditional equity managers maintaining a list of favorite stocks among which they have a smaller list of ready-to-buy candidates. These data are increased with new funds supplied by word of mouth and personal contacts, as well as by marketers who represent hedge funds and market their clients to institutional investors, family offices, and funds of funds. For those investors who want to invest with managers who are fresh out of their former jobs as star portfolio managers or traders with big investment banks, only personal contacts with these new managers allow early access to them.

Overall, to a significant extent, personal contacts are still the modus operandi for access to and information about hedge funds managed by well-known portfolio managers. This is especially true with regard to emerging managers, managers who have closed off their funds to new investors, or managers who open up new funds or open their funds to new investors because some existing investors have left for nonperformance reasons.

In recent years prime brokerage firms have begun to host capital introduction events to introduce both established and relatively new managers who are their brokerage clients to new investors. These firms include global banks like Citigroup and Deutsche Bank, and brokers and investment banks such as Goldman Sachs, Morgan Stanley, and Bear Stearns. By invitation only, these meetings provide an occasion for about half a dozen managers, in the course of a few hours, to make presentations to a small group of accredited investors.

Less-connected investors, however, have to contend with other less-efficient venues. One is through web sites such as www.hedgeworld.com. The readers need to certify that they are accredited investors and register for free access to the web site. This free-of-charge service allows investors to conduct "simple searches" listing four pages of funds with 25 names on each page. A recent search of "convertible arbitrage" turned up 100 managers, of which 66 have been in operation for at least three years and 26 have five-year track records; 12 funds were closed to new investors. Some of the funds that were still open to investors were quite large, with assets close to or exceeding $1 billion and a five-year track record in the mid-double-digit percentage rates of return. A search for long/short equity managers stopped in the middle of the letter B upon yielding the 100-manager limit, with 27 of them having five-year track records. For a fee of several hundred dollars, subscribers can have "unlimited" access to the hedge funds in the database. However, if investors want more than a fund's name and summary of returns from inception, a payment of $50 is required per hedge fund.

Likewise, for an annual subscription fee of a couple of hundred dollars, the HedgeFund.net web site (www.hedgefund.net) will allow access to hedge funds in different strategies. A search of convertible arb turned up 69 managers. The long/short equity search yielded 584 funds. The list does not rank by asset size. However, it does supply a list of "most visited" funds as well as last-calendar-year and year-to-date returns. To narrow down the list in terms of asset size and length of track records, investors can cull from the individual funds reports to obtain such data as basic overview about the funds, monthly and average rates of return, risk statistics, and contact information.

Well-heeled investors can pay annual subscription fees of a few thousand dollars for access to these databases and the use of PerTrac (www .pertract2000.com). Combining access to databases such as HedgeFund.net, PerTrac subscribers can obtain a full array of information about individual hedge funds, their rates of returns, risks, and, most interestingly, a vast arsenal of analytical tools and figures about their investment track records. They can compare any hedge fund's performance to traditional benchmarks as well as examine its performance relative to other funds within a strategy given investment criteria such as returns, geography, and risk statistics.

Clearly, efforts required to obtain information about hedge funds are far more cumbersome than analyzing individual stocks, not least because there is no central repository of hedge fund data nor are there requirements for disclosure standards. Nevertheless, the current state of affairs is an improvement over years past when less-connected would-be hedge fund investors had to rely on occasional tips from friendly brokers or friends working at hedge funds.

PRELIMINARY SCREENING

Several preliminary screens can be used to further narrow down the number of hedge fund candidates.

New versus Established Funds

Investors who have limited experience in hedge funds may feel more comfortable investing with larger and more established funds. Even professional investors would rather invest with firms that have established track records.

However, the term *established* has a relative meaning in the hedge fund world. Firms that have three-year track records can be considered established. More established firms have longer track records to be analyzed, and more developed infrastructure as to personnel, accounting, and compliance processes and systems. They also have shown an ability to survive and remain viable as a hedge fund manager and business entity in different market conditions. In contrast, new funds usually have a small amount of assets under management and are more prone to operational problems. Thus, institutional investors tend to shy away from hedge funds with less than three-year track records.

Nevertheless, investors have allocated some of their investment dollars to new or emerging managers. This is because they believe that new managers can generate alpha. This is especially true in the case of managers who have impressive track records in their prior jobs, and now spin off to establish their own funds. Academic research has also indicated that such funds tend to outperform older funds at least during the early stage of their corporate life.

Indeed, in one study, Amenc and Martellini (2003)[1] divided their 581 hedge funds into two groups, one- or two-year-old funds and older funds. The average alpha of the new funds exceeded that of the older funds by a wide margin, 2.76 percent per annum. Various methods to measure the performance differences yielded similar results.

More dramatic results were found in Howell (2001)[2] from the TASS/Tremont database covering the 1994–2000 period. These hedge funds were divided into deciles in terms of their age. The youngest funds reported a return of 23.2 percent, while the median of the group was 13.4 percent. However, young funds may have greater proclivities to fail. For this group, the failure rate of funds in business for one year or less was a low 7.4 percent, increased to 20.3 percent for two-year-old funds, 18.6 percent for funds of three years or less, 15.8 percent for four-year-old funds, and 12.9 percent for five-year-old funds. Also, the failure rate appeared to reach a maximum level at 28 months and then declined at a constant rate of 2 to 3 percentage points per annum. Adjusting for these probabilities of failure of survival into the future, the youngest funds still showed a return of 21.5 percent compared to the 13.9 percent median for the group.

In more research on the risk of failure of young funds, Gregoriou (2002)[3] reviewed 1,503 live funds and 1,273 dead funds in the Zurich Capital Markets database for the 1990 to December 2001 period. He found that the median life span of hedge funds as a group is 5.7 years. The median life expectancy declines between years 1 and 3 and improves thereafter, but peaks at 5.7 years in year 5. Looking at the statistics from a different angle, new funds face high risk of failure during the first three years, but their chance of survival steadily improves thereafter.

In the previously cited Morgan Stanley study[4] of the 1990–June 2000 period, starting with 112 funds and increasing to 1,003, younger funds outperformed older funds by wide margins, but outperformance decreased as they grew older. Similarly, Herzberg and Mozes (2003)[5] reported from a study of some 3,300 hedge funds dating back to 1990 that funds in operation for less than three years produced annualized returns higher than those with longer histories by approximately 3 to 4 percent. Their analysis over the 1990 to 2001 period also indicated that the return differential was consistent over time. However, risk-adjusted performance as measured by the Sharpe ratio exhibited no differentiation between young and older firms.

Thus, at the very least, it would be useful to monitor young firms. Should any of these firms continue their strong performance, they certainly would be viable candidates when they reach the maturity threshold. Furthermore, early investing with new managers preserves the ability to increase allocations at a later date, especially if the managers become very successful and close off investments to new investors. With a so-called soft close, such funds would still accept investments from their existing investors. This option can be obtained by investing a relatively small amount, say the minimum amount of $1 million that most hedge funds require. For an allocation of, say, $100 million to hedge funds, this is indeed an insignificant amount, considering the flexibility that may prove useful at a later date. Also, as noted earlier, if the new managers come with impressive pedigrees, competitive pressures may motivate some investors to accept the risks normally attributable to new ventures.

The belief that emerging managers have a tendency to outperform more established hedge funds has been accepted widely among fund of funds managers. Accordingly, they have used it to justify setting up funds that only invest with new managers. As one fund of funds executive put it, "I don't want to be cornflakes."[6] He believed that emerging hedge funds, which he defined as those launched by experienced managers, are the best sources of high returns. And typically the funds he selected were those niche players with small amounts of assets, such as a trader of precious-metals mining stocks who was not interested in growing assets, or a distressed fund focusing only on companies in German bloc countries.

However, the actual experience with emerging hedge funds by the fund of funds managers in my sample has been mixed. Some new managers have worked out very well, while others have turned out to be mediocre or ended in huge losses. One manager stated that his fund of funds, which invested solely in new managers, had not performed up to his expectations. Several other fund of funds managers, however, reported satisfaction with their new managers. It appears that this state of affairs reflects the varying luck or ability of the different fund of funds managers in selecting emerging hedge funds, which are, as expected, more difficult to evaluate due to their lack of track records.

Small versus Large Funds

Institutional investors, especially endowments and pension plans, prefer that their investments not constitute an overwhelming part of a hedge fund's assets under management. They also prefer that those funds with which they invest have a certain infrastructure in place, which would require a certain amount of assets under management. Size also suggests a viable performance track record, the ability to handle significant amounts of assets, and the presence of other investors. Some prime brokers would not handle accounts of hedge fund managers with assets under $10 million. Also, some hedge fund strategies such as distressed securities would benefit from "first call" or close relationships with brokers who would usually place their best and most active clients on first-to-call lists for impending deals or market news. Therefore, the amount of assets under management conveys advantages. Naturally, this minimum amount varies with the hedge funds' strategies as well as their styles.

At the same time, some research has indicated that the smallest funds have been the best performers and the largest funds have also performed well. In the Morgan Stanley study[7] cited earlier it was also found that the smallest funds, with net assets of less than $25 million, and the largest funds, with more than $200 million under management, have produced the highest returns, in terms of both absolute as well as risk-adjusted performance. During the period 1994–2000, the study calculated the annual return of the smallest funds to average 19.5 percent and the largest funds to average 18.0 percent. Funds with assets under management between $25 million to $50 million had annual returns of 15 percent. Lagging behind were the returns of funds with net assets between $50 million and $200 million, averaging 12.7 percent annually. Similarly, Harri and Brorsen (2002)[8] tracked a group of funds, from a couple of funds in 1977 growing to 1,209 funds in 1998, and came to an intuitively plausible conclusion that returns decline when fund size increases. Based on the premise that the hedge funds' goal is to exploit market inefficiencies, and that inefficiencies do not last forever or exist in inexhaustible amounts, the large size of a fund tends to hamper performance.

Somewhat differently, Herzberg and Mozes (2003)[9] found from their study of 3,300 funds that size does matter, but only if assets do not increase dramatically. They reported that funds with assets under $50 million outperformed larger funds in terms of risk-adjusted return measured by the Sharpe ratio; however, the difference in nominal returns was only marginal (1.1 percent vs. 0.98 percent per month). At the same time, if asset inflows increased substantially over short periods of time, performance deterioration ensued. The authors suggested, "This may be due to the fact that additional assets are often placed in cash equivalents until additional ideas can be generated for their use, or even worse, they are invested in lower probability positions."[10] Furthermore, when the data were segregated into large and medium-size funds, their Sharpe ratios did not differ significantly. This suggested that "given a minimum amount of assets under management accompanied by stability in asset size, larger and medium-sized funds perform comparably."[11] However, it is not clear that the possibly negative effects of large size on performance would show up over a short span of a few years. In other words, as a fund gets larger, its performance may lag gradually, but clear deterioration of performance may show up only after prolonged periods.

Contradicting the notion that smaller is better, Amenc and Martellini (2003)[12] found larger was better. They examined 581 hedge funds dating back to 1996, and divided the data into two groups by asset size. They employed 10 different methods to compute performance, including the standard capital asset pricing model (CAPM). They reported that the mean alpha of the larger funds exceeded the mean alpha of the smaller funds; the differences ranged from 1 percent to more than 3 percent. The dispersion of alphas among larger funds was also somewhat smaller, indicating larger funds were more uniform in their alpha-generating capability.

Given that studies on this issue and anecdotal observations are still inconclusive, investors should not be deterred because of a fund's size, other things being equal. Observations of funds in operation suggest that small funds tend to perform better, if they are managed by established managers or managers who have a compelling investment strategy and are experienced portfolio managers. A practical consideration is that funds that have become successful and raised large amounts of assets often close off investments to new investors. At the same time, the size of large funds is a sign of their success and performance track record.

Lockup Period

For certain event-driven strategies involving very illiquid securities or private equity, a lockup of a year or more may be needed to give the fund time to set up investments. For many hedge funds, a lengthy lockup period is not necessary for any investment purpose. Nevertheless, some still demand a lockup period in order to discourage so-called hot money and short-term investors. For this reason, a reasonable lockup period, say six months, may work to the benefit of both investors and managers. Investors who do not approve of lockup periods or who agree to only short ones may exclude funds with lengthy lockup requirements at the beginning. It is noteworthy that funds of funds tend to require longer lockup periods of up to one year in order to satisfy the varying lockup periods required by their underlying hedge funds.

Redemption Notice and Liquidity Gates

Illiquid securities are thinly traded in low volume, sometimes on a negotiated basis. Public securities are traded daily and can always be bought or sold at a price. However, in market dislocations, such securities may not be priced appropriately and forced sales would unnecessarily hurt the fund. In any case, it would benefit investors who seek to disinvest as well as those staying that planned sales are executed under more normal market conditions or in an orderly fashion where prices more fairly reflect the securities' underlying values. Additionally, many hedge fund strategies consist of complex transactions including options, derivatives, and hedges of different combinations. To unwind just one side of the trade would be detrimental to the fund. For these reasons, monthly redemptions (which allow investors to redeem at the end of any month) with advance notice of 30 to 45 days may not be wholly unreasonable. At the same time, some funds with relatively straightforward strategies should not need much time to unwind positions to raise cash. In such cases, redemption notices are a vehicle to retain investors or to discourage short-term ones.

Furthermore, funds of funds may impose liquidity gates, which would limit the amounts of redemptions by investors in any period. One fund of funds has a liquidity gate of 7.5 percent. This means that if all investors wish to redeem at the same time, each would receive only 7.5 percent of his or her stake in the fund. The liquidity gate is intended to allow funds of funds to dispose of their investments in an orderly fashion in extreme circumstances such as large losses or mass defections by investors. It also would help to minimize the impact on the remaining investors if a large investor decides to leave. From an investor's viewpoint, however, the liquidity gate is merely an additional layer of restriction.

For these reasons, investors should decide early in the evaluation process if redemption conditions are acceptable with regard to their liquidity requirements.

Fees

Hedge funds' fees are considerably higher than those charged by mutual funds, and some are significantly higher than the average. Critics have complained that hedge funds' fees are too high. They predicted that as competition increased, fees would necessarily decline. As it turns out, not only have fees not come down, they have actually increased. This is because of capacity shortage in the industry. Although new hedge funds set up shop every day, good managers who can generate alpha and produce good returns in diverse and fast-changing market conditions are difficult to find. They therefore can command higher fees. If high fees are objectionable to investors, it should be noted that while emerging managers may give discounts to early investors, the best-performing hedge funds typically do not discount or reduce their fees.

Most hedge funds charge a management fee of 1 to 2 percent per annum plus 20 to 25 percent for performance incentive. This performance fee may be subject to a hurdle rate. For example, if a fund returns 11 percent with a hurdle rate of 6 percent, an incentive fee of 20 percent is assessed on the 5 percent above the hurdle rate. Without the hurdle rate, the incentive fee would be higher. Funds of funds are increasingly doing away with incentive fees, or are instituting a hurdle rate based on the London Interbank Offered Rate (LIBOR) or the Treasury bill rate.

Transparency

Many hedge funds still do not disclose their underlying investment positions in stocks, bonds, and derivatives and their trades in these securities. Funds of funds rarely disclose the names of the hedge funds in their portfolios. Most individual investors acquiesce to hedge fund managers' desire for secrecy. Institutional investors such as pension plans, however, are increasingly insistent in their demands for transparency. The issue remains controversial, for hedge fund managers continue to maintain that secrecy is a part of their edge. They are concerned that providing transparency only allows third parties in the market to copy—or worse, front run—their trades. The questions investors should ask themselves are to what extent transparency is important to them, how they would put to use the information on individual security positions that would be made available by hedge funds, and what action they could take as a result.

For some investors, transparency of individual holdings may not be that useful, for it does require a substantial amount of analysis to translate such data into meaningful information on portfolio strategy postures, risk profiles, sources of alpha, and return prospects.

However, large institutional investors able to afford these expenses could improve on portfolio construction and risk management. But more importantly, detailed knowledge of security positions would enhance investors' ability to detect shifts in portfolio strategies, the risks undertaken, and the sources of return. For investors in funds of funds, without the knowledge about the underlying hedge funds, it is pretty much like investing in a so-called black box.

Background Investigation

At the beginning, investors would do well to verify that the hedge fund managers being considered are willing to allow their backgrounds to be investigated. Some established and successful managers, however, are not willing to put up with this distraction. Nevertheless, at the very least, investors should make sure early on that the managers have no criminal or securities violations in their records, and no discrepancies in their resumes of work history. Such information is now easily and inexpensively obtainable from securities watchdog agencies such as the National Association of Securities Dealers (NASD). Reference checks are also critical, for it remains a risk that resumes and such written documents do not reveal the full extent of a candidate's background and character.

STRATEGY ALPHA

At the heart of the hedge fund evaluation process is the effort to assess the future performance of the managers being considered. An obvious place to start is their track records, though they can be incomplete and potentially misleading.

Track Records

As discussed earlier in the book, recent studies of hedge funds have begun to record certain observable patterns about their returns and risks. First, hedge fund returns, on average, do not seem to persist for prolonged periods. Funds producing superior results tend to continue this outperformance for a few months or a few quarters, but not much longer. More importantly, funds that exhibit high volatility of returns tend to continue to produce high risks. Practitioners have also observed that poorly performing funds are unlikely to sustain improvements in returns for any significant period.

Past Returns   A key issue in the study of past returns of hedge funds is whether superior performance in the past is a predictor of future results. In the jargon of hedge fund research, is there persistence in hedge fund returns?

As has often been warned, past performance is indeed not indicative of future results. Well, actually, perhaps it is a little bit, or to be precise, maybe it is for the next few quarters.

Indeed, when Amenc, Bied and Martellini (2003)[13] examined the quarterly returns of the CSFB/Tremont hedge fund indexes, they found that a previous period's performance has a strong continuity in the next period's results. They observed that "positive excess return is more likely to be continued and therefore the next period's performance is likely to remain above average."[14] Similarly, Agarwal and Naik (2000)[15] found that there was persistence at the quarterly level, but persistence weakened in yearly returns. This means that a hedge fund's outperformance in one quarter may be repeated the next quarter, but it is unlikely beyond that. Also, outperformance in one year may not be repeated in the following year, much less in the third year.

In the Morgan Stanley study,[16] funds that were ranked in the top 20 percent did outperform the lower-ranked funds if the funds were reranked every month. In the real world, this means that investors would have to rebalance their portfolios on a monthly basis. This is not an option that is often available because most hedge funds require a lockup period and/or redemption notices of as long as six months to a year. When the rebalancing is set more realistically on an annual basis, the winning streaks displayed by the top-performing funds virtually disappear.

Persistence of Risks   Though past returns are not indicative of future performance for long, risky funds tend to remain risky. In a study of 324 hedge funds in five strategies including funds of funds from the TASS database between June 1994 and May 2001, Kat and Menexe (2002)[17] did not detect any persistence of performance from one period to the next. However, they observed very strong persistence of risk as measured by standard deviation. They also found persistent correlations of all fund strategies with the S&P 500, but few with bonds.

Herzberg and Mozes (2003)[18] came to similar conclusions in their study of more than 3,000 hedge funds. They commented, "The implication is that the more risky funds continue to be more risky, funds that are more highly correlated with equity markets continue to be more highly correlated with equity markets, and performance is as likely to mean revert as to persist. The persistence of a fund's correlation with the [Lehman Aggregate Bond Index] is positive but considerably weaker than that of a fund's correlation with the [S&P 500] and [Russell 2000] indices, while the persistence of a fund's correlation with the [Goldman Sachs Commodity Index] is very weak."[19] These observed relationships "may be explained by the fact that volatility, drawdowns, and correlations to markets are a function of a fund's investment *style*, [italics in the original] and investment style persists over time. For example, a fund that operates by taking large market bets tends to continue to take large market bets. Similarly, a fund's tolerance for risk and its risk management disciplines are also behavioral in nature and likely to persist. Returns, on the other hand, are a function of the *success* [italics in the original] of a particular investment style, and the success of a particular investment style varies over time. That is, the fact that a fund's market bets were successful in the past is not a strong indication that those bets will be successful in the future."[20]

Accordingly, preliminary statistical analysis of hedge funds should seek to identify two groups of funds for early elimination: (1) poorly performing funds and (2) funds that exhibit high risks.

Poorly Performing Funds   While the study of hedge fund performance is still evolving and researchers as well as practitioners are still trying to establish sound methods to evaluate hedge funds' returns, it is relatively simple to detect poor performers.

One handy benchmark is the hedge fund index applicable to the strategy under consideration. If a hedge fund's past returns are significantly below those of its peer group, it is unlikely its future performance will improve on a sustained basis. Furthermore, on a practical level, since there are funds of similar strategies that have provided better performances, it is in these funds that investors' resources should be concentrated.

Risky Funds   Funds that exhibit an unusually high level of volatility are likely to continue to do so. We have previously examined a number of risk statistics. Two statistics will prove useful in the early round of elimination: standard deviation and maximum drawdowns. While neither statistic alone nor both when combined are sufficient to fully evaluate the risks of hedge funds, those funds exhibiting standard deviations and drawdowns that are outside the normal ranges of their peers or beyond the ranges accepted by the investors warrant elimination from further consideration at the outset.

Strategy Alpha

Equity investors have long recognized that there are all-weather stocks that have such strong fundamentals they are able to maintain value or even manage to go up when the overall market declines. The search for hedge fund managers of such resiliency is even more critical in hedge fund investing. For alpha is the very reason that justifies investing in hedge funds. Experienced investors are willing to allocate money to hedge funds whose managers are perceived to be exceptionally talented even when these funds' strategies are not actively contemplated. The chief investment officer of a $2 billion foundation said, "We always have room for a talented manager regardless of his strategy."

This approach makes sense in the context of fierce competition for exceptional managers, not unlike the bidding frenzy for a hot initial public offering (IPO). As assets flowing into hedge funds increase and capacities of existing managers reach their limits, investors make quick commitments of capital in new firms started by managers with impressive pedigrees. Very recently, a $1 billion fund of funds director of research recalled with relief and a touch of pride that his fund was among three funds of funds that were "selected" to invest with a star trader from a big investment bank setting up his own firm to invest in the utilities industry. With a target initial capital of $500 million, the new fund was quickly oversubscribed.

Inasmuch as hedge funds' returns are supposed to be driven by alpha or manager talent, a manager's ability to navigate diverse markets while generating absolute returns can indeed be a sound basis for selection. From this vantage point, it is easy to understand investors' intense interest in Long-Term Capital Management with its stable of big-time traders and Nobel laureates. In this vein, it is worth noting that research into the alpha-generating capability of hedge funds has produced at best mixed conclusions.

Alpha Generation Amenc and Martellini (2003)[21] investigated this critical issue in their study of the 581 funds from the CISDM base. Previous research into this question employed different methodologies to estimate alpha produced by hedge funds. Some authors used single-factor models to calculate excess return over and above that provided by single factors such as the S&P 500. Others looked at the influences from a variety of factors such as U.S. and global equity and fixed income market risks, as well as commodity and currency risks. As can be expected, these studies differed in terms of the data and study periods. Additionally, they used different methods to adjust for the asymmetric or nonnormal distribution of returns characteristic of hedge funds. Unsurprisingly, these studies resulted in different and sometimes contradictory conclusions. Amenc and Martinelli tried to reconcile these differences by analyzing the 581 funds using an almost exhaustive set of pricing models to assess the risk-adjusted performance or alpha of hedge funds.

As it turned out, the authors found that hedge funds indeed did generate alpha in the context of the traditional CAPM world against the S&P 500 as the market proxy. Recall that alpha as postulated in the following expression assumes symmetric distribution of returns and standard deviation fully reflecting the risk spectrum of hedge funds.

$$\alpha_i = (\bar{R}_i - r_f) - \beta(\bar{R}_M - r_f)$$

In this formulation, the majority of hedge funds produced positive alpha, and about a third were statistically significant. Very few funds had negative alphas. The average fund in the study population also showed little correlation with the equity market, with the average beta at 0.37 and the majority having betas ranging between 0 and 0.70. These findings were not changed significantly when the S&P 500 was replaced by nonequity economic indicators, including yield on 3-month Treasury bills, dividend yield, term spread between 3-month and 10-year Treasuries, and default credit spreads. The analysis was also modified by using such obscure statistical methodologies as Power Utility and Payoff Distribution functions to factor in the asymmetries of hedge fund returns. Again, the evidence of alpha presence in hedge fund returns was strong and significant.

These findings would confirm the notion that hedge funds produce superior risk-adjusted performance and investors would do well by investing in hedge funds.

However, the naive assumptions embedded in CAPM fail to take into account the complex trading strategies employed by hedge funds. One is that hedge funds invest in illiquid or thinly traded securities. This strategy results in stale prices used to mark portfolio values to market. In the same study, Amenc and Martellini found that adjusted for this factor, the average alpha of the 581 funds was still positive, but no longer statistically significant; in other words, the positive alpha was random. Furthermore, the number of funds with statistically positive alphas dropped from one-third to 16.9 percent. Also, the number of funds with alpha between minus 10 percent and zero increased. Second, while hedge funds take limited risks from the stock and bond markets, hence their reported low correlations with stock and bond market indexes, they take other kinds of risks, including volatility, credit or default risks, and certainly liquidity risks. When these risks were taken into account, the average fund's alpha dropped to a negative 1 percent. However, the number of funds with alpha greater than zero rose to 44 percent from 31 percent under CAPM. Third, the analysis shifted to performance vis-à-vis styles claimed by the funds. In this case, the average fund's alpha was not significantly different from zero. In other words, a fund extracts alpha by not adhering to its self-proclaimed strategy. For example, a market neutral fund, equity or fixed income, achieved positive risk-adjusted performance by taking on market or beta risks.

Furthermore, the returns in the preceding analyses included survivorship and backfill biases, which resulted in overestimates of returns approaching 4.5 percent. The average alpha of the different methods of calculations was only 4.07 percent. This means alpha was a negative –0.43 percent, indicating that the average hedge fund did not generate risk-adjusted return. A bit of good news is that about half of the 581-fund population had alpha greater than the amount of overestimation bias (4.5 percent), indicating that at least some hedge funds did produce positive risk-adjusted return, even after accounting for overestimates of returns from data biases. Another interesting finding was that, despite the different methods used in estimating alpha and the different levels of complexities, there was a better than 50–50 chance that funds would be ranked in the same way regardless of which method was used to rank them. In other words, good funds would still rank at the top and poorly performing funds would fall to the bottom, regardless of the ranking methodologies.

The preceding findings are thus consistent with the notion that hedge funds are exposed to a variety of risk factors, some of which are not observable from hedge fund return data. Among these factors are leverage and illiquid securities. Investors have recognized that hedge funds traverse the traditional stock and bond markets, but they use different strategies to generate returns. They go long and short stocks and bonds, but they use all kinds of strategy maneuverings to reduce, increase, or transfer the risks of the underlying securities. At times, their trades produce positive, sometimes extraordinary, returns though the markets they are involved in perform poorly. Their winning streaks may last for some time. However, except for the very best funds, outperformance would be unlikely to last beyond the following year.

Alpha versus Beta: Hedges versus No Hedges   Hedge funds are supposed to generate alpha, independent of the market, whatever the "market" is, by engaging in short selling, that is, using hedges to offset their long positions. But not all hedge funds and hedge fund strategies hedge their long positions. While equity market neutral managers come closest to neutralizing the stock market's systemic risk and thus are fully hedged, long/short equity funds use only partial hedges; they are long the stock market to the extent of their net long exposures and are correspondingly exposed to beta risks. Event driven funds may use hedges in varying degrees depending on their market niches, whether distressed securities or merger arbitrage. Convertible arbitrage funds short sell stocks to hedge their bond positions, but some managers may choose to rely mostly on credit analysis and leave many of their positions unhedged. Global macro and multistrategy funds have great flexibility to be mostly long, short, or market neutral in the strategies they employ.

Fixed income arb funds may hold zero-duration positions, but are exposed to the risk of credit spreads. Emerging markets managers are mostly long, and short sellers are mostly short. Managed futures funds are long and short in different market segments so that in aggregate these positions may offset one another, depending on how they do the accounting, but they may not and therefore are making directional bets on both the long and the short sides in multiple markets. In some cases, a fund is more suitably considered an alternative investment, in a sense similar to private equity or real estate. An example is loan origination, which is essentially lending to subprime credits, or private investments in public entities (PIPE), which have more to do with investment banking than investing.

Funds that hedge away in varying degrees their markets' systemic risks and use hedges on an ongoing basis as a fundamental part of their strategies can be viewed as "hedges" funds. In addition to alpha generated from specialized skills such as stock picking or credit analysis, "hedges" funds also obtain alpha from taking beta risks by varying it—increasing it as the market goes up and reducing it on market declines. However, funds that have little or no hedging are predominantly long and therefore are dependent on their market or beta factors for returns, be it the stock market or interest rates; they are vulnerable to losses if their markets decline. Their returns are highly correlated to their beta factors.

If beta dominates a fund's return streams, the fund is indistinguishable from a long-only fund and would be best treated as such. Additionally, when a fund makes two-directional bets on both the long and short sides, they are exposed to the risk of double jeopardy.

Understanding Hedge Fund Strategies   It is critically important that investors gain a thorough understanding of what the hedge fund managers do. Investors want to determine the basis whereby excess return or alpha would be generated such that absolute return is produced regardless of the market condition. In other words, what is the alpha-generating thesis embedded in the investment strategy and process? Is it from timing the market by varying the beta exposure, or from specialized skills such as stock picking, credit analysis, or short-term trading? Is it sound and viable? Is it sustainable over time?

Unfortunately, acquiring this understanding is not always possible, as the head of one fund of funds manager who founded his firm in 1995 complained: "By definition, we cannot always understand the manager's strategy!" The complexities of the strategies, opaqueness of disclosure, and hedge fund managers' proclivities for secrecy certainly play a role here.

An effective practice is to spend time with the managers in their offices, watching what they trade, how they trade, and the process of how these decisions are made, as well as the risk-control mechanisms put in place to record and manage the flows of transactions. Some funds of funds in our sample adopt this practice as part of their due diligence process. Not all, however, practice this time-consuming and labor-intensive yet critical and possibly illuminating exercise. Nor are all hedge fund managers willing to accede to this level of disclosure.

It would be helpful if the investors are familiar with the types of strategies under consideration. Funds of funds claim their investment staffs have had experience in these hedge fund strategies. However, the chief executive officer of a $400 million fund of funds was not joking when he said, "I know we are still novices at this." For sometimes even the managers themselves are not aware of the risks they are taking. Certain strategies such as fixed income arbitrage that take advantage of narrowing credit spreads would become losers if spreads were to widen. It has been known that some such managers actually piled up on the amounts of leverage to maintain return when spreads were at their lowest, taking on risks that led to large losses when interest rates moved suddenly and prompted credit spreads to widen. Indeed, fixed income–related strategies such as mortgage-backed securities arbitrage are difficult to analyze and their correlation with the capital markets is not readily predictable. Also, Commodity Trading Advisors (CTAs) who use trend-following techniques or computer-generated buy and sell signals are often hard-pressed to explain what their edge is, other than the returns of their performance records. As hedge fund managers migrate to hedge funds from proprietary trading desks of investment banks where they made profits from trading actively in obscure niches of the capital markets and often benefited from having an edge in competitive information and deal flows, what they do to generate and maintain returns is not always easily discernible to investors of any stripe.

Furthermore, hedge fund managers are not always what they claim to be. A fund with about $20 million of assets called itself a global macro manager whose strategy is "to generate excess returns (alpha) through forecasting interest rates on a monthly basis. The manager establishes the fund's monthly directional positions, either long or short, through investing in 10-year Treasury futures." Though it charges high fees, it is difficult to see how this fund's strategy of directionally taking on interest rate risks is meaningfully different from a traditional bond manager. A self-proclaimed equity market neutral manager said he generated alpha by buying puts and calls in the distant months while selling offsetting puts and calls in the nearby months. Clearly this strategy depends on the time decay and volatility factors in the valuation of short- and long-dated options, not on stock-picking skills. Another fund with close to $200 million of assets claimed its primary strategy is fixed income arbitrage, but it also "participates on both the long and short side in various securities . . . [depending on] where the most favorable risk/reward profiles may reside." Investing in this fund, investors should not expect interest rates and credit spreads to be the only factors driving its performance and risks.

In this context, it is understandable why "integrity" has been the most prized character in hedge fund managers as cited by large investors, institutional or fund of funds. As in hiring employees or taking on new partners, investors want managers who did what they said they did and will do what they say they will do, or will at least try to, in the future. The history of these managers' past performances is merely a testimonial that the strategies they professed did in fact produce the desired risk and return profiles, and that they performed well with low correlation with the directions of the stocks and bond markets.

Investors should try to assess if these successes could be repeated in the future, the so-called repeatability of the strategies. For this purpose, the investors should look at the size of the niche markets in question; the amounts of transactions and deal flows; the types of investors and issuers, that is, the supply and demand sides of the market; and critically, the excess profits that could be extracted on an ongoing basis, as well as the strategies that are used to extract these profits. However, investors often lose sight of the prospect that as the number of players increases and assets flow into the strategies, the excess profits cannot be maintained for long, and hedge fund managers have to take increasingly larger risks to preserve their historical returns, even as the individual funds are closed to new investors.

ALPHA GENERATION AND MANAGER TALENT

Part of the "repeatability" question is related to the experience, education, and skill sets of the lead portfolio managers and the investment staff directly involved in trading the strategies. Some hedge fund strategies require specialized analytical skills even to analyze publicly available information, such as distressed securities, where superior legal expertise in bankruptcy proceedings, as well as experience in structured finance, capital structure, deal making, and the like would constitute an advantage over less-experienced competitors. At the same time, short-term trading is usually not part of the skill set of traditional long-only managers; being a successful traditional manager hardly qualifies one as a short-term trader.

Therefore, the relevance of the experience and skills of the hedge fund managers is critical in evaluating whether the strategies can be successfully carried out in the future, to produce the expected returns. Those with the most attractive pedigrees are the most sought after, such as former portfolio managers with well-known hedge fund firms and traders at global investment banks with respected proprietary trading desks. After accumulating a track record of having made impressive profits for their former employers, these traders become attractive when they spin off to set up their own hedge funds.

Statistical Evidence of Alpha

At this time, a more detailed quantitative analysis of the hedge fund's performance would be in order in the hedge fund evaluation process. This analysis would review its past historical record in terms of the absolute return as well as in comparison with its peers, the hedge fund indexes, the stock and bond major indexes, and the hedge funds already in the investors' portfolios. Statistics such as alpha, beta, correlation coefficients, skew, kurtosis, drawdowns, and other risk measurements can be used to highlight and focus the issues of interest. Views of the portfolio managers and their outlooks, prospective strategy changes, and portfolio compositions are key topics that will help further the understanding of the hedge funds' strategies, potential risks, and the managers' approaches in taking advantage of opportunities.

While this review uses historical data, the purpose must be to assess the prospective returns and risks of the hedge funds and their strategies going forward, and how they would fit in and add value to the investors' existing portfolios. Importantly, investors would wish to determine that the sources of excess return claimed by the hedge funds were in fact detectable from the data. Useful information would include leverages and how they changed over time, portfolio composition, turnover, and credit ratings of the portfolio's holdings. Investors would want to differentiate alpha generated from a manager's skills in security selection, credit analysis, market timing, trading, or risk management discipline, as opposed to gains from making large market bets, taking on the risks of illiquid securities, or excess leveraging. A good hedge fund track record would show evidence of excess return in diverse market environments, including times of unusual stress. It certainly would have an alpha-positive statistical risk and return profile. Drawdowns would be well contained within limits acceptable for such types of strategies, and the average returns would not be dominated by a few large gains among strings of losses.

As noted, performance among managers varies widely. This has been cited as evidence of differences in the ability of hedge fund managers. This is even more remarkable since managers are increasingly following similar strategies as the number of hedge funds explodes and assets under management skyrocket. In the previously cited Morgan Stanley study,[22] the research team found a low correlation among the managers within any individual strategy, between 10 and 20 percent, far below the correlation among mutual fund managers. This is understandable since mutual fund managers typically follow the stock markets in making stock selection. Later studies, however, suggest that correlation among managers has increased markedly. Capocci, Corhay, and Hubner (2003)[23] looked at almost 3,000 hedge funds for the period 1994–2002, covering the most recent bull-and-bear market cycle. They found that the correlation among managers is generally greater than 25 percent, and gets closer to 50 percent (and higher) among select strategies. In the Bridgewater study previously cited (Table 5.2, Chapter 5), the data included the period to June 2003. The authors found that correlation among managers is around 50 percent or higher.

DUE DILIGENCE

The preceding screening procedures will have reduced the number of hedge funds the investors can manage comfortably and go to the next step. For an individual investor venturing the first time into the hedge fund world, it may be that at this stage only a few funds qualify for further consideration. At most a few dozen hedge funds will make the cut if more than one strategy is considered, because many qualified funds may have closed to new investors. Even a large institutional investor seeking to allocate hundreds of millions of dollars for the first time may wish to undertake screening as described above, even though these investors usually engage consultants to do their searches. This is because no one database is large and thorough enough at the present time to cover all the bases. Personal contacts might turn up some new managers who are worth considering or other managers who are not in the loop or aware that a search is being conducted. Remember that even large funds of funds still rely to a significant extent on word of mouth to discover talented managers.

Once the candidate managers are identified, the most consuming part of the manager search and selection process begins: due diligence.

In a nutshell, due diligence has to do with making sure that the hedge fund being considered for an investment is what it is supposed to be, that is, what is claimed in its marketing material. In mergers and acquisitions, and other such business deals, due diligence is an integral part of the negotiation and a condition before deals are consummated and ready for closing. In investment, due diligence is a recent phenomenon prompted by the burgeoning interest in hedge funds. Part of the reason is that many hedge funds are new and small with little in the way of business history. Most of them also are generally reluctant to reveal much about their businesses and investment processes. Concerns about potential fraudulent practices also underlie the need for due diligence.

Overall, due diligence seeks to address the issues that are most important to investors. The first ones concern the soundness of the investment strategy and the relevant experience of the principals and lead portfolio managers. Other important issues include back-office operations, especially fund accounting and security pricing or marking to market. One should also review and assess the viability and sustainability of the fund's business organization, operation, and practice, as well as the risk management and controls in place to ensure fairness and integrity in portfolio management, fund accounting and reporting, and client servicing, including timeliness of reporting and responsiveness to inquiries.

Several critical due diligence issues are highlighted in the following sections.

Risk Controls

Hedge funds seek superior returns by being active traders of complex strategies in highly competitive markets and by using leverage. Though the management fee is handsome, the bulk of managers' earnings comes from the incentive fees on their fund returns. In this fast-paced environment laden with incentives to take risks with investor capital, how can risk be controlled and mitigated, and imprudence curtailed?

Certain risk monitoring mechanisms are usually in place at the individual hedge funds' levels. For equity funds, there are the usual limits on position size, sector concentration, amounts of exposure to the equity, and stop-loss levels beyond which the positions would be liquidated. Fixed income arbitrage funds would have limits on the portfolio duration to limit exposure to the direction of interest rate moves and to the range of credit risks. Leverage is a key component of risk in fixed income funds and managed futures, less so in equity-oriented funds. Therefore, a thorough understanding of the individual managers' definitions of leverage is critical, whether leverage is measured by the total of the notional long and short amounts or these amounts are option- or duration-adjusted, or both. This is a question to which investors must devote much attention, for these adjustments would understate the magnitude of the risks during times of sudden moves in interest rates and credit spreads.

Furthermore, different strategies have different risk management procedures. For example, automatic stop-losses are necessary for managed futures managers, but are not always as strict for long/short equity funds. Some funds follow well-defined technical rules in picking entry prices for buy and sell orders. Others, such as quantitative funds, are less sensitive to entry prices and usually execute portfolio changes at the beginning of each month. Still others buy or sell at closing prices and ignore intraday price movements. Short-term traders may close their positions at day's end. As such, being able to pick the right entry prices at which to buy and sell is critical to their success. Depending on strategies, it is important that the hedge funds are able to articulate the risk control procedures that are embedded in their strategies, and such procedures are sufficiently robust to allow early detection of the sources and causes of the risks. Without rigorous risk management, surprises are bound to happen and unexpected losses would surely occur over time.

Operations and Accounting

According to an industry consulting firm, Capital Markets Company (Capco), half of the hedge fund failures have been caused by operations-related problems.[24] Marking to market of securities' prices and accounting for fund values count as most important. Errors or omissions in handling these tasks lead to misstating of the hedge funds' performance and the values of the investors' accounts, thus causing harm to new investors as well as to those who redeem or remain with the funds. The crisis of investor confidence at the huge Clinton Group in 2003 was prompted by a portfolio manager's resignation citing his disagreement with management on the pricing of mortgage-backed securities.

There are effective ways to make sure that operational matters are handled adequately for hedge funds. These include on-site visits with back-office staffs, administrators, and custodian banks, and reviews of the paper flows and procedures for mark-to-market pricing and fund accounting. Examination of statements of assets under management, direct verification with third-party administrators, and audit reports are also necessary to ensure that assets under management claimed by a hedge fund are true.

Investors cannot be too careful in this aspect of the due diligence process. Cases have been reported whereby respected financial institutions were defrauded by self-proclaimed hedge funds. Witness the judgment against Manhattan Investment Fund and its manager, Michael W. Berger. As ruled by the judge on the case, "Berger commenced his fraudulent scheme almost immediately after the Fund began its operations in mid-1996. Judge Cote further found that, as a result of Berger's trading strategy, the Fund consistently suffered losses which ultimately totaled nearly $400 million. Instead of accurately reporting the losses the Fund was experiencing, however, Berger created fictitious account statements which substantially overstated the market value of the Fund's holdings. Judge Cote found that Berger caused a fictitious account statement to be forwarded to the Fund's administrator in Bermuda every month for 39 consecutive months. The Fund's administrator then calculated the Fund's net asset value and the market value of each investor's shares in the Fund based on Berger's fabricated figures, and sent monthly account statements based on these calculations to the Fund's investors."[25]

Nevertheless, experience has shown that audited financial statements contain fewer inaccuracies than those that are unaudited. A senior executive at a $3 billion fund of funds insisted, "You never hire a manager without audited returns done by a firm you respect and, if possible, know." Bing Liang (2002)[26] has documented that auditing makes a clear difference in hedge funds' data quality; audited funds had much less return discrepancy than nonaudited funds. Furthermore, large funds tend to be audited while small funds tend not to be. It is noteworthy that a foundation with $2 billion of assets actively invested in hedge funds armed itself with a team of lawyers and accountants dedicated to doing operations due diligence at on-site visits with its candidate hedge funds as well as those already in its portfolio.

Overall, investors would need to ascertain that back-office staffing is adequate to perform the necessary marking to market and fund accounting in accordance with generally accepted accounting principles. The head of the accounting function should also demonstrate evidence of competency in accounting and related functions. Preferably this individual should be independent from the portfolio manager of the hedge fund. However, this may not be possible in a small firm. In this case, an independent third party such as an outside administrator may fill this role.

One indication of this adequacy or lack thereof is the lead time required to provide mark-to-market portfolio values and rates of return to investors. Any such delays in reporting may be symptomatic of difficulties in obtaining securities prices. This may be due to any number of reasons. Possibly the securities are so rarely traded that fair prices are difficult to determine. In this case, investors should question the fairness of reported returns. Or it may simply be due to a temporary disruption in back-office functions because of personnel turnover. However, if staff turnover is high, especially in the case of resignations of senior executives, investors may be well advised to make further inquiries for any indication of adverse effects on the future performance of the firm in question.

RISK AND PERFORMANCE MATRIX

To summarize the preceding discussion, Table 6.1 shows the Risk and Performance Matrix designed to capture the factors that differentiate different hedge funds and highlight their relative importance and contribution to a hedge fund's attractiveness as an investment.

The Matrix has been distilled from the practices and considerations found at large funds of funds as well as institutional investors. As a checklist, it encapsulates the hedge fund data that need to be reviewed by investors. Each factor is scored and weighted according to its importance. There are 30 factors on the Matrix. Each is given a score of 0 to 10. The first 12 factors deal with the information that purports to shed light on the future performance of the hedge fund. They are given a weighting of 3. The next six factors deal mostly with the past performance track record and are assigned a weighting of 2. The remaining 12 factors relate to operations issues and each has a weighting of 1. The perfect score is 600. However, a passing score would probably range between 450 and 500.

TABLE 6.1 Evaluation Factors: Risk and Performance Matrix

Scoring Range: 0 to 10

	Factors	Score	Maximum Score/ Weightings
	Strategy Alpha		
1	Lead PM strategy experience	10	30
2	Viability of strategy	10	30
3	Alpha-generating thesis	10	30
4	Sustainability of alpha thesis	10	30
5	Degree of leverage	10	30
6	Sell discipline	10	30
7	Security/sector diversification	10	30
8	Overall portfolio liquidity	10	30
9	Risk controls	10	30
10	Style drift/discipline	10	30
11	Volatility bias	10	30
12	Capacity constraint	10	30
	Track Record		
13	Lead PM experience	10	20
14	Transparency	10	20
15	Volatility of past returns	10	20
16	Past returns	10	20
17	Depth of management	10	20
18	Marking to market	10	20
	Operations		
19	Technology contingency	10	10
20	Counterparty risk	10	10
21	Custody/prime broker	10	10
22	Audit checks	10	10
23	Regulatory compliance	10	10
24	Investor communication	10	10
25	Interim NAV estimates	10	10
26	Back office operations	10	10
27	Employee turnover	10	10
28	Growth plan	10	10
29	Fee structure	10	10
30	Lockup/redemption/notice period	10	10
	Total Score		600

BEYOND DUE DILIGENCE

While the preceding discussion provides a discipline for a requisite assessment of a hedge fund before money is placed with it, it should be recognized that the potential ramifications of a hedge fund are not always easy to be fully appreciated from statistical analyses of its past records, a few meetings, or even extended periods of tracking and observation.

There are very good hedge funds that generate superior returns, can sustain performance over time, and are usually able to navigate difficult market environments. However, some funds may frequently resort to style drifts or significant departures from their self-proclaimed strategies to exploit perceived market opportunities. In the process, they make take on risks outside the range of their normal tolerances, such as larger market bets, higher concentrations in illiquid securities, and excessive short-term trading. They may also engage in markets they may not have much experience with, such as a U.S. equity specialist trading in foreign stocks. Or like Long-Term Capital Management, a fixed income arbitrage manager may decide to dabble in the equity market. Since hedge funds report their returns monthly, investors would be ill-equipped to discern these out-of-the-ordinary trades and their effects if they are put on and taken off during the month.

Worse, some fund managers fudge the books during market downturns by using questionable values in security marking-to-market, in the hope of the market returning to more favorable conditions, allowing their portfolio holdings to return to fair values. In stressful times, some have resorted to fraudulent practices, as such cases have been reported time and again in the press.

Most hedge fund managers did not start out with the intention of defrauding investors. But many hedge funds do not practice transparency while they engage in complex strategies that navigate in multiple markets, use exotic derivatives, and/or employ shifting strategies. The more complex a hedge fund's strategy is, the more difficult it is to properly assess its sources of alpha and risks. Importantly, in times of market stress or when mistakes are made, only the most scrupulous managers would face up to the consequences and be forthcoming with their investors. However, some could not resist the temptation and, as the records have shown, resorted to deception. Lack of transparency is an unintended assist in these circumstances.

As a result, oftentimes a large investor would invest the required minimum with a potentially attractive hedge fund only to gain the ability to analyze the hedge fund up close and to gain insight into its trading and business before making any meaningful commitment. If the hedge fund turns out to be less than it appeared, hopefully the investor would not suffer much of a loss. Anyway, whether the initial investment is large or small, the tasks of assessing and evaluating a hedge fund must be ongoing until the relationship with it is terminated. These issues will be explored in greater detail in the following chapters.

CONCLUSION

In this chapter we have discussed how investors interested in investing in hedge funds must follow through on a disciplined process to research, analyze, and evaluate hedge funds, to capture this ephemeral characteristic called alpha, and to overcome the lack of data and lack of transparency— all of which contribute to the difficulty of identifying the best-performing hedge fund managers. At the end of this process, a few hedge funds would be selected and money allocated to them. The issues related to this task, how best to construct a hedge fund portfolio capable of achieving the investor's investment objective, are the subjects for examination in Chapter 7.

CHAPTER 7

Constructing a Portfolio of Hedge Funds

A large public retirement fund recently embarked on a new program to invest in hedge funds. As is the usual practice, it hired a well-known consulting firm to analyze its investment requirements and select the managers for its billion-dollar allocation to hedge funds. The objective of the fund is to diversify away from traditional stocks and bonds, and raise the allocation to hedge fund strategies to 15 percent of its assets. In the process, it hopes to achieve its long-term return target of 8 percent, which it has failed to meet in the past five years. The fund ended up hiring five funds of funds, achieving a broad diversification across managers. But it also added three hedge funds engaged in multitudes of trading strategies and markets. Two of them are a global macro fund and a multistrategy fund; the third specializes in market neutral strategies across global markets. The fund believes that these funds will give it access to a wider range of investment opportunities, and allow the potential for high return.

At the other end of the spectrum of investors' assets, an executive working for a hedge fund organization decided to put aside $2 million for investment with hedge funds. Approaching retirement, the executive has set his objective to achieve an overall return for his portfolio to be at least 6 percent with minimal risk of losses. After several months of research and conference calls, the executive placed $300,000 with his firm's fixed income arbitrage fund specializing in mortgage-backed securities. Clearly his intimate knowledge of his firm's hedge fund was a key influence. Furthermore, unlike similar funds that hedge the interest rate risk by shorting Treasury securities, this mortgage fund sought to arbitrage between "rich" versus "cheap" and conforming versus nonconforming mortgage securities while holding interest rate duration neutral. Though still exposed to sudden interest rate shifts, the portfolio minimized its exposure to a key risk in mortgages, the prepayment risk. The remaining $1.7 million was divided between two funds of funds.

Though vastly different in size, the two investors share a common goal in structuring their hedge fund investment programs: diversification. In fact, diversification is as crucial—some argue that it is even more so—for portfolios of hedge funds as for portfolios of stocks and bonds. As investors should not concentrate in one stock, they should not invest with just one hedge fund.

EFFECTIVE DIVERSIFICATION TO REDUCE RISKS

In hedge fund investing, the primary purpose of diversification is to reduce the risks from following the wrong strategies and from picking the wrong managers. Diversification across a variety of hedge funds can be achieved by investing in a number of hedge funds across a variety of strategies, or in funds of hedge funds.

Size of Capital

Though some hedge funds accept investments in the range of a few hundred thousand dollars or less, most funds, especially the more successful ones with track records lasting several years, require minimum investments of $1 million or more if they are still open to new investors. As a result, investors with a relatively small allocation to hedge funds may have difficulty in assembling a diversified portfolio of hedge funds. In this case, an effective strategy is to invest with a fund of funds that allocates capital to a number of hedge funds across a variety of strategies. This is following the same practice as investing in a mutual fund rather than buying a basket of individual stocks.

Like hedge funds, established funds of funds with billions of dollars under management require a minimum of $1 million or more. However, they typically have larger capacity; that is, they can manage a greater amount of assets, in billions of dollars, than a typical hedge fund, many of which close their doors to new investors after a few hundred million dollars. As a result, funds of funds can continue to accept new investors years after their initial launches. Additionally, index funds and funds of funds that require much smaller minimum investments have been recently made available to retail investors. One such fund is the index fund Lyxor, which accepts as little as $100,000. Lyxor is offered to U.S. investors by Paris-based Société Générale, which mimics Morgan Stanley's MSCI Hedge Fund Investable Index, and offers liquidity on a weekly basis. At the time of this writing, Lyxor had $2.2 billion under management, and planned to close to new investors once it reached $5 billion. Another retail platform is offered by Merrill Lynch. Investors who are able to invest at least $300,000 can place amounts of $100,000 or more with about a dozen third-party hedge funds and funds of funds selected by Merrill Lynch. As can be expected, retail platforms such as Merrill Lynch levy another layer of fees on top of those charged by the funds of funds, which are of course in addition to the management and incentive fees of the underlying hedge funds.

Though one fund of funds may be sufficient to achieve investment diversification, it may make sense to invest with more than one. One reason is the liquidity restriction placed by many funds of funds as discussed shortly and in Chapters 6 and 10.

Once the amounts of investment capital get larger, say, to a few million dollars, the opportunities to achieve diversification with single-strategy hedge funds would increase. In such cases, a couple of well-placed funds of funds plus a few well-chosen single-strategy hedge funds would allow the portfolio to tilt toward higher return as the previously discussed institutional investor had done. Or, the single-strategy hedge funds may gear toward lower-volatility strategies, thereby further reducing the overall risk profile. Alternatively, the single-strategy hedge funds may be those that are managed by particularly talented managers employing very specialized niche strategies. However, it should be noted that postinvestment monitoring and evaluating of manager performance can get complicated and require that a significant amount of time be devoted as the number of hedge funds increases. Therefore, it may be impractical for individual investors and small institutions to properly manage a portfolio with more than a few hedge funds.

Uncorrelated Assets

Merely assembling a number of hedge funds or funds of funds may not lead to effective diversification to reduce the risk. As discussed previously, low-correlation assets, when combined into a portfolio, could result in portfolio risk that is lower than the risk of the individual assets. Portfolios with highly correlated assets would have the risk approximating the weighted average of the risks of the individual assets. In practical terms, highly correlated assets go up in value or decline together. In contrast, a portfolio of low-correlation or negatively correlated hedge funds would allow some part of the portfolio to rise in value if the market conditions turn unfavorable while other parts may fare less well. This is the essence of hedge fund investing.

The requirement of low-to-negative correlation has important implications. In evaluating hedge funds of similar risk/return profiles, the preferred ones are those that exhibit the lowest correlation to stocks and bonds as they would add less risk to existing portfolios and might even reduce it. Even hedge funds operating within the same market—convertible arbitrage, as an example—may exhibit low correlation with each other. Some of these funds may specialize in credit analysis and use little leverage, while others resort to stock hedging and trade more actively. These different styles should lead to lower correlation among the individual funds. Their presence in a portfolio would therefore help produce a lower risk profile than those funds that employ similar styles.

Furthermore, low correlation does not necessarily mean "good" correlation. As previously discussed in Chapter 5, most hedge fund strategies exhibit "poor" correlation with the stock market in the sense that they follow the stock market down (that is, they are more correlated when equities perform the worst); they trail the equity market or are less correlated when the latter performs the best. One exception is the equity market neutral strategy, which has exhibited consistently little correlation with equities in both up and down markets. Another strategy that has shown consistent correlation is short selling. But unlike equity market neutral, this strategy acts countercyclically to the stock market; that is, it gains when stocks are down, and vice versa. Also, its historical return record consists mostly of losses, versus gains close to 10 percent by equity market neutral.

Fund of funds managers in our sample place special emphasis on selecting uncorrelated hedge funds for their portfolios. For this purpose, they prefer to line up managers who have different skill sets even if the managers employ similar strategies. An example in long/short equity is a high-frequency trader versus a stock picker. In fixed income arbitrage, an example is a yield curve arbitrageur alongside a mortgage-backed securities fund. In either case, the influences of the equity market and interest rates on the underlying funds, and the responses of the managers, can vary very substantially. Over time this lineup of dissimilar strategies should help reduce correlation with the traditional markets in times of stress and yet be positioned to take advantage of opportunities in more favorable market conditions.

Additionally, in hedge fund investing, diversification has several practical purposes. One is liquidity. Hedge funds require lockup periods, redemption notices, and waiting periods of at least 30 days; some also impose liquidity gates. As a result, a hedge fund portfolio needs to be structured so that redemptions can be accomplished with the greatest flexibility possible. This approach is similar to a bond portfolio with laddered maturities whereby the securities would come to maturity at different intervals, allowing investors more flexible access to liquidity.

Other practical considerations are a hedge fund's capacity and age. Except for early seed-capital investors in new funds, institutional investors often prefer not to invest more than a certain percentage of a fund's assets. Also, investors in general favor established funds over new funds. However, of importance is the consideration of the relative performances of small versus large and new versus established funds. As discussed in Chapter 6, new funds have been shown to outperform established funds, and small funds have greater flexibility in deploying assets than large funds. Accordingly, some diversification in terms of fund size and age may enhance returns—in other words, achieve higher alpha—without incurring commensurate risks.

HOW MUCH IN HEDGE FUNDS?

Brokers generally recommend that the right amount of allocation to hedge funds is about 10 to 20 percent, partly because this allocation is small enough to monitor and also because research at large investment banks has concluded that such allocations would significantly improve the risk/return trade-offs of the traditional stock and bond portfolios.[1] However, an examination of published hedge fund index data suggests a much larger percentage.

Thus, as shown in Figure 7.1, a data provider indicated an optimal allocation of 60 percent to hedge funds from a traditional portfolio of 60 percent in the S&P 500 and 40 percent in the Lehman Aggregate Bond Index. Calculating the efficient frontier from the CSFB/Tremont Hedge Fund Index produces similar results. This is shown in Figure 7.2. With 60 percent allocated to hedge funds, the resulting portfolio would contain only 24 percent in equities and 16 percent in bonds. It is also the optimal portfolio as it has the most favorable risk/return trade-off. Its Sharpe ratio is 0.78 compared to a ratio of 0.46 for the stock and bond portfolio and 0.32 for the S&P 500.

The reason for these high-allocation estimates is embedded in the data of the hedge fund indexes' returns. As is now clear, index data shows hedge funds to produce returns similar to the equity market and higher than bonds. Yet hedge fund risks as measured by standard deviation are lower and they have low correlation to the stock and bond markets. Applying this input to the mean-variance optimization analysis would automatically result in high allocations to hedge funds.

Some large institutional investors such as endowments have invested

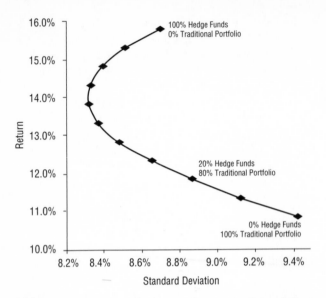

FIGURE 7.1   Impact of Hedge Funds on a Traditional Stock and Bond Portfolio
Notes:
Hedge fund statistics based on the 1Q1988–3Q2003 Van Global Hedge Fund Index data.
Traditional Portfolio = 60 percent S&P 500, 40 percent Lehman Brothers Aggregate Bond Index.
Source: Van Hedge Fund Advisors International, LLC and/or its licensors, Nashville, TN, USA.

more than 20 percent of their total assets in hedge funds. In 2003 the University of Virginia had half of its endowment in hedge fund investments, and planned to increase the allocation to 60 percent in 2004. Vanderbilt University's endowment, at the end of 2003, had a hedge fund allocation of 37 percent. The endowment at Yale University has increased its hedge fund allocation steadily during the past 10 years from 14 to 26 percent in 2003. A consulting firm reported that in aggregate endowments and foundations averaged 20 percent allocations to hedge funds as early as 2003.[2] A well-known hedge fund executive said on national TV that 80 percent of her net worth was invested in hedge funds.

Rhetorically, a strategist whose job at a global investment bank was to advise wealthy investors asked, "Why not 100 percent hedge funds?"[3] He then enthused, "The high risk-adjusted returns attainable via hedge fund investments make them an ideal product for leveraging. Rarely do hedge funds report negative returns. . . . For this reason, and because hedge fund

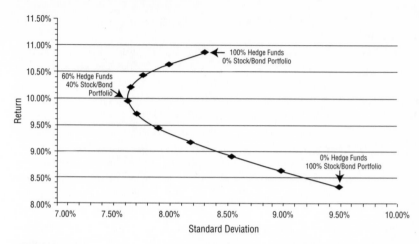

FIGURE 7.2 Asset Allocation of Hedge Funds and Stock/Bond Portfolios
Notes:
"Hedge Funds" are the CSFB/Tremont Hedge Fund Index.
"Stock/Bond Portfolio" consists of 60 percent in the S&P 500 and 40 percent in the Lehman Aggregate Bond Index.
Data are from January 1994 to June 2004.
Sources: CSFB/Tremont, Standard & Poor's, PerTrac.

returns are higher than bond returns and less risky, leveraging hedge funds represents an unadulterated profit opportunity."[4]

Academic research has also suggested that a very significant allocation would be necessary for hedge funds to begin to have a material impact on a traditional portfolio of stocks and bonds. Amin and Kat (2002)[5] examined monthly returns net of fees of 1,195 live hedge funds and 526 dead funds in the TASS/Tremont database. They constructed hedge fund portfolios with randomly selected funds, which included dead funds before these funds were closed down in order to correct for the survivorship bias. The resulting hedge fund portfolios were then added in varying portions, from zero to 100 percent, to equal-weighted stock and bond portfolios to create diversified stock/bond/hedge fund portfolios. As it turned out, the mean return of the diversified portfolios rose consistently and linearly with increasing allocations to hedge funds. Portfolio standard deviation also improved but reached its lowest point where hedge funds made up 50 percent of the diversified portfolios, then moved up with larger allocations.

However, generalizations about hedge fund investing should be tempered by considerations for the relatively short history of hedge funds, the paucity of the information available about them, their vast differences, their asymmetric return, and their "left tail" risks or negative skew, and high kurtosis.

The issue of how much is the optimal hedge fund allocation suffers from similar limitations. Ray Dalio, president and chief investment officer of the hedge fund firm Bridgewater Associates, suggested that because of the risk of selecting the wrong hedge funds (selection risk), a prudent allocation to hedge funds should not exceed 20 percent.[6]

In the previously cited study by Amin and Kat (2002)[7] which bore the subtitle "Not a Free Lunch," it was shown that although returns would increase linearly when hedge funds are added in increasing increments to equal-weighted stock/bond portfolios, risks in terms of standard deviation increased once allocations to hedge funds exceeded 50 percent. Furthermore, adding hedge funds to a stock and bond portfolio would reduce (worsen) the skew of the combined portfolio, thereby increasing the chances of abnormal losses. Skew would deteriorate with additional allocations to hedge funds, reaching the worst levels at 55 percent allocation, then turned up with higher hedge fund increments, but never returned to the zero-hedge-fund level. In contrast, kurtosis would increase with higher additions of hedge funds, indicating greater odds of large returns, but most of the rise took place with hedge fund allocations between 25 to 65 percent. The increase in kurtosis was relatively limited with allocations less than 25 percent. However, the combination of declining skew and increasing kurtosis at hedge fund allocations of greater than 50 percent also indicated increasing chances of higher mean returns aided by a few larger gains and accentuated by potentially large losses. This is possibly a dangerous situation but typical of strategies that exhibit negative skew and high kurtosis, such as distressed securities.

Amin and Kat also found that the results were not different when hedge funds replaced the bond component in stock and bond portfolios. When the stock allocation remained constant and hedge funds substituted for bonds in increasing portions, average portfolio return increased; standard deviation also rose, but only modestly. More importantly, skew of the portfolios declined sharply and kurtosis was substantially higher. Thus, mixing hedge funds with equity portfolios would improve return without significant increases in standard deviation, as compared to an equal-weighted stock/bond portfolio, but at the cost of a much higher probability of large losses and a lower probability of higher return.

These findings should not be surprising. As noted previously, hedge funds have outperformed stocks in equity bear market conditions, but underperform in bullish stock markets. Additionally, their returns are asymmetric and exhibit negative skew and excess kurtosis. Combining hedge funds with traditional stock and bond portfolios would increase average return and lower standard deviation up to a point. At some point, perhaps when hedge fund allocations exceed 50 percent, asymmetric return distributions characterized by a few large gains and fat tail risks begin to reduce the benefits of lower standard deviation. And the probability of earning large returns would be reduced. In economic terms, "the data suggest that when things go wrong in the stock market, they also tend to go wrong for hedge funds. . . . A significant drop in stock prices will often be accompanied by a widening of a multitude of spreads, a drop in market liquidity, etc. . . . As a result, many hedge funds will show relatively bad performance as well."[8] Thus, excess allocations to hedge funds would lead to larger give-ups on the upside and increased risks of large losses on the downside.

From a different perspective, Amin and Kat (2001)[9] examined the diversification benefits of hedge funds with consideration for the high fees and their potential inefficiency for diversification across asset classes. Their analysis argued that because of the return and risk profile of nonnormality and left tail risks, hedge funds would make inefficient investments on a stand-alone basis, that is, 100 percent invested in hedge funds. However, as a diversification from traditional portfolios of stocks and bonds, most hedge funds and hedge fund indexes would prove to be efficient. And the maximum benefit was achievable with allocations ranging from 10 to 20 percent.

Evidently, to achieve the benefits of hedge fund diversification, allocations to hedge funds should be upward of 10 percent. At this low level, it matters little whether the cutback should come from stocks or bonds; the Sharpe ratio would rise in either case. As the hedge fund allocation increases, the portions devoted to stocks and bonds should correspondingly be reduced. At the same time, the risk of selecting bad hedge funds increases. When the amounts of hedge funds approach 50 percent, especially when the fixed income component is replaced by hedge funds, the left tail risks become dominant without further gains in returns or reductions in volatility. Furthermore, large allocations to hedge funds increase the manager selection risk and complicate the tasks of monitoring and evaluating individual funds, as well as inevitably firing and hiring managers.

HOW MANY HEDGE FUNDS?

How much diversification is appropriate? Diversification can be viewed from two points of views: strategies and managers. Thus, how many strategies and how many managers? In traditional long-only equity portfolios, many actively managed funds contain a hundred or more stocks. Many others claim to be sufficiently diversified with 30 or fewer stocks. In theory, the residual risk of a portfolio resulting from the diversifiable or nonsystemic risks of the individual stocks falls off quite rapidly such that a 20-stock portfolio will have diversified away 95 percent of the individual stocks' risks. A 100-stock portfolio will have diversified virtually all of the nonspecific risks of the individual stocks such that the portfolio's risk as well as return is that of the market.

A concentrated portfolio with only a few stocks retains the specific risks of the stocks, but also the potential for outperformance. An example is the hugely successful hedge fund ESL Investments, which holds fewer than 10 stocks in its portfolio. So goes the belief that a hedge fund portfolio that seeks to outperform should contain only a few hedge funds. Since a large number of stocks would result in a diversified portfolio of which the expected return would be that of the market, a hedge fund portfolio with numerous hedge funds would resemble that of an index like the composite CSFB/Tremont Hedge Fund Index.

Academic research also has supported the notion that a diversified hedge fund portfolio does not need to contain a large number of funds. Lhabitant and De Piante Vicin (2004)[10] used quarterly data of 6,985 hedge funds from several databases to generate thousands of portfolios of different sizes. The portfolios were constructed from two approaches. The first was "naive" or "within style" diversification whereby assets are evenly divided among a number of randomly chosen funds. The second was "smart" or "across style" diversification in which assets are also equally weighted among the randomly selected funds, except that each of the various hedge fund styles is represented. Thus, if there are 13 styles, a portfolio needs to have at least 13 funds that equally share the available assets. As it turned out, a portfolio of 10 funds chosen within or across style would capture most of the benefits of diversification. Average return did not change much with the number of funds. Approximately 10 funds would be enough to reduce volatility; adding more funds would produce only marginal gains. However, skew tended to deteriorate as the number of funds increased, most dramatically in managed futures and fixed income arbitrage; excess kurtosis also increased sharply in fixed income as well as event driven. The authors suggested that these hedge funds tended to invest in similar assets, such as distressed companies that went bankrupt; diversifying among them would be a sure way to capture the systemic risks they are exposed to. In terms of other risks—specifically largest monthly loss, value at risk, and maximum drawdowns—most of the benefits can be achieved with 10 funds. Adding more funds would still increase the benefits but only marginally.

Similarly, Amin and Kat (2002)[11] found that most diversification benefits could be achieved with portfolios containing not more than 20 hedge funds; increasing the number of funds would only marginally increase the benefits. In a study of 1,721 live and dead funds from the TASS/Tremont database, they found that, as expected, a portfolio's standard deviation declined with increasing numbers of hedge funds and approached that of the population as a whole when the portfolio contained 20 hedge funds. Correspondingly, the portfolio's skew also degenerated with larger numbers of hedge funds, indicating the tendency of a portfolio containing a large number of hedge funds to suffer when hedge funds are in general decline. However, most of the improvement in kurtosis or the odds of large gains could be obtained with 10 hedge funds; after that, there was little change. Correlations with the S&P 500 rose with the number of funds, but correlations with the Salomon Brothers Government Bond Index declined; in any case, the changes became increasingly marginal when the number of funds got close to 20.

From a somewhat different perspective, Davies, Kat, and Lu (2004)[12] indicated that portfolios of hedge funds specializing in a single strategy would achieve optimal diversification with about 20 to 30 managers. As the number of funds in a portfolio increases, both standard deviation and skew decrease, suggesting that volatility improves but the probability of large losses also rises. The declines in these risk measures, however, occur at a declining rate. As the number approaches 30, skewness falls off rapidly and the portfolio's skew depends on the individual funds' co-skew, or how the individual skews interact. (Skew and co-skew is similar to the concepts of variance versus covariance.) Economically, this mathematical result makes sense because of the exposure to common risk factors that the individual funds are subject to as well as their correlations to one another. Directional strategies such as global macro or emerging markets are susceptible to common risk factors and experience increasing co-skew and lesser diversification benefits as their number in a portfolio increases. Lower-correlation strategies—say, convertible arb and merger arb—would be less affected by co-skew because they are exposed to multiple risk factors.

Notwithstanding the above studies, besides measures of volatility and losses, there are other issues to be considered in terms of the optimal number of hedge fund managers. Thus, if the selection risk and liquidity issues are considered, a greater level of manager diversification is required. Long-only diversified portfolios contain many more than 20 stocks, especially if they are small-capitalization companies, which typically have low-volume trading. A large diversified portfolio would do well to limit its position in any of these stocks individually, as a percentage of the stock's market value, the number of shares outstanding, as well as the daily trading volume. Liquidity issues also concern hedge funds, from the size of a hedge fund to the securities they buy and sell as well as their lockup and redemption provisions.

CSFB/Tremont divides the universe of hedge funds into 13 subindexes. Allowing for possible duplication, 8 to 12 managers are needed to achieve some modicum of diversification. Some funds of funds in fact have around 10 managers. One fund of funds with close to a half-billion dollars under management placed 13 percent with Beacon Hill, which lost all of its capital.

This incident has badly damaged this fund's otherwise pretty strong performance track record. Trying to avoid similar mistakes in the future, the fund placed an 8 percent limit on any individual investments, thereby increasing the number of funds in its portfolio to around 15 from as few as 8. Thus, while large concentrations in a few funds may be sufficient to reduce volatility over time, they open up the possibility of catastrophic large losses in times of market stress that can prompt the underlying funds to suffer disastrous losses or collapse altogether. This potential has been taken to heart by most funds of funds in my sample. As pointed out by the previously quoted executive of a $3 billion fund of funds, "Diversification lowers risk in traditional ways, but mostly by insulating the total fund from a meltdown."

Therefore, consideration of liquidity and selection risks suggests smaller bets on each of the managers. With two managers for each strategy, a portfolio needs to have 15 to 20 managers to begin to address the range of risks inherent in hedge funds. If a constraint of 5 percent maximum is placed on each manager allocation, the number would likely surpass 20. Because of these considerations, most fund of funds portfolios contain about 20 to 30 hedge funds. Leveraged funds may have 50 managers or more, spread over upward of 10 different strategies. With an average of 2 percent allocated to a manager, a 3:1 leverage fund would risk losing 6 percent or more in a market freeze when most hedge funds would lose money and some would just simply collapse. A loss of this magnitude would have a far greater impact on a leveraged fund of funds with, say, 25 managers.

One other consideration particular to hedge funds is that, to the extent that hedge fund returns come from alpha, adding one or more hedge funds with alpha-generating capability to an existing hedge fund portfolio should not dilute its future return, just as adding a positive number with a value greater than the average of a series causes the resulting average to increase. Thus, if a hedge fund that is managed by a manager of superior talent can be found, adding it or others like it would only help the performance of the portfolio. In contrast, adding stocks to an already well-diversified stock portfolio should not make any difference, for its expected return will always be that of the market.

In other words, the critical issue in constructing a hedge fund portfolio, in theory and in practice, is to find superior managers with alpha-generating capability and low volatility, as well as low correlation with one another.

Next are considerations of liquidity and selection risks. Of secondary importance is the exact number of funds to be included in the portfolio.

KNOW YOUR OBJECTIVES

As suggested in the previous discussion, a broadly diversified portfolio of hedge funds may contain funds of funds plus single-strategy hedge funds. Any of the constituent funds may tilt toward higher return or lower risk. This type of decision can be made only in the context of a defined investment objective. In fact, setting a well-defined investment objective is a crucial part in constructing a hedge fund portfolio or any investment program.

An investment objective can be expressed quantitatively in terms of rate of return and risk targets, as it often is among professional money managers. At the same time, by itself, risk is not an unambiguous concept. Also, while standard deviation is commonly used to measure risk, it, too, is not without ambiguity. During the bear market of 2000–2002, the S&P 500 lost cumulatively 37.6 percent. However, few investors would realize that the S&P's standard deviation during this three-year period, which is longer than the lives of many hedge funds, was only 18.8 percent, just slightly higher than the historical average in the 17 percent range. In terms of standard deviation, the bubble period of 1997–1999 was only a touch less risky, at 16.75 percent, yet the S&P rose more 100 percent.

To account for this drawdown risk, investors should place a maximum drawdown limit on any fund being considered. Thus, if a fund experienced a maximum loss or drawdown in any month or cumulative period that exceeds this limit, that investment should be eliminated from consideration.

Other less quantifiable expectations can be part of the consideration in constructing a hedge fund portfolio. Some funds of funds expressly rule out mortgage-backed arbitrage managers and the cited reason is that they are concerned with the mark-to-market pricing of illiquid securities and derivatives in MBS portfolios.

The critical aspect in deciding on investment objectives is establishing an acceptable level of risks; it is not about setting up a target rate of return. In the world of U.S. equities, volatility has been relatively stable in the range between the low teens to the high teens but rates of return have varied substantially from period to period. In hedge funds, it has been shown that while returns are not persistent, risks are; that is, past returns are not indicative of future performance, but risky funds will remain risky.[13] Also, it has been documented in extensive academic research that forecasts of future return are subject to large estimation errors; that is, expected future returns are difficult to estimate.[14] Furthermore, risk can be controlled by such moves as increasing cash holdings to reduce it or leveraging in order to increase it. At the same time, it is more difficult to manage return. Thus, targeting a low-risk level has a likelihood of being achieved, while aiming for a high return may prove disappointing.

Volatility Target

A question of the first order is: how much risk? In traditional long-only investments, bonds are considered safe investments for conservative investors. A commonly used index for fixed income is Lehman Government Credit Bond Index. This index covers a wide range of maturities in the fixed income market, from Treasury bonds with 30-year maturity to shorter-term bonds issued by corporations. Historically, it has a long-term standard deviation of 5 percent. Another commonly used fixed income index is Lehman Aggregate Bond Index (Lehman Agg), which includes mortgage-backed securities, in addition to the securities included in Lehman Government/ Corporate Bond Index. It has a long-term volatility of 6 percent. However, in the last decade, bond volatility has come down significantly so that the standard deviations of these two indexes have been cut by about one-third. Over all, the Lehman Agg's volatility was about 5 percent during the S&P 500's ascent between August 1982 and August 2000. In contrast, this bond index's volatility was significantly higher during 1979 to October 1987, at 9 percent. This period started with Paul Volcker as chairman of the Federal Reserve and the shift to money supply targeting as the guide to the Fed's conduct of monetary policy. The period ended with the stock market's October 1987 crash. Bond volatility was even higher, at almost 12 percent, during the period from 1979 to July 1982, which ended with the start of the stock market's two-decade ascent.

On the other end of this risk spectrum is equity risk. The S&P 500's standard deviation has historically averaged around 17 percent. During the bull market of 1994–1999, its volatility fell to less than 14 percent. The stock market's decline between 2000 and 2002 led to a return to the historical average volatility levels.

In the hedge fund world, lower volatility has been associated with arbitrage or relative value strategies. However, during the 2000 to 2003 period, the volatilities of these strategies have dropped below the averages of between 3 to 6 percent as recorded during their brief histories between 1994 and 2004. This is shown in Table 7.1.

For Fixed Income Arbitrage, corresponding with the drop of interest rates during the equity bear market, its volatility has declined to 2.5 percent from its 10-year historical average of almost 4 percent. This was about the same as the volatility of the Lehman Aggregate Bond Index during the same

TABLE 7.1 Hedge Fund Volatility in Different Periods

Index	2000–2003	1994–1999	1994–June 2004
CSFB/Tremont Hedge Fund Index	5.71%	9.87%	8.31%
Convertible Arbitrage	4.40	4.95	4.74
Dedicated Short Bias	18.24	18.00	17.67
Emerging Markets	11.04	21.17	17.41
Equity Market Neutral	2.06	3.59	3.04
Event Driven (E.D.)	4.19	7.01	5.91
E.D. Distressed	5.48	7.84	6.84
E.D. Multi-Strategy	4.17	7.49	6.23
E.D. Risk Arbitrage	3.95	4.75	4.37
Fixed Income Arbitrage	2.50	4.69	3.88
Global Macro	6.07	14.89	11.83
Long/Short Equity	9.71	11.56	10.78
Managed Futures	13.19	11.46	12.26
Multi-Strategy	2.75	5.36	4.46
HFR Fund of Funds	4.08%	5.69%	5.04%
Lehman Aggregate Bond Index	3.95	3.99	4.01
S&P 500	17.84	13.65	15.47

Sources: CSFB/Tremont, Standard & Poor's, Hedge Fund Research, PerTrac.

period. The volatility of Equity Market Neutral also experienced similar declines while remaining lower than the Lehman index. The volatilities of other arbitrage strategies remained above the Lehman index, though they, too, have seen lower levels recently. As all of these arbitrage strategies are exposed to interest rate volatility, though differently from long-only fixed income strategies, it can be construed that the relative value strategies are bound to continue to experience volatility similar to that of the bond market. As such, their volatilities are likely to increase to a range of about 5 to 10 percent, or even higher.

Directionally biased strategies such as Long/Short Equity and Global Macro have also seen lower volatilities, compared to the historical ranges upward of 10 percent. Volatility of long/short strategies in U.S. equity or global markets should remain below the volatility of long-only equities. However, long/short volatility will be hard-pressed to stay below 10 percent as these strategies are also exposed to interest rate volatility as well as the equity markets.

Overall, going forward, an average hedge fund index like the CSFB/Tremont Hedge Fund Index or diversified hedge fund portfolios can be expected to experience volatility of upward of 10 percent, buttressed on the lower end by arbitrage strategies with volatility around 5 percent or higher, and on the high end, directionally biased strategies, like emerging markets, with volatility as high as upward of 20 percent.

Thus, investors who prefer bondlike volatility in the range of single-digit percentage points will have to contend with arbitrage strategies and attendant left tail risks and large drawdown potential. The exception is Equity Market Neutral, which has provided a track record of lower volatility and competitive return, while being free of negative skew and excess kurtosis and large drawdowns. Investors who are more agreeable to greater volatility (10 percent or higher) in exchange for potentially higher return can look to long-biased strategies such as Long/Short Equity and Global Macro. To achieve volatility in the range of 6 to 10 percent, a diversified hedge fund portfolio would need to include Equity Market Neutral and other arbitrage strategies, in addition to higher-return directionally biased strategies.

Return Expectations

How much return should be expected from hedge funds? The history of hedge fund indexes provides some hints. Historical returns collected by the different database providers suffer biases such as survivorship bias as had been discussed previously, suggesting that if these biases had been corrected, hedge fund returns might on average have been historically lower than indicated by the indexes. Also, diversified indexes such as multistrategy and fund of funds have reported returns below the overall composite indexes. For example, the HFR Composite Hedge Fund Index showed an annualized return of 14.5 percent from 1990 to June 2004 while its Fund of Funds Composite Index had a return of 10.8 percent. CSFB/Tremont Multi-Strategy component underperformed its composite Hedge Fund Index. Furthermore, CSFB Fixed Income Arb produced an annualized return lower than the Lehman Aggregate Bond Index, 6.35 percent versus 7.59 percent. The other strategies, which exhibited a greater equity exposure component, have produced return in line with the equity market.

This track record, combined with research indicating a correlation of hedge funds with the returns of the capital markets higher than indicated by correlation data, points to the boundaries of prospective returns that hedge funds can generate. And these boundaries are limited by the expected returns of the traditional stock and bond markets.

Even professionally and actively managed hedge fund portfolios like funds of funds and multistrategy funds tended to produce higher returns in periods that the stock market trended higher, and weaker returns in periods of weakness and high volatility. In 2003 when the S&P 500 registered a strong recovery of 28.68 percent, in 1998 when the global markets were hit by the Asian crisis, and in 1994 with the Fed rate hike and the ensuing bond market sell-offs, multistrategy and funds of funds returns were scant evidence of any ability to avoid the consequences of these market dislocations or take advantage of opportunities available to them. Likewise, although the Lehman Aggregate Bond Index produced a return of 10.1 percent during the 2000 to 2002 period due to sharp interest rate declines, the returns of the CSFB/Tremont Multi-Strategy and HFR Fund of Funds Composite indexes were modest in comparison.

If the prognosticators turn out to be right in predicting that the equity market will produce returns much lower than during the bubble years—say, in the high single digits or in the low teens, to be on the high side—the stock market will not provide much of a return booster to actively managed diversified funds. Against this modest return expectation, risk of equity hedge funds is likely to return to historical levels. At the same time, credit spreads and interest rates, having been at historic lows, are set likely to rise, providing little relief in both return and risk to fixed income–oriented hedge strategies. For sure, there will be strategies that from time to time will produce significantly higher returns, as convertible arbitrage and distressed securities have done in the past few years. Capturing these return opportunities will, however, require an exceptional ability to change asset allocations and/or pick top-performing hedge fund managers that has not been entirely evident in the track records of funds of funds or multistrategy funds, on average.

With these considerations, it is probably prudent for investors to expect no more than a 6 to 8 percent return from a diversified unleveraged portfolio of hedge funds. However, this return, which is comparable to expected returns of stocks, would come with a volatility that is lower than stocks but higher than historically experienced by hedge funds. Nevertheless, the return-to-risk ratio of hedge funds would still be significantly better than those of traditional bonds and equities.

HEDGE FUND PORTFOLIOS IN PRACTICE: CASE EXAMPLES

We now look at the composition of two major types of hedge funds. The first type, the low-volatility portfolio, would target a low standard deviation. The second type is the absolute return portfolio, which seeks to achieve a higher rate of return. As will become evident, the low-volatility portfolio is more concentrated in fixed income and market neutral strategies. As the risk range increases, directional strategies play a greater role in the absolute return portfolio's composition.

Low-Volatility Portfolio

Figures 7.3 and 7.4 show the low-volatility portfolios of two funds of hedge funds. They both reported five-year volatility of around 1.7 percent. Noteworthy is the absence or very low content of long/short directional equity and global macro funds.

The predominant strategies in these two portfolios are fixed income arbitrage, relative value arb, and equity market neutral. When directional funds are included, they are often short-term traders, who trade in and out of the market rather than holding on to positions for any length of time. As such, they are positioned to generate profits whether the markets go up or down. Also note the significant presence of subprime lending in Portfolio B, labeled "Loan Origination," to the tune of 7 percent investment. Perhaps it is thanks to this investment that it reported a five-year return of almost 10 percent, compared to Portfolio A's reported return of around 7.5 percent.

Thus funds of funds follow the footsteps of traditional investors in using fixed income strategies to achieve low volatility. When venturing into the equity market, they would emphasize strategies with a fixed income

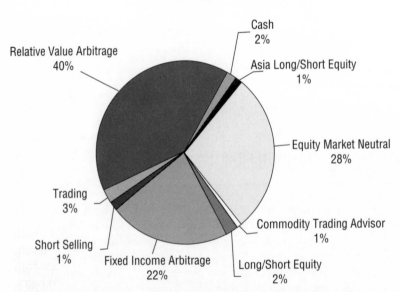

Low-Volatility Portfolio A

Cash 2%

Asia Long/Short Equity 1%

Relative Value Arbitrage 40%

Equity Market Neutral 28%

Trading 3%

Commodity Trading Advisor 1%

Short Selling 1%

Long/Short Equity 2%

Fixed Income Arbitrage 22%

FIGURE 7.3 Low-Volatility Portfolio of Hedge Funds—7.5 Percent Return

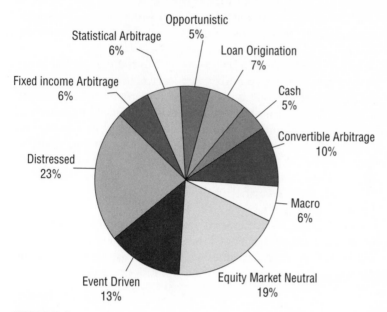

Low-Volatility Portfolio B

- Opportunistic 5%
- Statistical Arbitrage 6%
- Loan Origination 7%
- Fixed income Arbitrage 6%
- Cash 5%
- Convertible Arbitrage 10%
- Distressed 23%
- Macro 6%
- Event Driven 13%
- Equity Market Neutral 19%

FIGURE 7.4 Low-Volatility Portfolio of Hedge Funds—10 Percent Return

component such as convertible arbitrage and distressed securities, or invest with equity market neutral funds where the equity market's risk is hedged away.

Historically the CSFB/Tremont indexes in these strategies have shown volatility in the low to mid single digits. During the past few years, volatility in these strategies has come down even further, concomitant with interest rates trending lower as a result of easing by the Federal Reserve. Table 7.1 shows annualized monthly volatility of the CSFB/Tremont indexes from 1994 to June 2004.

Volatilities of directional strategies such as Long/Short Equity, Managed Futures, Short Sellers, and Emerging Markets remain high. In contrast, arbitrage strategies have experienced very stable periods, with volatility lower than even that of fixed income arbitrage. As a result, Multi-Strategy and the composite CSFB/Tremont Hedge Fund Index both saw their volatilities decline to below their historical 10-year averages. Even Global Macro, which has benefited from the steady decline of the dollar, registered a decline of volatility to 6 percent from a 10-year average of 12 percent. The skew and kurtosis statistics also showed lack of instances of unusually large gains or losses. Even Fixed Income Arb, which had negative skew of −3.25 and excess kurtosis of 16.6 during the 1994–2003 period, saw these statistics decline to virtually zero during the past three years.

Thus, it will be interesting to see if low-volatility funds of funds can continue to maintain the low volatility they have enjoyed in the past few years, if volatility in the stock and bond markets increases leading to higher volatility in hedge funds. In fact, in expectations of higher stock and bond volatilities, a number of funds of funds have increasingly resorted to highly illiquid strategies such as subprime lending, labeled "Loan Origination" or "Private Credit Arbitrage," to keep their funds' volatilities low. In justification for this strategy, some of them argue that they would not sell these securities in times of market stress, so illiquidity should not be an issue. Clearly, this argument ignores the requirement that such illiquid securities still need to be marked to market, whether or not they are sold, unless these fund managers plan to disregard the marked-down market values and instead use some formulaic figures more applicable to normal market conditions in order to value these securities.

Leveraged Portfolios

Leveraged portfolios deploy from two up to four times the amount of base capital. They are often clones of low-volatility portfolios offered by the same firms. In this case, the allocation to each of the managers in the leveraged fund would simply be in multiples of the investments with the same managers in the low-volatility fund. The volatility of the leveraged fund would be equal to the risk of the original fund multiplied by the leverage. The return is similarly leveraged; additionally, the cost of borrowing for the leverage would reduce any gains, but add to losses.

Stand-alone leveraged funds typically employ low-volatility strategies, but not necessarily so. They usually have a larger number of managers; whereas nonleveraged funds of funds might have 20 to 30 managers, leveraged funds usually contain upward of 50 managers. One fund of funds invested with more than 200 managers. The large number of managers is aimed at reducing the manager selection risk. If the allocation to a manager is 5 percent in a nonleveraged fund, the maximum total loss would be 5 percent of the fund's assets. The same allocation in a 4-to-1 leveraged fund means a potential loss of 20 percent, enough to put it out of business.

Absolute Return Portfolio

Absolute return portfolios distinctly contain a significant allocation to directional strategies as in Figure 7.5, which shows the composition of Absolute Return Portfolio A.

This fund of funds was predominantly invested in long/short equity managers, with a smattering of long-biased or outright long-only funds. However, the long-biased allocation of 6 percent was well offset by short-selling exposure of 10 percent. The portions labeled "Opportunistic" and "Trading" were also directionally biased. However, this fund's five-year standard deviation was less than 4 percent, with annualized return of 12.5 percent (ending first quarter 2004). These statistics compared very favorably with the CSFB/Tremont Long/Short Equity index as well as HFRI Fund of Funds Composite Index. One interesting aspect about this fund is that it has 55 managers, with 22 in long/short equity. Apparently, the large number of managers did not hurt its performance, providing a case example that a large number of managers does not necessarily lead to lower performance.

Figure 7.6 shows another absolute return portfolio whose strategy allocation somewhat resembles that of Absolute Return Portfolio A. Its

Absolute Return Portfolio A

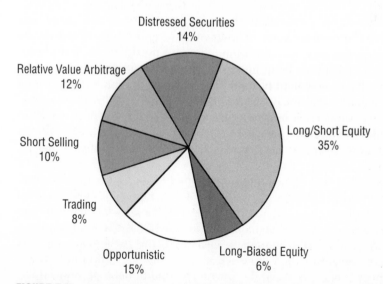

FIGURE 7.5 Absolute Return Portfolio of Hedge Funds—12.5 Percent Return

Absolute Return Portfolio B

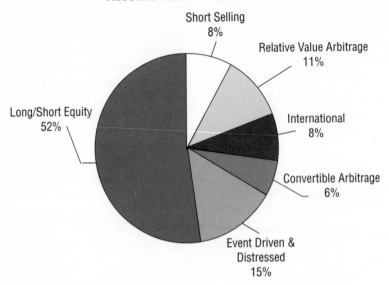

FIGURE 7.6 Absolute Return Portfolio of Hedge Funds—11.5 Percent Return

hedge fund managers, however, number only 23 while its risk and return statistics are somewhat less favorable than those of Portfolio A; it registered volatility at 4 percent and five-year annualized return at 11.5 percent. Note also the large allocation of 52 percent to long/short equity managers.

Figure 7.7 shows a balanced absolute return portfolio that has a long-term target of 60 percent allocated to equity-oriented managers and 40 percent to fixed income hedge funds. Note the large presence of directional long/short equity funds, including global managers. While there was a significant presence of fixed income arbitrage, the fixed income managers in this portfolio engaged in a variety of strategies, from convertible arbitrage to distressed securities, capital structure arbitrage, and special situations as well as event driven.

Unlike its absolute return rivals, this fund of funds eschewed the practice of significantly changing asset allocations to opportunistically capture changing trends in the markets. Instead it has stayed close to a split of 60/40 between equity and fixed income strategies, just like the traditional 60/40 stock/bond balanced portfolio. This is why this fund is characterized as a balanced portfolio.

As readers might recall, in the wisdom of traditional long-only investing, market timing has never been considered a profitable strategy. Over

Balanced Portfolio

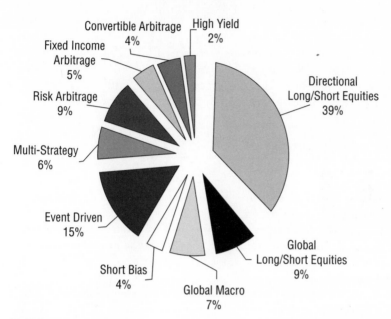

FIGURE 7.7 Balanced Portfolio of Hedge Funds—10 Percent Return

the years, market timing funds have invariably underperformed stock index benchmarks. Thus, there is no prima facie reason why funds of funds would have better chances of profiting from market timing by being opportunistic, which is the term often used by such funds to describe what they do to take advantage of changing market conditions. This is especially so considering the redemption and lockup restrictions imposed by hedge funds, which limit funds of funds' flexibility to move their assets around. The managers of this balanced portfolio believe that they are better off concentrating on selecting managers who can deliver alpha, rather than trying to anticipate which strategies possess anomalies and inefficiencies and then selecting managers who can exploit these opportunities. As it has turned out, this fund of funds has achieved volatility around 4.5 percent while generating returns close to 10 percent in recent years.

Also somewhat unusual in this balanced portfolio is the presence of a truly global macro manager who invests in stocks and bonds on a global scale as well as engaged in trading currencies and commodities. However, these global managers are U.S-domiciled, not foreign-based.

Most noticeable among many funds of funds is the low content and often absence of global macro managers. Part of the reason is there are only a few outstanding ones. By necessity truly global macro managers need expertise if not physical presence in a number of foreign countries, which few hedge funds can muster resources for, because of expenses. On the part of funds of funds, if they want to invest with non-U.S. managers, they may not have the resources for travel and research. This shortcoming is particularly acute among smaller funds of funds.

QUANTIFY YOUR JUDGMENT

Portfolio construction is a most vexing issue in investment, yet it is also most important in terms of the impact on performance results. No matter how well you select your stocks, bonds, or hedge funds, if you put too much in an underperforming asset and too little in winners, your portfolio will not produce the expected returns. Often enough, a few well-placed investments will bail out an otherwise mediocre portfolio.

In the preceding paragraphs we have discussed how professional hedge fund investors, notably funds of funds, go about assembling hedge fund portfolios. Modern portfolio theory has sought to address this portfolio construction issue by way of a procedure whereby a set of optimal portfolio combinations are depicted on the efficient frontier. First-year MBA students know that any portfolio on this curve has the highest expected return for a given level of risk; any other portfolio with the same amount of risk would have a lower expected return. All an investor would have to do is decide on the acceptable level of risk, and voilà, the right portfolio is there to be selected, with the appropriate amounts to be invested in each of the securities included in the portfolio. The difficulty of this seemingly simple procedure is in estimating future expected returns and standard deviations of the assets in the portfolio, as well as how these assets are correlated with each other. In practice, long-only managers have little interest in using this optimization procedure to build their portfolios.

In hedge funds, the principles as posited in the efficient frontier are in wide practice and quite applicable to the issue of constructing a portfolio of hedge funds, although the application is performed differently.

Among funds of funds, low-volatility funds set specific and often narrow ranges of volatilities at the outset. They avoid high-volatility hedge funds and seek to invest with those that have low correlation among themselves. For other funds of funds, optimization with mean and variance is one of the later steps in constructing a portfolio of hedge funds. Experienced practitioners would use these optimization results to set the approximate boundaries of the weightings in each of the hedge funds and in setting what might be called a "risk budget" for the portfolio. Their judgment about the stock and bond markets, the opportunities going forward, and the returns and risks of the individual funds set the stage for selecting the funds to be included in their funds of funds. They would then calculate the resulting standard deviation of the resulting portfolio, based on the historical data of the hedge fund managers available to them. If the calculated standard deviation exceeds their expectations, they might modify the amounts they plan to invest in any of the managers. They would also perform stress tests by running a series of random simulations, typically using the Monte Carlo technique and historical data, to chart the odds of potential losses.

Thus, well-run funds of funds explicitly recognize the return and risk profiles of their managers and the correlation among these managers. They also set the diversification and volatility targets, as well as seek to assess the potential of large losses using stress tests. They use the mean-variance framework for portfolio optimization as a way to quantify the potential risks, but rely on qualitative judgment to assess anomalies, which in the end dictate the final makeup of their portfolios.

However, in recent years it has been widely recognized that standard deviation is inadequate as a measure of risk for hedge funds. Since mean-variance asset allocation is derived from an underestimation of risk, it follows that the efficient frontier derived from mean-variance optimization results in an overallocation to hedge funds. Favre and Signer (2002)[15] demonstrated that investments with negative skew and high kurtosis, which indicate higher risks, would have lower weightings in an optimal portfolio.

In order to account for the asymmetry, research in recent years has emerged to explore methods that incorporate skew and kurtosis into the mean-variance framework. This involves substitution for standard deviation with a measure that emphasizes the downside risk. Lamm (2003)[16] investigated the relative merits of different techniques that factor in the downside risk in portfolio optimization. Table 7.2 is a summary of the essential features of the various approaches to constructing optimal hedge fund portfolios.

Investors with a low tolerance for downside risks would avoid or substantially underweight funds with negative skew, such as distressed securities and mortgage-backed securities arbitrage. The Cornish-Fisher, mean semivariance, and mean downside risk optimization procedures would capture this feature, resulting in portfolios with positive skew

TABLE 7.2 Portfolio Optimization with Downside Risks

Optimization Approach	Abbreviation	Description	Risk Measures
Mean Variance	MV	Symmetric bell-shaped distributions.	Squared deviations. Large deviations are more penalized.
Mean Semivariance	MSV	Downside risk metric with lower-half bell-shaped distributions.	Same as MV.
Mean Downside Risk	MDR	Similar to MSV, but downside deviations are relative to a minimum acceptable return.	Same as MSV.
Mean Absolute Deviation	MAD	Deviations are weighted equally. Otherwise similar to MV.	Large and small deviations are equally penalized.
Mean Absolute Semideviation	MASD	Deviations are weighted equally. Otherwise similar to MSV.	Large and small deviations are equally penalized.
Mean Absolute Downside Risk	MADR	Deviations are weighted equally. Otherwise similar to MDR.	Large and small deviations are equally penalized.
Cornish-Fisher	CF	Allows for both skew and kurtosis.	Asymmetry of returns is considered explicitly.

Source: R. McFall Lamm Jr., "Asymmetric Returns and Optimal Hedge Fund Portfolios," *Journal of Alternative Investments,* Fall 2003, pp. 9–21.

and low kurtosis. In contrast, the traditional mean variance method and mean absolute deviation would place substantially more funds with distressed securities, and less with equity-oriented managers.

However, though theoretically appealing, none of these methods has gained wide acceptance, not least because their effectiveness is yet to be demonstrated. As Lamm observed, "There is no straightforward and elegant mathematical solution to the portfolio optimization problem."[17] Nevertheless, explicit recognition of the risk factors would go a long way toward constructing portfolios that are better positioned to achieve the desired risk levels.

CONCLUSION

In the previous two chapters, we have examined the factors and the processes of evaluating and selecting individual hedge funds. In this chapter, we discuss the considerations to assemble a hedge fund portfolio. For investors with small allocations to hedge funds, funds of funds offer a practical means to diversify. The most important consideration in assembling a hedge fund portfolio is the correlation among the managers. Lower-correlation managers result in a lower-risk portfolio.

But few benefits are visible with a small hedge fund allocation—say, less than 10 percent. At the other end of the spectrum, there is unlikely to be much, if any, increase in the benefits of lower volatility and higher return with hedge fund allocations of greater than 50 percent. Rather, such large allocations tend to result in higher probabilities of large losses.

For diversification with hedge funds to be effective, a lineup of 20 to 30 hedge funds is needed to address the full range of risks, from volatility of the resulting portfolio to the liquidity risk or the flexibility of withdrawing funds when needed, and the risk of selecting bad managers. But the critical issue here is manager talent, not a set number of managers. A talented manager should always help to reduce risks or increase returns, but adding a bad manager is an invitation to disaster, not risk reducing.

In the end, it is important to "know your objectives," whether to have low risks with a low-volatility portfolio or to achieve performance with an absolute return portfolio. The former would be dominated by fixed income and relative value strategies, while the latter would prefer high-volatility and higher-return-potential managers in long/short equity, global macro, or such directionally biased funds. To aid in the construction of these portfolios, quantitative methodologies can be helpful—not in their strict application, but in the explicit recognition of the different aspects of the risks of hedge funds and in the formulation of a risk budget, that is, how much volatility is acceptable.

Having selected a lineup of hedge funds and allocated money to them, investors now need to monitor and evaluate on an ongoing basis their performance and risk profiles, in order to make sure that the portfolio and the managers continue to perform as expected, and, more importantly, that they continue to meet the investors' investment objectives. These issues will be discussed in Chapter 8.

Three

Evaluating Performance and Risks

Now that a portfolio of hedge funds has been assembled, the investors will need to periodically review, evaluate, and assess the performances of the funds in the portfolio, including their rates of return, volatility of these returns, and how these investment results were produced. The purpose, in a nutshell, is to make sure that the portfolio and its hedge funds perform as expected. The issues related to monitoring and evaluating hedge fund performances are discussed in this Part Three.

In traditional investing, risk management is an afterthought if any thought is given to it at all; the focus is on beating market indexes, not managing risks. In contrast, risk management can make or break a hedge fund. It can be said that hedge funds begin where long-only managers leave off: Hedge funds are about managing the systematic risk of the market and managing the risks of the long and short positions, not only picking the best stocks. Long-only equity managers accept the risk of the market as a given and little attempt is made to manage it. A great many long-only managers proclaim that they do not time the market and that they are always fully invested even as the market declines. Furthermore, by holding a large basket of stocks, these managers actually diversify away the risks and potential returns specific to the individual stocks, and depend on the fortune of a rising market to generate returns. No wonder the majority of mutual funds cannot outperform the S&P 500 even as they take greater risks by venturing into riskier stocks not contained in the index.

Equity market neutral hedge funds, however, seek to neutralize this market risk and extract alpha from the returns of specific stocks. In addition to alpha from specific stock risks, long/short equity managers hope to ride on the back of a rising market by having the long positions larger than the short side, and conversely reduce the longs and increase the shorts as the market declines.

As such, evaluating hedge fund performance is first of all about measuring and assessing the risks of hedge funds. The performance results of a hedge fund can be properly evaluated only in the context of the risks that it takes. And its risks go beyond the usual statistics of standard deviation or losses, but must be evaluated and understood in terms of the strategy or strategies that it utilizes to produce the performance and risk figures. We have discussed the issues of hedge fund strategies and their evaluation in Part One and Part Two. Chapter 8 of this part focuses on evaluating performance. Chapter 9 is a discussion of the evaluation and the management of the risks of hedge funds. Chapter 10 is especially devoted to funds of hedge funds. The book ends with a practical guide to investing in hedge funds in Chapter 11.

CHAPTER 8

Evaluating the Performance of Your Hedge Funds

In assessing hedge funds' performance, not only rates of return are important, but risks, or, more accurately, changes in the risk profiles of the funds, are crucial. Among funds of funds, it is a well-known practice that sometimes a fund is terminated after a period of generating extraordinarily large gains. In traditional investing, such results would be lauded as exceptional talent. In contrast, a fund of funds manager might look at such instances as signs that the hedge fund managers were taking exceptional risks.

As a result of the evaluation of performance and reassessment of the risk profiles, the underperforming funds would be shed. At this time, the cash raised from redemptions from poorly performing funds may be reinvested in new funds, or simply new investments need to be made. Accordingly, new managers need to be identified and selected and portfolio construction issues arise regarding the risk and return to be expected from the newly reconfigured portfolio. For investors who are active in hedge fund investing, the three-step process of manager evaluation, portfolio construction, and monitoring are continuous, overlapping, and integral.

HOW WELL IS YOUR HEDGE FUND PORTFOLIO?

Most individual investors who invest in stocks and bonds would be happy if their investment advisers produce a 20 percent return when the stock market goes up by, say, 25 percent, and they would be content even if their accounts increase somewhat less. In other words, these investors are mostly content if their investments increase in value. They would be happy to have the bragging right of seeing their portfolios outperforming the market; but usually this is not how they view the performance of their managers. On the other hand, they become very concerned if their investments lose value, even if their losses are less than those of the market. Furthermore, they are reluctant to fire the managers who incur losses worse than the return of the market, hoping to recoup when the market recovers. At this time, they may contemplate redeeming from the managers if the underperformance continues.

Thus, individual investors are inclined to achieve some sort of absolute returns from their managers. Institutional investors, by contrast, are mostly interested in relative performances. If the market is up by 25 percent, as desirable as this return might be as viewed in the context of the market's historical averages, they would still prefer to see their investment managers go up by more, even if the managers take on unusual risks to achieve these returns. Not only that, they would reward those managers who exceed the market as well as most of their peers with rewards in the form of allocating more money to these managers. They still would reward these managers, or at least not punish them by termination, if these managers lose less than the market and most of their peer groups.

Thus, in contrast to individuals who are apt to seek absolute returns, institutions prefer to evaluate their managers relative to the market.

Unfortunately, whereas in traditional investing the "market" is commonly equated with the S&P 500, Russell 3000, or similar indexes, "market" is a more elusive concept in hedge funds. Hence, a market benchmark for hedge funds is more difficult to define.

The lack of an objective measurement benchmark for hedge funds is further complicated by the tendency of institutional investors to continue to be influenced by the return of stock market indexes like the S&P 500; that is, "The market rose 28 percent last year and my fund gained only 15 percent!" They often forget that hedge fund investing is about achieving an absolute and positive rate of return regardless of the condition of the market, up or down. For the uncommitted investors who entered into hedge funds because of concerns due to the prolonged bear market, periods of strong market returns coupled with lower returns by hedge funds may have an influence on how hedge funds are evaluated.

Hedge funds themselves hardly help the matter due to high portfolio turnover and the lack of transparency in their investment strategies and processes as well as changes thereof. They also are apt to cite their positive returns when the market indexes go down as proof of their talent, or alpha. In the absence of relevant information and mixed signals from their hedge funds, investors often resort to the convenience of market benchmarks to judge their managers.

BASIC CONCEPTS OF PERFORMANCE MEASUREMENT

The fundamental approach to measuring a fund's performance is to adjust its return for the risk it incurs. Modern portfolio theory defines risk as the fund's total risk measured by its standard deviation. This gives rise to the familiar Sharpe ratio. The higher the Sharpe ratio, the better the fund. In the hedge fund world, the Sharpe ratio has become the standard for performance measurement of risk-adjusted returns.[1]

The advance of the capital asset pricing model, which relates the return of a risky asset to the market by a factor called beta, led to another method of measuring risk-adjusted performance by using beta as the measure of risk. To the extent that a fund's return exceeds the return of a market benchmark after adjusting for beta, the excess return or alpha, represented by the familiar Greek letter α, measures the outperformance of the fund. This relationship is expressed in the familiar equation:

$$\bar{R}_i = \alpha + [r_f + \beta_i(\bar{F}_j - r_f)]$$

In this equation, a hedge fund's excess return over the Treasury bill rate in a time period t can be explained by some factor F_j (and there can be more than one factor) in the same period, adjusted by a coefficient beta. Accordingly, the methodology is to regress the fund's excess return over the one-month Treasury bill rate onto a single factor such as a stock market index, or a set of multiple return-generating factors. The fund's performance is then evaluated on the basis of the significance of the term α. Its risk would be judged to be low if beta is small or close to zero. Once a fund's beta takes on values in excess of 0.5, it is considered long-biased.

It is obvious that the most crucial issue in evaluating hedge fund performance is the definition of the F_j term. In long-only equity investing, the term is often equated with the S&P 500. Though approximate, this index is not as applicable to a fund trading in, as an example, small-cap stocks as to a large-cap stock fund. It is of course far less relevant to a hedge fund. Furthermore, the equation assumes that the term beta would stay constant. This is not an unreasonable assumption as it applies to traditional long-only portfolios, whose managers normally stay invested in their respective markets—say, large-market capitalization stocks—whether their markets go up or down.

The assumption, however, is not realistic with regard to hedge fund managers who are apt to adjust their strategies to cope with the changing market conditions by reducing or increasing risks from exposures to different market factors. Finally, the significance of alpha would vary with the time period, for example, one quarter, one year, or five years. As discussed previously, research has shown that alpha has a tendency to degenerate over time (after an initial rise) and older funds tend to do worse than young funds.

ISSUES DIRECTLY RELATED TO HEDGE FUNDS

Hedge funds follow certain styles. They just do not go long on the market, whatever the market is. They also short the market, sometimes by as much as the long position. Thus long/short equity funds go long certain stocks and short others, whereas equity market neutral have equal long and short positions. Similarly, fixed income arbitrage funds buy and sell securities in the fixed income markets. However, they may change their strategies in a number of different ways, all of which have great bearing on their investment results as well as risks.

Changes in Leverage

A fund may increase the amount of leverage. Fixed income arb funds typically use greater leverage than equity-oriented funds. It is not unusual for such funds to have leverage 20 times or more of their capital bases, although Long-Term Capital Management was a very unusual case. These leverages can change not only during the year, but as often as during any monthly period. For fixed income funds, such as fixed income or convertible arbitrage, shifts in the amounts of leverages can occur not only with greater frequency, but also by greater amounts.

   The use of leverage clearly has a great impact on the return and risk of a fund. Suppose it is a diversified stock fund, and its performance is assessed against the S&P 500. If such a fund is leveraged by 50 percent, should its return not be compared to 1.5 times the return of the S&P 500? Yet, it is a common practice that the leverage amount is not explicitly factored into the performance assessment.

Changes in Hedging Techniques

An equity market neutral fund is supposed to be zero-beta or long and short stocks by equal amounts. The short side can be accomplished by short selling the stocks such that if the short stocks decline by 1 percent, the overall short position will gain 1 percent times the amount of the short position. But short selling can also be accomplished by using derivatives such as put options. The return/risk relationships of options are much different from a long or short stock position. If you buy a put option, you have to pay a premium, which is only a fraction of the price of the stock. If the stock goes down, the gain depends on the so-called delta, which is the extent to which the value of the option responds to the changes in the stock's price. However, if the stock keeps on increasing in value, the maximum loss would be the premium. A long/short equity or an equity market neutral fund that buys put options in lieu of direct short selling of securities would participate in a rising overall stock market to a greater extent than those managers who directly short sell securities. But also the risks of such funds are much different: In a down market a put option would provide less protection than outright short positions; a deep out-of-the-money put has little protection.

Style Drifts

Style drifts are a common problem both in long-only traditional managers as well as in hedge funds. Managers who specialize in certain sectors of the markets, such as large-cap stocks, may start buying small-cap or mid-cap stocks when they perceive that large-cap stocks begin to lag the others, or vice versa. Mortgage-backed securities traders may likewise begin to dabble in nonconforming mortgages to increase yields and leverage. Thus, when strategies drift, the original factors F_i are no longer appropriate to measure manager performance.

Portfolio Turnover

This is also a common change seen in both traditional and hedge fund managers. In fact, during the 2000–2002 bear market and as the stock market recovers, traditional managers have sharply increased their portfolio turnovers to unprecedented levels.[2] For hedge funds, rapid-fire trading in periods of market instability is not an unusual activity. In fact, they take advantage of such volatility in order to generate excess returns.

Once a hedge fund begins to change its strategy, its risk factors and sources of alpha also change. To the extent that a hedge fund is hired because of the manager's expertise in that particular strategy, any changes will have an effect on the fund's risk/return profile. Thus, any excess return generated from the new strategies may be a random event, perhaps due to luck. At the same time, market conditions do change and the ability of a hedge fund to tactically modify its trading strategies, perhaps by shortening the holding periods of its positions, which would cause higher portfolio turnover, may be a sign of strength.

MARKET AND HEDGE FUND INDEXES

Although market indexes may not be entirely depended upon to judge hedge fund performances, they are not wholly irrelevant, either. We will examine these benchmarks in some detail.

Market Indexes

To assess hedge fund performance, the relevance of market indexes is limited. Some of the reasons were discussed earlier. Also, hedge funds have low correlation to market indexes. Previously we have shown in Table 2.4 the correlations of the various CSFB/Tremont indexes versus the S&P 500. Table 8.1 examines the correlations of several CSFB/Tremont strategies against major market indexes.

Hedge funds that navigate the bond markets by using fixed income or convertible arbitrage or trading distressed securities might be presumed to be more correlated to the bond market than to equities. As it turns out, the correlations of these CSFB/Tremont strategies have significantly higher correlation with the market when the market is defined as the Merrill Lynch High Yield Index than with either the Lehman Aggregate Bond Index or the S&P 500. In fact, the Merrill index explained 64 percent of the returns of Distressed Securities, 40 percent of Convertible Arbitrage, and 30 per-

TABLE 8.1 Correlation of Select Hedge Funds with Major Market Indexes

| | CSFB/Tremont Hedge Fund Index | | |
Market Index	Fixed Income Arbitrage	Distressed Securities	Convertible Arbitrage
Lehman Aggregate Bond Index	0.176	0.068	0.144
S&P 500	0.029	0.546	0.126
Russell 3000	0.041	0.571	0.147
Merrill Lynch High Yield	0.296	0.640	0.401

| | CSFB/Tremont Hedge Index | | |
Market Index	Long/Short Equity	Equity Market Neutral	Global Macro	Emerging Markets
S&P 500	0.583	0.400	0.231	0.480
Russell 3000	0.649	0.398	0.238	0.510

Sources: CSFB/Tremont, Standard & Poor's, PerTrac.

cent of Fixed Income Arb. These correlations are higher than when the S&P 500 was the market proxy and indicate a significantly greater dependence by these hedge funds on their markets to generate returns.

In the equity space, Long/Short Equity is shown to have greater correlation with the Russell 3000 than with the S&P 500, reflecting the fact that these funds extensively troll the market of less-researched small-capitalization stocks in their search for alpha. However, the Russell 3000 does not explain the performance of Equity Market Neutral and Global Macro any better than the S&P 500 does.

From this limited evidence, it appears that if market indexes are used in evaluating hedge funds, broad-based indexes such as the Merrill Lynch High Yield Master for fixed income funds or Russell 3000 for equity-oriented funds can better capture the performance of hedge funds. More likely, a combination of indexes would have higher correlations with hedge funds than any individual index. In this respect, academic research on mutual funds has shown that multifactor models do a better job than any single index at explaining the returns of mutual funds.[3]

Furthermore, while market indexes cannot entirely explain the returns of hedge funds, market returns demarcate the boundaries of the returns that can be expected from hedge funds. A hedge fund that produces return streams outside of these boundaries may demonstrate manager talent, unusual risk taking by the manager, or simply a mere random event that is not repeatable. In any case, such outlier returns may be indicative of the need to investigate the sources of the unusual returns, positive or negative.

Hedge Fund Indexes

Obviously hedge fund indexes such as the CSFB/Tremont Hedge Fund Index and its components are more reflective of hedge funds than market indexes are. This is more so since correlations among managers have been shown to be fairly high.[4] If the hedge fund index is a category index like Fixed Income Arbitrage or Long/Short Equity, it has a basis for performing peer analysis.

However, even in this situation, there still are significant differences between a hedge fund's strategy versus the strategies embedded in the category index. One example is the mortgage-backed securities strategy, which is only one of a variety of fixed income strategies underlying the CSFB/Tremont Fixed Income Arbitrage index. Thus, comparing the performance of a mortgage-backed securities manager against the index does not even allow a comparison between the fund and its peers. And it certainly does not give any clue as to how well it does in terms of the exact strategy that it employs to generate the returns.

Furthermore, there are also aspects relating to the construction of the hedge fund indexes that require caution in using them for performance evaluation. Some of these are listed in Table 8.2. For these reasons, hedge fund indexes would be useful to the extent that they set the boundaries of returns, helping to detect potentially unusual activities at a hedge fund that generates exceptional returns outside of these boundaries. Yet, these indexes can be misleading as a basis for evaluating a hedge fund's alpha or ability to generate excess returns.

Positive Risk-Free Rate

The risk-free rate has been recommended by consultants and used by many institutional investors as a benchmark for hedge fund performance. A variation of this measure is to add a margin from 300 to 600 basis points.

It has been argued that the risk-free rate indicates investors' requirement for positive return, independent from the market. Also, arbitrage strategies have short positions that earn a "short" rebate linked to the risk-free rate.

The justification for using the risk-free rate is the notion that arbitrage strategies are supposed to be neutral to the market. Therefore, the expected return from such strategies should be the risk-free rate. Adding a few percentage points to this rate reflects the expectation that hedge fund managers have skills to generate excess return and they are well compensated for it. And this expectation should be built into the benchmark for performance measurement. Exactly what this margin is depends on the institutions.

TABLE 8.2   Hedge Fund Index Data

Data shortcomings:

- Fund listing is up to individual hedge fund managers.
- Indexes include many small funds and miss some large funds.
- Data from hedge funds are not verified by index publishers.

Questionable statistics:

- Funds in index are subject to turnover.
- Survivor and backfill biases may overestimate returns.
- Presence of large funds that are closed to new investors creates under/overestimate bias.
- Autocorrelation may significantly underestimate volatility.
- Track records are still relatively short.

The hedge fund strategy that comes closest to pure risk-free arbitrage is equity market neutral. However, as discussed previously, market neutral does not mean risk free. A dollar-neutral strategy is certainly not market neutral even though it has equal amounts in long and short positions. A zero-beta portfolio may not be market neutral, either, because we don't know what the "market" is. Even if the "market" is known, the portfolio's weighted beta shifts in the interim reporting periods. Thus, the portfolio is never truly zero-beta. And it is certainly not risk free. If the portfolio is not well diversified, the company-specific risks of the stocks in the portfolio are not diversified away, leaving a residual risk in the portfolio.

If the readers are inclined to accept the risk-free rate plus a margin as a practical and acceptable approximation of a true benchmark for equity market neutral, other strategies hardly qualify as risk-free arbitrage. Fixed income arbitrage takes advantage of the differences in the yields of two fixed income securities. On the long side, the security is one that has a higher yield, and the short side is one that has lower yield. The net difference is the spread. Typically, spreads are relatively small, such as spreads between U.S. Treasury securities and investment grade corporate bonds. But spreads can be several hundred basis points in cases of Treasuries versus high-yield or junk bonds. Against mortgage-backed securities, spreads above Treasuries average about 100 basis points. In order to achieve high-single-digit or double-digit rates of return, fixed income arbitrage managers engage in leverage. Leverages of 20 times the base capital are not unusual.

Thus the risks of fixed income arbitrage funds come from the leverage as well as the potential widening of the spreads. In times of unusual market volatility, the combination is explosive, as in July 2003 when it contributed to the collapse of Beacon Hill as well as unusual losses at other fixed income arb firms. Risk free plus a safety margin hardly qualifies as a measurement benchmark for the return of fixed income arb hedge funds.

KNOW YOUR HEDGE FUND MANAGERS OR KEY DRIVERS OF RETURNS

Underlying the preceding discussion is the fact that hedge fund strategies are vastly different, even among funds with similar styles. Application of some universal benchmark, no matter how well constructed, is unlikely to capture the essence of all hedge funds' performances. Evaluation of hedge fund performance therefore requires an intimate understanding of how returns are generated by individual funds, from the amount of leverage to trading style and proclivity to take risks by the lead portfolio managers.

Such individual variations cannot be captured by just looking at a benchmark index of some kind. Furthermore, hedge fund investing is about capturing an absolute positive rate of return even when the market, whatever it means, goes down. As the market experiences periods of unusual volatility, different management styles will produce different results. Understanding these styles would greatly enhance the ability to judge the performance of hedge fund managers. In the following, we discuss what can be expected from different investment styles and strategies.

Equity-Oriented Hedge Funds

There are three principal hedge fund equity strategies: long/short, market neutral, and short bias. In terms of dollar amounts, long/short is net long, short bias is net short, and market neutral has close to equal amounts. Using dollar amounts as measures of the equity market exposures most certainly would misestimate the amount of market risk, leaving aside the nonsystematic risks specific to the underlying securities.

A better measure of the market risk is the weighted average beta of the individual securities. This is the sum of the securities' beta multiplied by the percentage weightings of the securities. This sum is then divided by the number of securities. The result is not the same as the *ex post* return of the portfolio, which is correlated to the market's return to arrive at a calculated beta.

A portfolio's weighted average beta of individual securities would then be correlated to the return of the market to arrive at its expected return. An equity hedge fund's expected return calculated from weighted average beta would then be compared with its actual return. A fund's excess return or alpha is the difference between its actual return and its weighted average beta return. The use of weighted average beta in performance and risk analyses will be discussed in greater detail in Chapter 9.

Fixed Income Funds

For fixed income funds, the amounts of leverage are the key to their return and risk profiles. When credit spreads narrow, fund managers tend to increase leverage in order to generate returns. However, increasing leverage would increase the funds' risks.

Thus, in evaluating fund performance, it is essential to assess the attendant risks due to the use of leverage. A simple way to gauge leverage is to add the long positions to the short side to find the total face value of all positions. In normal market conditions, these nominal amounts need to be adjusted for their exposures to interest rates in terms of duration and implied options. However, in times of market dislocations, these adjustments can lead to underestimation of the interest rate risk.

One approximate method of estimating the expected return of a fixed income arbitrage fund is to multiply the amount of credit spread by the amount of leverage.

A more elaborate method of estimating the return of a fixed income arb fund as suggested by Hsieh and Fung (2002)[5] is to use changes in the credit spread during a given period. Thus, for the 1990 to 1997 period, this methodology would yield the following formulas for estimating the return of the HFR Fixed Income Arbitrage strategy:

HFR Fixed Income Arb return = 0.0096 − 5.37 * [Change in credit spread]
(10.0)   (6.6)

$$R^2 = 0.32$$

If this relationship holds true in any period, the estimated return can be compared to the actual performance of a fixed income arbitrage hedge fund's returns, and inferences can be made as to whether the fund generates any excess return, or it simply follows the market, which is the credit spread.

HEDGE FUND BENCHMARKS IN PRACTICE

To incorporate the ideas that hedge funds seek market neutrality or at least protection against market downturns while at the same time being exposed to market factor risks, some combination of the risk-free rate and market indexes have been used by leading institutional investors as benchmarks for their hedge fund investments. Some of these benchmarks are:

- Related market index: Russell 3000 plus a margin.
- Hedge fund index: Return on a pool of hedge funds of different or same styles.
- Market-linked absolute return.
  - Risk-free rate plus a spread:
    30-day Treasury bills + 5%
    60% of Salomon Global Equity Index + 20% of J. P. Morgan Global Bonds + 20% of (LIBOR + 5%)
  - Minimum return plus some market upside:
    60% Wilshire 5000 + 40% Treasury bills + 3%
- Others have suggested an absolute target such as 10 percent or a target that is linked to the inflation rate, such as the consumer price index plus a margin.

Clearly any absolute target may be unachievable in the short term, while it may be too lenient at other times depending on the market conditions, such as the inflation rate and the general level of interest rates. Furthermore, a performance benchmark should be one that can be used to judge the performance of the hedge fund. A benchmark that is applied to all hedge funds in a portfolio is not as much a performance benchmark as the investment objective of the investors. A hedge fund that fails to meet the objective of such a benchmark may not necessarily fall short because the fund is a poor performer given its strategy, although it may justifiably be eliminated from the portfolio because the fund and its strategy are no longer suitable for the portfolio.

EVALUATING PERFORMANCE: A HEURISTIC PROCESS

In evaluating hedge fund performances, it is useful to keep in mind that hedge fund managers operate within the constraints of the capital markets. Though they have specialized skills to discover and profit from anomalies in certain segments of the broad stock and bond markets, such opportunities must exist for them to exploit. When the conditions in these market niches are favorable, these hedge fund managers are well positioned to earn excess returns. If they take additional risks by leveraging in multiples of the capital base, the excess return would be extraordinary. In times of sudden shifts in the direction of the broad markets, it is likely that these market niches would experience dislocations. Only the most talented managers are positioned to cope with these inflection points in the markets. The average manager, however, would likely record excess negative returns, as the hedge fund indexes have shown. Less risk-averse managers, those who put on additional leverage to maintain returns as the opportunities in their market niches dwindle, such as when credit spreads have narrowed to historical lows, would likely endure unmitigated losses.

Therefore, it is most critical to understand the market niches that the hedge fund managers operate in: the conditions, opportunities, and potential risks in these markets; the strategies that are employed to achieve returns; and the managers' predisposition to take risks. Some managers are more prone to take higher risks to take advantage of small opportunities, especially when they are falling behind in their return targets. Other managers are less willing to increase their risk exposures even when they believe that risk taking is warranted and would be handsomely rewarded by unusual opportunities.

Only when equipped with this understanding of the hedge funds' strategies can an investor properly evaluate their performances.

Shortcut approaches such as hedge fund indexes or peer groups can point out potential problem managers by identifying outlier performers. In such instances, more intense reviews of the managers' trades and strategies would reveal more information on the causes of these outlier returns. However, even when the hedge funds' returns are within some normal bounds, they may be extraordinary nevertheless if the risks taken to achieve them are relatively low. Conversely, normal returns may mask potential problems.

Hedge funds should generate positive returns in all market conditions. However, in cases of extreme market dislocations, a small amount of loss should not be considered poor performance. In this instance, a relevant index should provide a ready comparison. A strong performance relative to the peer group suggests the managers are still in top form.

Lagging behind a rising stock market is not necessarily a sin, especially if the market's rally is very substantial, as in 2003. However, if the fund manager gained only a few percentage points or incurred losses following prior periods of mediocre results, in 2001 and 2003 for example, it might be a signal that the manager was losing his touch. In this case, a focused review of the manager's strategy and investments would be in order. Another aspect of the use of a market benchmark is that in times of high volatility a fund may choose to reduce the exposure. Its return, though good, may as a result show underperformance relative to the benchmark index if the index registers strong results.

When a hedge fund navigates in multiple markets, it has the opportunity to take advantage of different market conditions to generate returns that are not available to funds that are focused on single markets or types of trades. The hurdle of expectations for these funds may be higher as a result. As such, a single absolute target or one-factor benchmark would not truly reflect the opportunities and risks available to them. Accordingly, a complex multifactor model of expected return and risk would more likely capture these funds' potential performance. Though the multifactor approach has weaknesses, mainly in the construction and identification of the relevant factors that drive returns, it captures more fully the range of possible returns and risks of multistrategy funds.

Strategy Review

Underlying the evaluation of the performance of a hedge fund is the need to assess the strategy it employs to achieve the reported rate of return. Therefore, the entire investment strategy and process of the hedge fund needs to be reviewed as part of the performance evaluation.

Funds of funds and large institutional investors typically follow monthly reports of investment results from their hedge funds with conference calls with the managers of these funds. They discuss a review of the market conditions, what accounts for the gains or losses, the good trades that generated the gains, and the adverse developments in the markets that led to disappointments in the results. Often only the most glaring mistakes are revealed by the hedge funds and the market usually is blamed for the losses. However, investors use this opportunity to glean from the conversations indications of any changes in strategies or any unusual trades that may exacerbate the gains or losses. On balance, it is in the interest of the hedge funds to attribute positive returns to talent, and losses to adverse conditions in the market. Typically, whether or not relevant, returns that exceed a hedge fund index would be seized upon as evidence of special skills. On the investors' part, a month with good returns, especially when the competition fares poorly, often dulls any urgent sense of need to delve into the behind-the-scenes trades that account for the good results.

Review of Investment Suitability

Whether a hedge fund is a star or an underperformer is not the only objective of performance review. An additional question is whether it continues to be suitable to contribute to the investor's investment objective. As we have seen in Chapter 5, not all hedge fund strategies perform equally well in all market environments. Furthermore, in times of high volatility in the capital markets or economic expansion, hedge funds may not add value, as suggested in Kat and Miffre (2002).[6] Also, a fund that seeks low volatility by investing in strategies such as fixed income arb may in fact find this leads to high volatility. This is because of the left tail risks inherent in fixed income arbitrage.

In such situations, the investor may be well advised to redeem from a fund that is performing well. Funds of funds often face this type of decision as the capital markets evolve, creating new profitable opportunities that funds of funds wish to take advantage of.

CONCLUSION

Evaluating hedge fund performance is a far more complex issue than simply comparing a fund's return with an index, whether the return is adjusted for volatility or for tracking errors vis-à-vis a market index. The difficulty lies in the fact that hedge funds navigate in a multitude of markets while often making strategy shifts and adjusting risks with leverage. Thus, hedge fund returns are not readily assessable against a market benchmark like the

S&P 500, or an aggregation of different hedge fund strategies like the CSFB/Tremont Hedge Fund Index. Nevertheless, market and peer group indexes can serve as the boundaries of returns or indicators of the ranges of average results. If a hedge fund's return falls in the tail ends of the distribution, either negative or positive, it might be a signal for review, to analyze and evaluate the circumstances whereby such returns are generated: Are new strategies being employed? Have unusual risks been undertaken? Or is it mere luck?

To improve on the relevance of an index to a hedge fund's particular strategy, special indexes can be constructed. Discussed in this chapter is an index relating fixed income arbitrage returns to credit spreads and a methodology using weighted average beta to evaluate equity market neutral and long/short equity funds.

However, no matter how well a performance evaluation benchmark is constructed, it cannot substitute for an intimate understanding of a hedge fund's strategy to generate the returns and risks. We have discussed evaluating returns in this chapter. We now turn to evaluating hedge fund risks in Chapter 9.

CHAPTER 9

Buyers Beware

Evaluating and Managing the Many Facets of the Risks of Hedge Funds

Long-Term Capital Management (LTCM) has been etched into the collective memory of investors and the history of Wall Street as the ultimate folly of hedge funds. Formed in 1993 by the former star trader John Meriwether of the now-defunct Salomon Brothers, and populated by celebrity Harvard professors and Nobel Prize winners, it made a big splash by raising $1.25 billion at the start, only to require a multibillion-dollar bailout organized by the Federal Reserve following its near collapse in September 1998. Postmortem analyses abound as to what and whom to blame for the disaster.[1] Yet it is an irony that the types of strategies that led to the LTCM disaster are now being employed every day at hedge funds, often successfully and profitably for their clients. LTCM itself has been reincarnated to become JWM Capital Management with close to $1 billion of assets under management.

LTCM engaged in a variety of fixed income arbitrage trades. Among the basic ones employed by the firm were going long off-the-run Treasuries and going short on-the-run Treasury bonds. Because the former have higher yields due to their relative lack of liquidity, the trade yielded a small price advantage of a few hundredths of 1 percent. In order to generate returns in the low teens, say 10 to 12 percent, leverages of 20 or 30 times and higher had to be used.

Two things went wrong. First, as success piled up, the firm ventured into trades that were drastic departures from the initial strategies. It began to arbitrage between dissimilar securities such as Italian bonds and German Bund futures or Danish mortgage securities. In 1997, according to newspaper accounts, the firm went into trading equity index options and stocks involved in takeover positions—that is, merger arbitrage.

Second, the firm took on huge amounts of leverage. At the beginning of 1998, LTCM had capital of $4.8 billion but a portfolio of $200 billion in securities, many of them illiquid, plus derivatives of $1.2 trillion in notional value. As arbitrage trades, many of these positions offset one another such that when market conditions returned to equilibrium, the price differences between these securities would return to normal, allowing LTCM to book large profits from its hugely leveraged trades. But the market did not return to normal. The price differences on LTCM arbitrage positions widened further, partly because of the flight to quality that was precipitated by the Russian crisis, and also because other market participants had taken positions opposite to LTCM, reportedly to take advantage of its overexposures. But it was the huge leverages that caused the losses that precipitated the firm's collapse. One of the trades that it had on its books was long/short on off-the-run against on-the-run Treasuries. At the end of September 1998, the spread between these two securities had widened from 5 basis points (0.05 percent) to 15 basis points. It was a big move, but not fatal on an unleveraged portfolio of $4.8 billion. The loss would have been a mere $4.8 million, or 0.1 percent. But multiplied by 100 times, the loss would be gargantuan. On August 21, LTCM reportedly lost $550 million. By September 21, the firm was said to have lost an additional $500 million.

The LTCM fiasco highlighted the need for understanding the risks of hedge funds before investments are made and for postinvestment monitoring and managing these risks. And certainly high returns should not lull investors into complacency. After all, in the first full year of operation, 1995, LTCM produced an eye-popping 43 percent after all fees and expenses. In the following year, it recorded profits of 41 percent. In fact, in its first two or three years of operation, LTCM would have passed with flying colors any of the standard tests of performance evaluation such as the Sharpe ratio.

However, alert and dispassionate investors might have noticed the low-returning nature of the markets LTCM was navigating, and the extraordinary results it generated, both of which should have served as warning signs of the kind of risks that LTCM had been taking with its investors' money. This lesson has been memorized by some experienced investors: Several fund of funds managers in my sample said that one of the reasons they redeem from a hedge fund is that it generates very unusually high returns. They believe such returns not only will not be repeatable in the future, but also are indicative of the unusual risks taken by these hedge funds.

However, extraordinary investment risks such as those taken at LTCM are not the only causes of hedge funds' collapses. In fact, according to Capital Markets Company, operations problems, including mispricing of securities, have been found to contribute to more than a third of hedge fund failures.[2]

Overall, having made the investments in hedge funds, investors would need to monitor closely the strategies and operations of their funds. Hedge fund investors are interested in making sure that their investments will perform in the future in the way they were led to believe they would prior to making the investments. They certainly would not want their money to be stolen or spent on the fund managers' personal habits. Furthermore, any individual hedge funds will see their investment performances vary over time. The market niches that have in the past produced superior returns may become crowded and opportunities to earn excess return may evaporate. Or the competition may become fierce, and the hedge fund managers may become complacent or their skills become less attuned to the new conditions in those market niches. "Further, the attractiveness of a particular strategy or manager is likely to vary over time, since a) many hedge fund strategies rely on niche areas of market imperfections, which may disappear over time, and as money seeks to exploit them, b) particular managers may lose their motivation over time, and their skills may become less applicable as market conditions change. For these reasons, [hedge funds] may be limited in the amount of money they can accommodate, and require close attention and monitoring."[3]

In this chapter we discuss the types of risks that necessitate close monitoring and the steps investors can take to minimize those risks.

THE MANY FACETS OF HEDGE FUNDS' RISKS

Risks of hedge funds come in many facets, not just in the volatility of returns. We distinguish three broad categories of risk that face hedge fund investors: fraud, operations risks, and investment risks.

Frauds

Newspaper accounts abound with stories about frauds in the hedge fund industry. Regulatory authorities also have taken punitive actions against those who claimed to manage hedge funds, but in fact used these vehicles to steal investors' money. The misdeeds usually included misrepresentation of managers' backgrounds, investment track records, assets under management, and circumstances that were designed to inflate the attractiveness of the investments. The end game was usually to misappropriate investors' funds for personal use and other purposes.

Such was the case in a complaint filed by the Securities and Exchange

Commission (SEC) against Ashbury Capital Partners and its 23-year-old president and portfolio manager Mark Yagala whereby Yagala was charged with misappropriating for personal use a substantial portion of the millions he had raised from 20 investors.[4] Or the case against Burton G. Friedlander whereby the SEC accused him of misrepresenting the value of investor assets in a fund and spending over $2 million of investors' money to pay for his company's operations and for his personal expenses, including country club dues.[5] The common thread in these fraudulent cases is that the perpetrators falsely represented their backgrounds and qualifications, and their investment track records. To detect these fraudulent activities, experienced practitioners insist on due diligence whereby a thorough investigation of the hedge fund managers and their operations is conducted. These investigations would include, as a minimum, verification of employment history, reference checks, and search of court records.

Sometimes the frauds arise from attempts to conceal losses and to attract new investors. That was the case against Michael T. Higgins of San Francisco, California, wherein the SEC charged in civil and criminal actions that he claimed to have produced returns of 54 percent in 1998 when in fact he had losses.[6] Sometimes the misdeed would be comic were it not for the losses that investors suffered as a result. Ryan J. Fontaine was a 22-year-old college student living with his parents who claimed to have $250 million under management and to have produced an annualized return of 39.5 percent for 13 years, including an average of over 21 percent for two years during the bear market.[7]

When investment results are extraordinary, whether or not these outsized returns are real, investors need to investigate how these returns were generated. In fraudulent cases, the returns are often claimed to have been generated in the context of some obscure investment strategies. Or the strategies are relatively straightforward, like trading S&P 500 index futures, but the returns are so great that investors might do well to recall the old saying "too good to be true." This is especially so when the portfolio managers are unknown to the investors.

But frauds can be committed by hedge fund managers whose backgrounds are beyond reproach, at least on the surface, and whose investment strategies are sound. In *SEC v. Beacon Hill Asset Management, L.L.C.* (November 15, 2002), the Securities and Exchange Commission charged Beacon Hill Asset Management with deliberate falsification of its investment results to investors.[8] For the month of September 2002, Beacon Hill reported to its investors that two of its mortgage-backed securities hedge funds suffered losses of 25 percent. Nine days later, the firm restated the losses to be 54 percent, including losses that had not been reported during prior periods.

In the complaint, the SEC charged Beacon Hill with fraud and named as defendants the firm's four principals: John Barry, the president; Tom Daniels, the chief investment officer; John Irwin, senior portfolio manager; and Mark Miszkiewicz, chief financial officer. The SEC alleged that the four principals of Beacon Hill together implemented a fraudulent scheme resulting in losses of more than $300 million to investors. The allegations were that from at least the beginning of 2002 through October 2002, Beacon Hill and its principals defrauded and made material misrepresentations to investors by way of the methodology Beacon Hill used for calculating the net asset values (NAVs) of the hedge funds it managed, the hedging and trading strategy for the purportedly market neutral funds, and the value and the performance of the funds.

The SEC also alleged that central to Beacon Hill's fraud was its method of valuing securities in the hedge funds to show steady and positive returns: that Beacon Hill manipulated its valuation procedures and thus allowed it to report steady growth and hide losses in its master fund, which was the core hedge fund that held and traded securities in its three feeder hedge funds.

According to the complaint, as the value of these Beacon Hill hedge funds decreased over the summer of 2002, the firm continued to report positive returns by inflating the prices of the securities in the master fund to maintain the appearance of positive returns. At the same time, contrary to what it was telling investors, Beacon Hill made an increasing and ultimately unsuccessful bet in the hope of profiting from interest rates rising in an attempt to cover its hidden losses. Additionally, Beacon Hill was alleged to have entered into a series of trades between the master fund and other accounts it managed for two institutional clients at prices that defrauded the master fund and allowed the managed accounts, whose performance had also declined, to reap substantial profits. The SEC argued that Beacon Hill was able to hide the losses resulting from these fraudulent trades by inflating the value of the securities in the master fund to an even greater extent.

As their situation started to unravel, in September 2002 three of the four principals liquidated an account in which they were the only investors by selling the securities in their account to the master fund without disclosure to investors. In early October 2002, when Beacon Hill's prime broker challenged the valuation of the master fund and they were forced to admit it had sustained losses, the principals misrepresented the magnitude of the actual losses in an attempt to save Beacon Hill's operations and make the losses appear to be the result of market conditions.

On October 17, 2002, Beacon Hill finally announced the full extent of investor losses, admitting that as of September 30, the NAVs of its hedge funds had declined 54 percent from the previously reported August 31,

2002, levels, and further acknowledged that it had mispriced securities in the funds prior to August. Clearly, this acknowledgment did not reveal the extent of the machinations alleged by the SEC that Beacon Hill and its principals had undertaken to defraud investors.

One thing that was different between Beacon Hill and LTCM was that LTCM did not hide its losses; everyone in the marketplace knew about them. However, both firms employed strategies that involved a high level of leverage, and these strategies traded illiquid securities and market sectors that were susceptible to stresses during market dislocations. Once the losses became substantial, Beacon Hill, as it was alleged, engaged in deception.

Operational Risks

Operational risks may be rooted in insufficiencies in resources, infrastructures, and technologies. They may result from lax supervision in trading that leads to unauthorized trading or violation of trading guidelines. Operational risks are also manifested in ways that often result in inflated valuation of securities, even with the possible absence of the intention to deceive. In the absence of fraudulent intentions, inflated valuations—inflated because there has never been any known case whereby a hedge fund or any investment fund gets into trouble due to *under*reporting of investment results—often originate with derivatives and illiquid securities that are traded in the dealer market, as opposed to the exchange-listed markets.

Exchange-listed securities, even if they are thinly traded, always have closing prices and tradable bids and offers that serve as verifiable bases for securities' valuation. However, securities that are traded in the dealer market, such as bonds and foreign exchange contracts among and between banks and their customers, are those that rely on quotes for bids and offers from dealers. Exactly the same securities, even those that are traded in large volumes by numerous dealers such as U.S. Treasury notes and bonds, can get different quotes from different dealers. Differences in quotes on U.S. Treasury securities, however, are usually no more than a few ticks or 32nds. (Bonds are quoted in 32nds. This means a dealer may quote a bid, that is, to buy, for a 30-year Treasury bond at $100^{25}/_{32}$ while another may quote the same bond at $100^{15}/_{16}$.) Quote differences among illiquid lower-rated securities are often much larger. In times of market turmoil, quote differences usually increase. Sometimes there are no dealer quotes at all. During the crisis of 1998, some dealers reportedly did not even pick up the phones to answer calls from longtime customers.

Many complex securities, such as derivatives, require dealers to make mathematical calculations involving different markets and different securities to arrive at fair prices. These calculations by necessity are based on assumptions that may be theoretically reasonable but are not realistic in the then-prevailing market conditions.

Often certain derivatives were constructed by one dealer for a particular client. To obtain a price, the client must go back to the same dealer. In this type of situation, it is very difficult to arrive at the fair market value for these securities. One example is a three-year note denominated in U.S. dollars, which would be pegged to the relationship between two currencies such as the British pound and the Japanese yen, and have a leverage of multiples of the face value of the note. One advantage of such securities is that it does not show up in the calculation of the leverage of the fund. In times when trading volume is low, such as in summer, or even in normal market conditions, the differences between bid and ask prices can be quite significant even from the same dealer. Under these circumstances, "put these natural, inherent difficulties in pricing complex or illiquid investments together with a powerful financial incentive to show strong (or hide weak) performance, and then situate these factors in an environment with minimal regulatory oversight, or without strict discipline and internal controls (still far too typical in the hedge fund industry), and there is potential for trouble."[9]

This was the situation that apparently happened at the big hedge fund Clinton Group. In November 2003, a senior portfolio manager resigned from the firm saying he disagreed with management about the way certain mortgage-backed securities were valued. This triggered a cascade of redemptions from investors, causing Clinton's assets under management to tumble from a high of $10 billion to $4.5 billion in December, then $2.2 billion as of January 2004.

Many securities are also subject to counterparty risks. This is the failure of any trading counterparty in a chain of intermediaries prior to settlement. This is prevalent in any transaction that is not exchange traded, such as derivatives, foreign exchange, and bonds. This issue has come to the fore after the collapse of Enron, which was of course a onetime dominant player in the energy market. A less serious risk, though one that nevertheless can be costly, is the transaction risk whereby a transaction fails to settle on the specified date. It has been estimated that 8 to 20 percent of cross-border trades involving non-U.S. stocks, bonds, and foreign currencies fail to settle on time.[10] While the impact of settlement failures is not as crippling as counterparty risk, when a hedge fund is involved in exotic emerging markets with a high level of leverage and use of derivatives, settlement failures may have snowballing effects on the entire fund.

Investment Risks: Ongoing Focus

Investors should want to make sure that the investment returns did not result from any unusually substantial risks that the managers were taking. As in the case of LTCM, its first two years' returns of more than 40 percent in each year partly stemmed from the extraordinary leverage that it piled onto its capital base.

Investment risks refer to the risks embedded in the strategies used by the hedge funds under consideration, their trading styles, the markets they operate in (stocks or bonds, U.S. or foreign, developed or emerging markets), and the kinds of securities they trade (small-cap or large-cap stocks, U.S. Treasury securities or mortgage-backed securities, high-yield bonds, foreign bonds).

Traditional long-only investment managers strive to stay within their stated strategies and styles. Hedge funds have much greater flexibility, especially with regard to broad-based strategies such as multistrategy, global macro, and fixed income arb. Multistrategy and global macro managers trade in all manners of markets and all kinds of securities. Fixed income arb managers navigate in a wide spectrum of the fixed income market. Even managers of seemingly narrowly defined strategies such as convertible arb can have distinctly different styles. Some rely on hedging by short selling stocks while others emphasize credit analysis to generate returns.

In the previous chapter we discussed the difficulties in measuring and evaluating hedge fund performance. The opposite side of the evaluation issue is the measuring and evaluating of hedge fund risks.

Short History of Hedge Funds   As in performance measurement, the issue is the lack of a benchmark for comparison. Additionally, when it comes to risks, the short history of hedge funds further complicates the measurement and management of risks. Even though the concept and strategy of hedge fund investing have been in existence for some 50 years, organized collection and presentation of hedge fund data have begun fairly recently. The CSFB/Tremont database of hedge funds has historical data going back only to 1994. Of the approximately 7,000 hedge funds, this database contains only a few hundred. Most of the HFRI indexes began in 1990, although a few include data since 1987.

Analyses of hedge funds and their risks thus rely on information that date no earlier than the late 1980s. This period happens to be relatively stable from the viewpoint of the long-term history of the financial markets, in spite of the sharp rise in interest rates in 1994, the Asian crisis in 1997, the Russian debt default in 1998, and the burst of the equity market bubble in 2000. As an example, although the equity bear market lasted for three years, Black Monday in October 1987 was far more traumatic in its shock effect. In the fixed income market, July 2003 was most unpleasant for fixed income arbitrage managers as interest rates rose and credit spreads widened, causing large losses at these funds. Even funds of funds that were supposed to be well diversified suffered losses as a result. The problems at the Clinton Group originated from this period. The July 2003 interest rate moves, however, were relatively small compared to late 1979 when the Federal Reserve Board under Chairman Paul Volcker shifted its policy to money supply targeting instead of setting interest rates at specific levels.

How would hedge funds perform and handle risks under those circumstances? To have a glimpse, and this is no more than a glimpse, at the risks of fixed income arbitrage hedge funds in times of stress, Hsieh and Fung (2002)[11] attempted to analyze the factors that determine the performance and risk of fixed income funds. They first reported that the biggest risks to these funds are credit spreads, which are the differences between U.S. Treasury securities and other types of bonds. They also examined the history of credit spreads dating back to the 1920s and found that in terms of credit spreads the 1990s was a friendly period to fixed income funds as compared to earlier periods such as the 1920s and the 1960s through the mid-1980s.

In the summer of 1998, between June and October, credit spreads widened by 110 basis points. Based on the authors' model for estimating the impact of credit spreads, fixed income arbitrage funds would have lost 4.95 percent in those months. It is interesting to note that the CSFB Fixed Income Arb index recorded actual losses of –11.32 percent during this period, or more than twice the model's estimate. In April 1932, credit spreads widened by 187 basis points, implying a loss of –9.08 percent for fixed income arbitrage funds if they had been in existence then. One can only wonder how much higher the actual losses to such funds would have been. In this connection, it is worthwhile to note that the model would estimate the loss suffered by LTCM to be –15.85 percent in July–August 1998. Its actual loss was –44.8 percent. Thus, it is only prudent to expect that in times of systemic stress, losses can be substantially much larger than anticipated.

Credit Spreads Also, historically, widening of credit spreads can last for prolonged periods. During these times, just as in stocks, there have been movements lasting for months or several years whereby credit spreads widened very sharply to be followed by short-lived calmer periods, only to be interrupted by sharp increases of spreads. One such period started in late 1963 from about 50 basis points only to keep widening to over 400 basis points in late 1974, punctuated in the meantime by shorter-term contractions of 100 to 180 basis points. By comparison, between 1984 and

1995, credit spreads widened by about 100 basis points, with relatively little fluctuations in the interim. How would fixed income arbitrage funds perform in periods of high volatility, which have been unseen in the past 10 to 15 years? How many funds would survive such an onslaught?

Fixed Income Arb Funds and Equity Risks   Another aspect of the risk of fixed income arbitrage funds that is not well recognized is its correlation with the movements of the stock market. The CSFB Fixed Income Arbitrage Index showed virtually zero correlation with the S&P 500, NASDAQ, Dow Jones Industrial Average, and the MSCI World Index. This suggests that fixed income arbitrage funds can perform well even when stocks performed poorly. And indeed these funds did produce on average high-single-digit rates of return during the three-year bear market of stocks. However, in their study, Hsieh and Fung (2002)[12] found that there was a significant correlation between the S&P 500 and credit spreads such that if the S&P 500 dropped by 10 percent, fixed income arbitrage funds would lose 1.5 percent. This implies that "there exists cyclical exposure to risk factors inherent in most fixed income arbitrage funds that may be masked by the short existence of the funds themselves."[13]

How can fixed income strategies lose if the stock market declines? Isn't it true that when stocks decline, signifying economic weakness, interest rates would be cut, benefiting fixed income securities? Such would be the case if the hedge fund managers are long high-credit-quality bonds such as U.S. Treasuries. But in arbitrage trades, in one form or another, managers go short Treasuries and go long lower-credit bonds. In times of economic weakness, lower-credit bonds experience declines in yields and higher prices, just as in Treasuries and high-credit securities, but by smaller amounts. In other words, credit spreads widen. Arbitrage managers owning such credit spread positions would suffer losses from their short side that are larger than the gains coming from the long side, which consists of lower-credit bonds. Some of the lower-credit bonds may in fact lose principal even when the overall level of interest rate declines. This happens when the corporations issuing the bonds suffer profit declines or losses, or even bankruptcies. Arbitrage managers holding such securities would suffer a double hit: losses from the short Treasury position and losses from the bonds that receive credit downgrades or go into default.

Stock Market Risks and Equity Funds   Switching to equity-oriented funds, a study by Capital Market Risk Advisors indicated that merger arbitrage funds take on more equity market risk exposure than the strategy may imply.[14] This explains why these funds produced greater returns than a pure merger arbitrage strategy. During the bubble period, defined as between

1998 and March 2000, merger arbitrage funds had a correlation of 0.55 with the S&P 500 compared with 0.46 by the pure strategy. After the bubble burst, merger arbitrage funds continued to be correlated with the stock market, though the correlation ratio had declined to 0.37. This correlation with the equity market brought returns on merger arbitrage funds down from 13.1 percent during the bubble to 3.8 percent, compared to 8.9 percent net from the pure strategy.

In the study by Asness, Krail, and Liew (2001)[15] previously discussed, it was found that hedge funds had greater exposure to equity risks than commonly assumed. A look at recent correlation data shows that the exposure to the equity market risk continues to be more significant than standard deviation statistics imply. For example, the CSFB/Tremont Long/ Short Equity index had a standard deviation of 11 percent during 1994– 2003. Equity Market Neutral showed a volatility of 3.07 percent during the period, while Risk Arbitrage's volatility was a bit higher at 4.4 percent. The two strategies' standard deviations are similar or lower than the standard deviation of Fixed Income Arbitrage, and much lower than Long/ Short Equity's. From these standard deviations, one would conclude that Long/Short Equity has much greater risk than the other two. The following correlation data, however, clearly indicate that Risk Arbitrage and Equity Market Neutral are significantly exposed to equity market risks, though less so than Long/Short Equity.

	Dow	MSCI World	S&P 500	NASDAQ
Risk Arbitrage	0.44	0.45	0.44	0.39
Long/Short Equity	0.45	0.61	0.58	0.76
Equity Market Neutral	0.39	0.36	0.39	0.29

Stock Market Risk Exposure The equity market exposure underlying those strategies that are seemingly neutral to equity market risks is an issue that needs to be understood by hedge fund investors. In some strategies, the equity market risk is in fact asymmetric to the detriment of investors. For example, Lo (2002)[16] found that strategies involving emerging market equities have an up-market beta of 0.16, seemingly market neutral, but a down-market beta of 1.49. Thus, these funds would decline more than their markets in downturns, but significantly lag behind in upturns. In funds that use relative value option arbitrage, betas for up and down markets are actually of the opposite signs: –0.78 in up markets and 0.33 in down markets. Since these funds would follow the S&P 500 on the way down and produce losses when the stock market was up, theirs is hardly a strategy that is market neutral. Additionally, they exhibit the undesirable characteristics of "poor" correlations, as discussed in Chapter 5.

Thus, there are reasons to believe that hedge fund arbitrage strategies, whether equity or fixed income oriented, actually have greater exposures to equity and interest rate risks than they may purport to have. Because of the existence of these common risk exposures, in times of market dislocations seemingly uncorrelated strategies such as long/short equity and fixed income arbitrage can move in the same direction. This occurred in August to October 1998 when both strategies had significant losses in the aftermath of the Russian debt default. The CSFB Long/Short Equity index recorded a loss for only one month, in August at −11.43 percent. The CSFB Fixed Income Arbitrage index had a loss totaling −11.75 percent, but it was spread out over three months, August through October. These losses were in addition to very lackluster performance since the beginning of the year.

Style Drifts   From an investment point of view, money managers for both traditional investments and hedge funds often get into trouble because they depart from their core competencies.

In favorable market conditions, taking risks by venturing into unfamiliar investment spaces or strategies may be rewarded in the short term. The additional risks thus are masked by results that are above historical norms. However, careful analysis of the risk/return trade-offs would indicate inferior risk-adjusted rewards for the risks these funds have taken on. When market dislocations disrupt normal relationships in prices across securities and asset classes, often precipitated by liquidity drains in low-credit sectors and illiquid securities and flight to quality and near-cash safe havens, the lack of expertise in these strategies invariably leads to above-normal and sometimes catastrophic losses.

Increases in Risk Taking   Hedge fund strategies differ in their use of leverage to boost returns. In a survey by HBV in June 2002,[17] the leverages used at the time by major hedge fund strategies range as follows:

Fixed income arbitrage	20 to 30 times capital base
Convertible arbitrage	2 to 10 times
Risk arbitrage	2 to 5 times
Equity market neutral	1 to 5 times
Long/short equity	1 to 2 times
Distressed securities	1 to 2 times

Thus, historically fixed income arb funds employ the highest amount of leverage. Typically, these funds' goals are to exploit credit spreads that are normally less than 100 basis points (i.e., less than 1 percent). To achieve rates of return in the double-digit range, they would have to leverage their funds 10 times or more. When credit spreads contract, the temptation to increase leverage rises in order to obtain high returns. If LTCM had adhered to a leverage limit of 30 times, the one-day loss on the spread widening would have been $150 million, or 3 percent, a severe blow but not systemically crippling. But its return would have been a fraction of what it reported in its first full-year results of 40 percent in 1995.

EVALUATING THE RISKS OF YOUR HEDGE FUNDS

It is now clear that risks of hedge funds go beyond such measures as standard deviation or beta. In order to have a successful hedge fund investment program, investors need to put a process in place to monitor and assess the risks.

As suggested in the discussion in Chapter 6, to pick the right hedge fund managers, the principle is "know your managers." The same principle is applied in monitoring your hedge fund risks: Continue to know your managers. It is only common sense that the job of evaluating hedge funds does not stop after the managers are selected and allocations of funds to them are made.

In a nutshell, risk management seeks to detect the yellow flags or the warning signs that signal potential trouble ahead. A best-practices risk management system would include an ongoing ability to (1) assess worst possible losses; (2) detect significant deviations from stated strategies; (3) evaluate the target versus potential risk/return profiles; (4) identify sources and causes of risks: manager skills, strategy changes, style drifts, or market dislocations.

Worst-Case Scenarios

Most investors can tolerate some degree of loss in the normal course of investing. But few investors can accept total or huge losses due to fraudulent practices, business failures, or catastrophic events in the market. It is therefore important for investors to realize the extent of worst-case loss potential of any investment. If the worst possible losses are beyond the ability or willingness of the investors to tolerate, such investments probably are not suitable.

As indications of potential worst-case losses, maximum drawdowns of different strategies were shown in Table 4.2. Remember that these were the *averages* of losses suffered by funds in these categories; *individual* worst-case losses could be worse or total. Looking at these numbers, it should be clear that investors unwilling or unable to accept losses more than 10 to 15 percent from any manager should not invest in strategies such as emerging markets or global macro.

Frauds and Operational Risks   Huge or total losses are usually the consequences of frauds or operational failures. For such risks, a thorough preinvestment due diligence is the first defense. Postinvestment due diligence will include monitoring for any changes in the circumstances surrounding the personal and business operations of the hedge fund managers that may point to potential risk areas.

Some fund of funds managers believe changes in the personal lifestyles of hedge fund managers are an issue that needs to be monitored. As is often the case, undue personal stress caused by events such as changes in marital status, extravagant personal spending, or financial or legal difficulties may create conditions for abnormal risk taking or business failure. They may even be the telltale signs of potential trouble that may have been missed during preinvestment due diligence. To achieve this awareness, fund of funds managers develop a network of personal and business contacts to pick up on information that is not otherwise available.

One obvious change that should be further investigated is any change in key personnel such as the chief financial officer, who has direct responsibility and supervisory authority over the compilation, collection, and dissemination of fund returns. In the non–hedge fund world, a change of the chief financial officer, especially at large public companies, is a significant event. In hedge funds it is more so, as it might signal irregularities in financial and accounting matters as well as distracting disagreements among key managers on business strategies.

The one person who is critical to the success or failure of a fund is the portfolio manager responsible for its actual day-to-day investment management. In hedge funds, the portfolio manager, the chief executive officer, and the owner are sometimes one person. However, portfolio managers should not play a direct role in determining the prices of securities in the portfolios they manage. This responsibility should reside with the chief financial officer, who should have the authority to make the final determination of the fair values of the securities. At hedge funds where this separation of authority is not in place, investors are denied a safeguard for accurate accounting and investor protection, and therefore face a greater risk of erroneous reporting of investment returns.

Sometimes changes of key personnel may be well justified. This appeared to be the case of the resignation of the portfolio manager of two funds at Stamford, Connecticut–based Andor Capital after the two funds that he managed, the Diversified Growth Fund with $1.5 billion of assets and the $250 million Diversified Growth Perennial Fund, suffered large losses in 2003. Even then, investors had already lost 17.5 percent in the Diversified Growth Fund, and 21.5 percent in the Perennial Fund, which would be liquidated.[18] Nevertheless, facing such losses, a fair question that should be asked by investors is: Why should the hedge fund be retained? A review of the circumstances of the investment losses, how such lapses can be prevented in the future, and the specific changes to be made are topics that investors should discuss with the firm.

At other times, a key resignation is a sign of impending trouble. The resignation of a senior portfolio manager at the Clinton Group was a classic case. Upon leaving the firm, the portfolio manager stated that his resignation was caused by his disagreement with management over the ways in which the securities in the portfolio he managed were valued. Those investors who redeemed their investments from the Clinton Group could congratulate themselves for taking timely action.

Audited Reports   Audited reports of returns and financial conditions, including the amounts of assets under management, are crucial to both pre- and postinvestment monitoring of hedge fund risks. While financial statement audits are naturally expected in public companies, not all hedge funds are audited. According to one study of hedge fund audits in 2000,[19] as much as 40 percent of hedge funds did not have auditors, or were not audited. And the audited funds reported distinctly more accurate return data than nonaudited funds; the data quality difference amounted to an average of 1.8 percent a year. Not surprisingly, defunct funds were more often not audited than live funds, and larger funds tended to be audited while small funds were less so. Also, the Big Four auditing firms produced fewer errors than smaller auditors. Thus, as common sense and evidence suggest, investors should demand that hedge funds supply audited reports, and the auditors should be reputable firms.

Deviations from Stated Strategies

It is not possible to understand and monitor the risk of a hedge fund without knowing what its investment strategy is. As with evaluating its performance, risk management needs to identify how the fund generates returns. But the focus of risk management is different: First, it seeks to anticipate the potential losses that this strategy can generate; and second, it seeks to recognize if the managers change the investment strategy.

Deviations from stated strategies invariably are manifested in a number of indicators. First are changes in the amount of leverage. Second, there are a number of statistics to detect changes in the investment styles of hedge fund managers. The variations among different managers in these figures indicate differences in styles. Here are the commonly used indicators.

Security and Sector Concentration   Expressed as percentages of the portfolio's holdings in individual securities and in different sectors of the broad market, these indicators measure the degree of portfolio concentration in these securities and sectors. The idea is that more concentrated portfolios are subject to greater risks. Thus, portfolios with 10 or 15 securities are supposed to be riskier than those with 50 or more stocks. Likewise, portfolios concentrated in one or two sectors, say, technology or biotech, are thought to be subject to greater risk than those invested in the broad market. At the same time, concentrated portfolios are more common in hedge funds than in traditional portfolios. Some very successful hedge funds with billions of dollars of assets have been known to hold only 20 to 30 stocks.

Price-Earnings Multiples   The idea behind price-earnings (P/E) ratios as a risk indicator is that presumably stocks with high P/E multiples are riskier than those with low multiples. They also indicate if the managers are value or growth oriented because high-P/E multiples are associated with growth styles.

For fixed income–oriented funds, there are similar measures of sector concentration, such as holdings in mortgage-backed securities, investment grade corporate bonds, high yield bonds, foreign bonds, and so on. The distinctions are also made in terms of the credit ratings, such as BBB or lower. A host of other measures related to portfolio duration are also used to assess market neutrality or lack thereof.

These indicators are then monitored over time to detect shifts in strategies. Their values by necessity will vary from period to period. As long as they remain within relatively small ranges, the shifts should not be deemed significant enough to suggest changes. However, if the variations are large and frequent, clearly style drifts become an issue for consideration and for review.

These indicators have been made popular to investors and fund managers in the context of traditional long-only investments. In hedge fund investing, where returns are supposed to be uncorrelated to markets and investments vary across time frames, securities, and sectors, fund of funds managers and other experienced investors tend to place much less reliance on these indicators in the assessment of their portfolios' risks. Part of the reason is that hedge funds' mission is to search for alpha wherever it exists. But also, not all hedge funds are willing to provide such detailed statistics to their investors, either directly to the investors or indirectly to a third-party risk assessment firm.

As a result of these limiting practicalities, experienced hedge fund investors place particular emphasis on frequent contact with their hedge fund managers, in telephone conferences, and, less frequently, in on-site visits. As discussed previously, these meetings are supposed to provide investors with insight as to the thinking of the hedge fund managers and their thoughts on changes in market conditions, shifts in trading strategies, where alpha can be found, areas of potential risks, expectations of prospective returns, and market rumors. These meetings are expected to provide a more insightful understanding of the hedge funds' strategies, risks, and any changes thereof than any available statistics.

Factor Risks

Unable to rely entirely on risks data specific to individual hedge funds, active hedge fund investors such as funds of funds look to macroeconomic and market information to guide their assessment of the potential risks, and potential rewards, of their investments. They hope to benefit from these analyses to make decisions in retaining or redeeming from their existing managers, as well as in hiring new managers whose specialties are in areas of attractive future rewards. In this respect, these funds of funds are supported by evidence presented in this book and elsewhere that in order to generate returns, hedge funds are dependent to a significant extent on market factors such as the broad equity market, credit spreads, interest rate directions, merger activity, and so on. They are more beta dependent than one might assume from correlation and standard deviation statistics. The ability to unearth the emerging promising trends in any of these markets would allow funds of funds to invest with hedge funds that are strong in these areas.

In fixed income, traditional long-only funds are exposed to the risk of interest rates rising. The extent of the impact depends on the duration of the funds. Additionally, they are subject to changes in the credit upgrades or deterioration of the underlying securities. These credit risks may result in lesser increases in the prices of the bonds if interest rates decline, as compared to U.S. Treasuries. However, those bonds that receive credit upgrades may experience higher prices even if the overall interest rates increase.

Generally, fixed income arbitrage funds have little duration risk, and therefore are little impacted by shifts in interest rates, although they are still affected by yield curve shifts due to rate movements. The key risks inherent in these funds stem from credit spreads. To estimate the effects of changes in credit spreads, in terms of both risks and potential returns, Hsieh and Fung (2002)[20] formulated, as cited previously, the following relationship for the HFR Fixed Income Arbitrage strategy:

$$\text{HFR FI Arb} = 0.0096 - 5.37 * (\text{Changes in Credit Spread})$$
$$(10.0) \quad (6.6)$$
$$R^2 = 0.32$$

This relationship can be updated and fine-tuned for more specific fixed income markets.

A similar approach can be used to estimate the impact of the stock market on equity-oriented funds. As can be readily recalled, one feature of hedge fund strategies is low correlation to markets or market neutrality. Thus, fund managers often cite low portfolio beta as evidence of low correlation. Beta that is used in this citation comes from the familiar equation:

$$\overline{R}_{Fa} = r_f + \beta_F(\overline{R}_M - r_f)$$

In this equation, β_F is the result of two time series; one is the *ex post* returns of the F hedge fund, and the other is the actual returns of the market factor. It thus shows the effect of portfolio strategies, not the sources and causes of portfolio returns. To understand the causes of portfolio returns— that is, to determine the extent to which the portfolio's return is generated by the market—a more insightful measure is the weighted average betas of the individual securities in the portfolio.

$$\overline{R}_{Fe} = r_f + waB_i(\overline{R}_M - r_f)$$

where $wa\beta_i$ is the weighted average of the individual securities in the portfolio F. It can be calculated by multiplying each security's beta by its weighting in the portfolio, summing them up, then dividing the sum by the number of securities in the portfolio. Mathematically,

$$wa\beta_i = \sum_{i=1}^{N} X_i\beta_i$$

Given the actual return of the market factor and the weighted average beta, the preceding equation would produce the *expected* return of the hedge fund, and it can be compared to the fund's *actual* return.

An equity market neutral fund is supposed to have zero beta because it generates returns independently of the market's moves. The portfolio's weighted average beta may tell a different story, however. In terms of weighted average beta, if it is long beta as the market rises, short beta as the market declines, and low beta in flat markets, it is not market neutral, although it may have a very low or zero portfolio β_F. Thus, changes in $wa\beta_i$ points to the fund riding on the market to generate returns. Unfortunately, due to the lack of transparency, these moves of shifting $wa\beta_i$ may not be detected by investors as the only data made available would be β_F.

Over time, changes in a fund's $wa\beta_i$ can be tracked to analyze the sources of returns generated by its portfolio, as well as to assess its risk profile. Thus, a fund's $wa\beta_i$ can be correlated to market returns. If correlation is high, it would indicate that the fund may have generated returns from taking market risks. It does not necessarily mean that the fund manager lacks stock-picking or market-timing skills. The opposite can be true if the returns are good. A positive excess return—that is, $\overline{R}_{Fa}$ is greater than $\overline{R}_{Fe}$—coupled with $wa\beta_i$'s high correlation with the market would suggest that the fund manager generates excess return by being exposed to the market at the right time. As such, since target $wa\beta_i$ can be compared to actual $wa\beta_i$, using $wa\beta_i$ can assess more accurately the amount of actual market exposure of a fund. Compared to β_F, $wa\beta_i$ is also a more revealing measure of the degree to which the portfolio is exposed to the market in its position taking. Further attribution analysis can then be used to assess the extent to which a fund manager relies on stock selection or beta risk taking to generate excess return. This information can be useful to determine the veracity of a fund manager's claim as a stock picker or a market timer, and the fund's strategy shifts over time.

"LEFT TAIL" RISKS AND OTHER QUANTITIES

Standard deviation measures the overall volatility around the average of a stream of returns. It does not differentiate between positive and negative deviations from the mean; any deviation from the average is treated as risk. Left tail risks, however, reflect greater concerns about the potential losses or the left tail of the normal distribution. When the return distribution is skewed to the left because of large losses and below-average gains, the distribution is said to have a fat left tail. In evaluating potential losses, investors should look at the left tail risk in addition to the standard deviation or volatility of returns of a hedge fund. There are a number of ways to measure the left tail risks. One is the maximum drawdown.

Maximum Drawdown

A drawdown is a loss. It is defined as the retrenchment in percentages from an equity peak to an equity valley. A drawdown is in effect from the time a retrenchment starts until a new equity high is reached (i.e., in terms of time, a drawdown encompasses both the period from equity peak to equity valley (length) and the time from the equity valley to a new equity high (recovery). Maximum drawdown is simply the largest percentage drawdown that has occurred in any stream of returns. Thus, the larger a fund's maximum drawdown is, the higher is its left tail risk.

A shortcoming of this maximum drawdown measure is that it does not give a sense as to the context and probability of such large losses. For perspective, between the near total loss of the Dow Jones Industrial Average in 1929 and the huge decline in the NASDAQ following the 2000 bubble burst, there was a time gap of 70 years of profits, sometimes extraordinary. However, most investors would shun any hedge funds that have experienced drawdowns approaching anywhere near such magnitude, and rightly so.

Value at Risk

Value at risk (VaR) is similar to maximum drawdown in that it is an indication of the largest possible loss, except that it is a probabilistic estimate based on past experience. The value-at-risk concept, pioneered at J. P. Morgan, seeks to estimate the maximum amount of losses with the highest possible level of confidence. Thus, the VaR estimate can be expressed as, "There is a 95 percent confidence that fund A will not lose more than X percent over the next year."

Although frequently touted, VaR is not widely used in hedge funds and funds of funds. For the latter, portfolio turnover or strategy changes in their hedge funds substantially reduce the quality of the value-at-risk measure. By itself, VaR is a statistical measure based on historical data; without additional information, it is hardly a reliable estimate for the future. Witness the data on the catastrophic losses of the stock market in the 1929 and 2000 bear markets. Also, from a technical standpoint, hedge fund returns are not normally distributed, a key prerequisite for the value at risk to be meaningful. Furthermore, some methodologies to calculate value at risk assume risks are either additive or reductive when in fact they may be multiplicative, such as the currency risk in foreign currency investments.

Nevertheless, risks of hedge funds tend to persist. From a practical viewpoint, it is fair to assume that hedge funds with large maximum drawdowns or high VaR in their records will remain risky. Investors with low tolerance for such risk levels might be better off looking elsewhere. Postinvestment, if any of the portfolio's hedge funds exhibit deterioration in these risk measures, it is probable that things have gone wrong at the fund. Perhaps the degenerating statistics may have been foretold by events such as the resignation of a key analyst. If so, it would be time for a detailed investigation and critical review of the fund's strategies and operations.

While drawdowns and VaR focus on the tail end of the left tail, the following statistics analyze the entire left side of the distribution. (For convenience, the definitions used here are from PerTrac.com. See http://support.pertrac2000.com/statistics2000.asp.) However, they all focus on the returns below a number, be it the average of the returns or a required minimum.

Loss Standard Deviation

While standard deviation analyzes both positive and negative deviations from the average, loss standard deviation focuses solely on the losses. However, the methodologies of both statistics are similar. Loss standard deviation calculates an average return for only the periods with a *loss* and then measures the variation of only the *losing* periods around this loss mean. As such, this statistic measures the volatility of downside performance.

$$N_L = \text{number of periods that } R_i < 0$$

$$\text{Loss Mean: } M_L = \left(\sum_{i=1}^{N} L_i \right) \div N_L$$

$$\text{Loss Deviation} = \left[\sum_{i=1}^{N} (LL_i)^2 \div (N_L - 1) \right]^{1/2}$$

where N = number of periods
R_i = return for period i
M_L = loss mean
L_i = R_i (if $R_i < 0$) or 0 (if $R_i \geq 0$)
LL_i = $R_i - M_L$ (if $R_i < 0$) or 0 (if $R_i \geq 0$)

Downside Deviation

This statistic is similar to loss standard deviation, except for the introduction of a minimum acceptable return (MAR). MAR is usually a positive number. Thus, the downside deviation considers only returns that fall below a MAR rather than the arithmetic mean of the losses, which is always a negative number, as in loss standard deviation. For example, if MAR is assumed to be 10 percent, the downside deviation would measure the variation of each period that falls below 10 percent.

$$\text{Downside Deviation} = [\Sigma(L_i)^2 \div N]^{1/2}$$

where R_i = return for period i
N = number of periods
R_{MAR} = period minimum acceptable return
$L_i = R_i - R_{MAR}$ (if $R_i - R_{MAR} < 0$) or 0 (if $R_i - R_{MAR} \geq 0$)

Sortino Ratio

This risk statistic is similar to the Sharpe ratio, except that it places emphasis on a required minimum rate. The numerator is defined as the incremental compound average period return over a minimum acceptable return (MAR). In the Sharpe ratio, the numerator is the return in excess of the risk-free rate. If MAR is equal to the risk-free rate, the numerator in both ratios would be equivalent.

Risk (denominator) is defined as the downside deviation below a minimum acceptable return (MAR). MAR can be (1) a user-defined value, (2) the risk-free rate, or (3) zero. In the Sharpe ratio, the denominator is simply the standard deviation of returns.

$$\text{Sortino Ratio} = (\text{Compound Period Return} - R_{MAR}) \div DD_{MAR}$$

where R_i = return for period i
N = number of periods
R_{MAR} = period minimum acceptable return
DD_{MAR} = downside deviation
$L_i = R_i - R_{MAR}$ (if $R_i - R_{MAR} < 0$) or 0 (if $R_i - R_{MAR} \geq 0$)
$DD_{MAR} = [\Sigma(L_i)^2 \div N]^{1/2}$

Obviously these downside risk measures focus on the concern for losses or returns below some required minimum. Investors who have lower tolerance for losses or require a minimum rate of return would find these statistics useful but at the expense of downgrading funds with higher average returns.

ONGOING RISK MANAGEMENT: RISK AND PERFORMANCE MATRIX

Overall, evaluating a hedge fund's strategy and performance postinvestment is the same as before the investment is made, except that most likely greater insight has been gained from more in-depth and frequent contacts with the manager. Nevertheless, hedge fund evaluation is an ongoing process whereas the key factors shown in Table 6.1, "Evaluation Factors: Risk and Performance Matrix," in Chapter 6 need to be continuously reviewed. Changes in these factors should be rescored and the viability of the hedge fund should be reassessed. The resignation of a key portfolio manager of the management team may or may not affect the fund's performance, but its prospects need to be reevaluated in the light of this event. Or when the chief financial officer is terminated, or there is high turnover in the back-office operation, or there is an unusual delay in the issuance of monthly returns and audit reports, questions should be raised about the fund's risk controls and security and portfolio valuation issues. If the fund has an unusually large return, positive or negative, the scoring for the style drift/discipline factor of the matrix may be downgraded if there is evidence of unusual risk taking.

CONCLUSION

Of the key issues confronting investors in hedge funds, risks and risk management are most important in determining the success of a hedge fund investment program. Management of hedge funds' risks requires not only a thorough understanding of the risks of the strategies, what they are, how they are generated, and if and how the managers manage them, but also the strategies themselves and how these strategies are executed over time. If "know your managers" is the key to selecting good hedge funds, "continue to know your managers" is the key to having a successful hedge fund portfolio. We have discussed these issues in this chapter. Now in Chapter 10 we turn to discuss funds of funds as an investment structure that allows hedge fund investors to delegate the resource- and time-consuming tasks of evaluating and selecting hedge funds and monitoring and evaluating them on an ongoing basis.

CHAPTER 10

Instant Diversification:
Funds of Funds

Funds of funds (FoFs) experienced explosive growth in 2003. TASS Research estimated the number of funds of funds has grown to 1,700 compared to 1,250 in 2002.[1] This figure is comparable to Hedge Fund Research's estimate that 500 funds of funds were launched in 2003, and fund of funds assets accounted for more than 38 percent of the hedge fund industry's total assets of $817 billion.[2] At the same time, the number of funds of funds that had $1 billion or more of assets under management grew from 61 in 2002 to 81 in 2003. Their assets leapt from $199.7 billion to $291.6 billion during the same period. Concurrently, each of the five largest funds of funds had more than $10 billion under management, and together they commanded $63.4 billion of assets, which was a 50 percent increase from the prior year. In 2004, Barclay/Global HedgeSource reported further growth in the FoF industry. Figure 10.1 shows the growth of assets of funds of funds since 1997, as reported by Barclay/GHS. From less than $100 billion six years earlier, the industry now was reported to command assets of almost $500 billion, as of the end of 2004.

As their assets grew, funds of funds also increased their presence and impact as they have become increasingly a primary source of investment capital for single-strategy hedge funds. For a large fund group like London-based Aspect Capital with $2.7 billion of assets under management, 70 percent or more of the assets managed by the firm came from funds of funds, such as Global Asset Management in London and Grosvenor Capital in Chicago.[3]

The growth in funds of funds reflects an increasing number of both institutional investors and individuals who were not previously hedge fund investors, but have now decided to gain access to hedge funds through diversified portfolios provided by funds of funds. With FoFs, investors can achieve instant diversification and invest with multiple hedge funds across

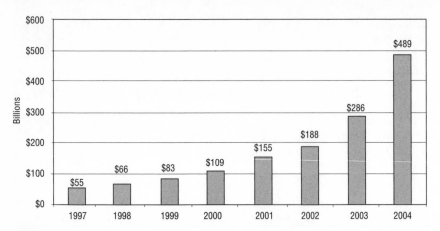

FIGURE 10.1   Fund of Funds Industry Assets under Management
Source: Barclay Trading Group, Ltd. (www.barclaygrp.com).

a variety of strategies and markets with different risk and return profiles. Rather than making investments directly with individual hedge funds, investors contract with FoF managers who have discretion in choosing which strategies and which hedge funds to invest in. Funds of funds may allocate assets to numerous managers within a single strategy, or with numerous managers in multiple strategies. Some FoFs design their strategies to target a relatively low level of risk or volatility. Others seek a high range of absolute return, often in excess of 10 percent, within a target band of volatility.

DIVERSIFICATION BENEFITS OF FUNDS OF FUNDS

While diversification is an obvious and important benefit to investors, funds of funds provide two services that on their own investors may find difficult to obtain: access to hedge funds and manager selection. Though the number of hedge funds has grown substantially, access to quality hedge funds has not been made easier, as demand for them has outpaced the capacity of best-of-breed hedge funds. Sometimes strong investor demand has allowed newly minted hedge fund managers with outstanding pedigrees to pick and choose their early investors. Established hedge funds, once closed, might accept new investments from only celebrity or well-known investors and large investors who have had a presence in hedge fund investing and can be expected to provide additional funds in the future. Typically, when these hedge funds are again open, only select investors are invited and are given a small time window to decide whether to invest. Thus, in terms of access, established funds of funds are likely to have advantages over smaller individual or institutional investors.

As a consequence, smaller or less-connected investors have to contend with a large universe of thousands of hedge funds that are likely to be smaller and less well known, and have shorter track records. Many of them are virtually invisible. That is, they are not listed with any database provider or the information available from the database publishers is sufficiently opaque to require much research and analysis. Worse, some managers actually set out to deceive investors from the start, by making false presentations on their managers' backgrounds, investment records, and the amounts of assets under management. Even the task of requesting and receiving information from hedge funds is a time-consuming process. And not all hedge funds respond to such requests from mail-in investors. Once investment data and other information have been received, they must be processed and analyzed as discussed in Chapter 6. Clearly, in evaluating and selecting hedge funds, established funds of funds are much more prepared to sort the wheat from the chaff than small or inexperienced investors.

Another service provided by funds of funds is postinvestment monitoring of performance and risks of the underlying hedge funds. As discussed in Chapter 9, scam artists abound and good managers can turn bad. When investment returns sour, even established fund managers might be tempted to resort to poor or illegal mark-to-market pricing procedures to boost their returns. Funds of funds are supposed to be alert and equipped to detect these practices in order to safeguard investor capital. They also perform periodic portfolio rebalancing, in order to take advantage of new opportunities and/or reduce portfolio risks. These tasks are achieved by redeeming from some hedge funds, while increasing investments in others or hiring new managers. As such, funds of funds provide the ongoing services of evaluating, selecting, and monitoring managers on behalf of investors who are unable or unwilling to do so.

In traditional equity investing, investors have encountered stocks that trade at very low volume, with investors having little knowledge about them and no analyst covering them. During the bubble years, hot IPOs have been known to double, or more, their prices during the first trading day. Such illiquidity, market inefficiencies, and expectations of excess returns entail premiums in a competitive market. It is the same in hedge funds. Funds of funds exact a price for providing information and access and for generating alpha, by charging management and incentive fees over and beyond the fees levied by hedge funds.

If performed effectively, these tasks should allow funds of funds to generate alpha or extract excess returns, from selecting and accessing leading hedge fund managers, from managing portfolio risks, and from portfolio rebalancing. As in mutual fund investing, investors would expect funds of funds to avoid disasters like Beacon Hill and to deliver consistent performance results, after fees and expenses.

FEES AND THE PRICE OF ACCESS

Management and incentive fees charged by funds of funds tend to be somewhat lower than those levied by hedge funds. Our sample of funds of funds charged a minimum of 1 percent for management fees and a maximum of 2 percent; many included an incentive fee of 10 percent or less. When the fee structure includes an incentive fee, it is always subject to a high-water mark. Sometimes the incentive fee is effective only above a hurdle rate.

These findings are in line with the results of a study by Ineichen (2002)[4] of 118 funds of funds of which 51 were in operation in December 2000. He found that 75 percent of the funds, or 88 funds, had a management fee between 1 and 1.9 percent. These funds had a median incentive fee of 10 percent, with an average of 12 percent. The author concluded that the most common structure is a management fee of 1 percent plus a 10 percent incentive fee. He also found that the hurdle rate ran the gamut from some sort of short-term interest rate like Treasury bills to the rate of return of the S&P 500. In my sample of funds of funds, the hurdle rate ranges from the London Interbank Offered Rate (LIBOR) without a margin to LIBOR with a margin added to it. The addition of a margin is associated with funds aiming at low volatility of returns. Funds that seek absolute return tend to use the LIBOR rate or similar short-term benchmarks without an added margin.

These findings are also in line with those from a study by Brown, Goetzmann, and Liang (2004)[5] of 328 funds of funds, of which 260 were live in March 2000, from the TASS database. The incentive fee was 10 percent, and the median management fee was 1.5 percent.

The management and incentive fees charged by funds of funds are of course in addition to fees from individual hedge funds. This double fee structure, especially the incentive fee, has been the main objection to funds of funds. Additionally, a retail platform like Merrill Lynch would add another layer of fees on top of the fund of funds fees.

REDUCED LIQUIDITY

Hedge funds in general are not liquid investments. Many single-strategy hedge funds impose a lockup period of six months to a year, especially those investing in illiquid securities. Additionally, they allow redemptions only once a month, and often as infrequently as quarterly. These redemptions must be preceded by redemption notices, usually 30 days in advance.

Funds of funds, like other investors, are subject to the same liquidity constraints from their hedge funds, although sometimes they can negotiate more liberal terms. As a result, they impose their own liquidity limitations, usually more severe, on their own investors. Their lockup periods tend to be longer than most of those of their hedge funds; one year is not unusual. Also, funds of funds' redemption and notice periods tend to be as restrictive as the terms imposed by their hedge funds, if not more so. In our sample, notices are 30 to 90 days and redemptions average around six months, but can be as long as annually. In one fund of funds, after the one-year lockup period investors can redeem their investments monthly, but with a 2 percent penalty. The only exception is at year-end. Only a few of the funds allow quarterly redemptions. Additionally, funds of funds may impose liquidity gates, which limit the maximum amounts of total investor redemptions in any given period. This restriction effectively would prevent mass defections by investors from failing funds.

These more severe restrictions would assure funds of funds the time windows that they would need to access liquidity from their own portfolios' hedge funds, whose requirements are varied. At the same time, they represent a further reduction in liquidity to investors.

REDUCED TRANSPARENCY

Hedge funds are notorious for their lack of transparency. While they profess certain trading strategies that would produce superior returns even if the stock and bond markets tumble, and hence charge high fees, many do not disclose to investors exactly what securities they buy or sell and how the securities are linked together in their portfolios.

Funds of funds are not treated much differently by their hedge funds. While funds of funds can obtain greater detail about the trading strategies of hedge funds owing to, among other things, frequent and periodic conversations and reviews of market conditions with hedge fund portfolio managers, they still do not have full transparency at the levels of the individual securities and strategies. A fund of funds manager said it is a "leap of faith" when investing with multistrategy funds because these funds make shifts in their strategies and the allocations of funds among them with little transparency to their investors. And at the security level, disclosure of individual holdings is still a rarity.

The opaqueness of hedge funds combined with liquidity restrictions have no doubt significantly contributed to the inability of funds of funds and other clients of failing hedge funds to liquidate their investments in time. As funds of funds hold dozens of hedge fund investments in their portfolios, the potential of double jeopardy caused by opaqueness and restrictive liquidity can only increase.

To make matters worse, funds of funds rarely disclose the underlying hedge funds in their portfolios. Before investments are made, few of them disclose the identities of their hedge funds to potential clients. Even postinvestment disclosure is highly selective. Like FoFs investing in multistrategy funds, investors in funds of funds just have to take a "leap of faith" when investing with funds that do not disclose their underlying managers. In such situations, investors are virtually in the dark about what, where, and how their money is invested.

GENERATING ALPHA: PORTFOLIO REBALANCING

Funds of funds are supposed to periodically rebalance their portfolios of hedge funds in order to take advantage of emerging opportunities and reducing risks in areas of rising vulnerabilities, and as such generating alpha. This is akin to stock or bond managers buying and selling securities at will in the open markets. Although they sometimes must deal with reduced market liquidity when trading volume is low or a security experiences sharp surges up or down in prices due to earnings surprises or such events, the trades can be executed, albeit possibly with sacrifices in prices paid or obtained.

In contrast, the market of hedge funds trades "by appointment only." Investors can sell their investments only after the lockup period has expired. Even then, investors must give redemption notices, in writing, sometimes months in advance, effectively increasing the length of the lockup period. Buying into hedge funds can be effected only at predetermined frequencies, mostly monthly. Participation is often by invitation only, especially with regard to high-profile managers. New managers who have attractive pedigrees select their clients, not the other way around. Because at the beginning of their operation the capacity of "hot" managers is limited, not all investors who wish to can get in. Once a hedge fund has a hard close, even existing investors cannot add to their investments in the fund. Furthermore, if a hedge fund has performed well, funds of funds might be reluctant to liquidate or reduce their investments in it, even if they believe the strategy will produce mediocre results going forward and there are more attractive opportunities elsewhere. This is because the hedge fund may not readmit a departing client, either as a retaliatory action or simply because the vacated spot is taken up by a larger or more valued customer.

Growing funds of funds have greater flexibility in dealing with these limitations. If a strategy is deemed unattractive, rather than liquidating existing investments, new funds from clients could be invested in other strategies, whereby reducing the weighting of the unattractive strategy in the portfolio. Large funds of funds, which may have multiple managers in the same strategy, can fire the poorly performing managers while retaining a presence in a strategy. New hedge funds are also created every day, with different twists in strategy.

Nevertheless, the difficulty of moving investments around has been felt across the board in our sample of funds of funds. One fund of funds manager was proud to point out that his fund was one of three funds of funds that were "allowed" to invest with a new hedge fund manager coming fresh out of a highly respectable proprietary trading desk at a leading global investment bank. Other managers have cited instances where they did not liquidate entire investments with established hedge funds for fear of being locked out later. One fund of funds has invested close to 50 percent of its assets with a couple of multistrategy funds, which are of course another structure of fund of funds except that the portfolio managers are in-house rather than third-party. The cited reason was that the manager could not find comparably good single-strategy hedge funds.

On balance, because demand is still strong as FoF firms have been growing, just as the entire hedge fund industry has experienced phenomenal growth, limitations due to access and liquidity constraints are matters of concern, but have not seemed to quite yet exert industry-wide observable effects on the ability of funds of funds to move assets around. At the same time, in my sample, smaller funds of funds have been observed to face greater rigidity in access than their more fortunate brethren, and they have experienced lower performance as a result.

Academic research has gathered some evidence suggesting that this may be an industry-wide phenomenon. Gregoriou and Gueyie (2003)[6] calculated the value at risk (VaR) and modified VaR (which takes into consideration skew and kurtosis) for 60 funds of funds, differentiated by size. The small funds showed significantly higher values for VaR and modified VaR than larger funds, indicating higher risks. They also demonstrated lower Sharpe ratios. The study's data, however, was dated December 2001, and the small fund group had assets of only a few million dollars. The validity of the study therefore can only be considered tentative.

Hilary Till (2004)[7] has attempted to calculate the capacity of the hedge fund industry. What if hedge fund investors expect returns in excess of 10 percent when the global stock and bond markets tolerate inefficiencies of 0.5 percent? Given a $55 trillion global market, this would suggest a hedge fund capacity of $2.75 trillion. Hedge fund capacity would quadruple if inefficiencies are increased to 1 percent and expected hedge fund returns are reduced to 5 percent. Of course, why should investors accept 5 percent returns from hedge funds given the availability of traditional investments generating higher rates of return? Even the concept of a permanent inefficiency, meaning there is always a risk-free excess return to be exploited by the average hedge fund manager, is questionable, given that hedge fund returns are a zero-sum game. On the other hand, the capacity varies substantially across strategies. The markets for long/short and arbitrage funds that specialize in publicly traded and highly liquid securities, including mid-cap stocks, government bonds, and currencies, are much larger than distressed securities and convertible arbitrage. Furthermore, many hedge funds package beta as alpha, taking market risks while charging fees as if they were alpha generators[8]. As such, the amount of assets managed by the hedge fund industry could be much larger than its true capacity may indicate.

All of this only points to an increasing differentiation among funds of funds, those that have the ability to discriminate among different hedge funds' strategies and to access top-performing hedge funds, and the rest. This two-tier system has already resulted in the top FoF firms amassing the bulk of the industry's assets while others make do with marginal operations and possibly less-competitive performance.

TYPES OF FUNDS OF FUNDS

Like single-strategy hedge funds, FoFs come in different sizes and shapes. In Chapter 7, investment objectives for hedge fund investors are generally classified as low volatility or absolute return. Many FoFs also similarly distinguish themselves. Absolute return FoFs typically invest in a wide variety of hedge fund strategies with the objective of maximizing return. Low-volatility FoFs prefer to concentrate in relative value and arbitrage strategies, especially in fixed income, although they may also venture into equities with strategies such as equity market neutral and short-term stock trading.

Hedge Fund Research divides its FoF indexes into four subgroups. The HFR Conservative Index consists of funds that invest in equity market neutral and fixed income relative value and arbitrage strategies. FoFs in the HFR Diversified Index also pursue a lower volatility objective, but invest in a wider spectrum of strategies. The HFR Strategic Index funds of funds seek higher total return by mixing in long-biased managers and higher-risk strategies such as emerging markets. The Market Defensive Index funds seek hedge funds that have negative correlation with the market or outright short selling, as well as managed futures funds.

Many funds of funds use the single-strategy approach, investing with hedge funds in a particular strategy such as long/short equity. Figure 10.2 shows the asset allocation strategy of a fund of funds investing primarily with event driven managers.

Figure 10.3 shows the strategy composition of a fixed income arbitrage fund of funds. Unlike multistrategy FoFs, specialized FoFs generally stay within their niche markets.

In the past few years, new hedge fund managers have gained popularity with FoFs as they are believed to generate greater alpha than more established hedge funds. Figure 10.4 shows the allocation strategy of a new manager FoF. As can be expected, new manager funds of funds comprise a fairly large number of managers to diversify their risks; depending on the size of the fund of funds, a 50-manager lineup is not uncommon. They further seek to reduce risks by way of investing in a wide spectrum of strategies.

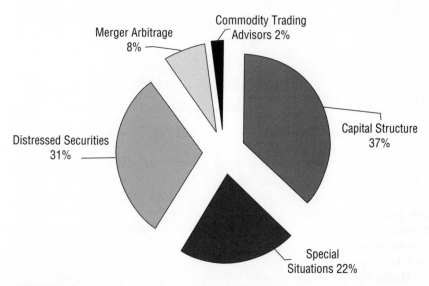

FIGURE 10.2 Fund of Funds: Event Driven Arbitrage

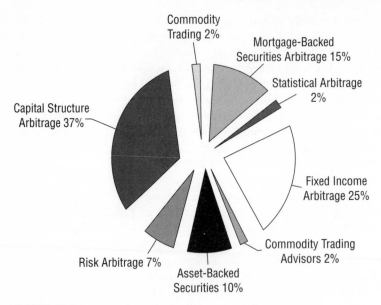

FIGURE 10.3   Fund of Funds: Fixed Income Arbitrage I

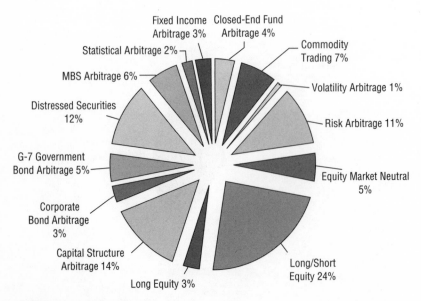

FIGURE 10.4   Fund of Funds: New Managers

Another type of fund of funds invests in a diversified range of strategies. Such a fund's allocation is shown in Figure 10.5. Like an absolute return FoF, diversified funds of funds seek higher return by mixing relative value strategies with equity hedge funds and possibly also predominantly long managers such as emerging markets.

To distinguish among different types of FoFs, investors would have at their disposal the return and risk objectives, and then the makeup of each FoF in terms of the number of managers and the strategies embedded in the funds of funds. As discussed in Chapter 7, the number of managers in a fund of funds bears consequences on the FoF's prospective return and risk. Figure 10.6 and Figure 10.7 show the strategy compositions of two additional funds of funds, one in fixed income arbitrage and the other in diversified strategies.

As shown, the two fixed income arb funds employ fairly different strategies. One, Fixed Income Arbitrage II, uses yield curve swap trades more extensively, while the other, Fixed Income Arbitrage I, is more involved in credit analysis for its statistical and capital structure arb trades. Among the two diversified FoFs, fund I is more involved with equity hedge strategies while fund II is more active in relative value and short-term equity trading.

After that, analysis of historical returns and risks in varying degrees

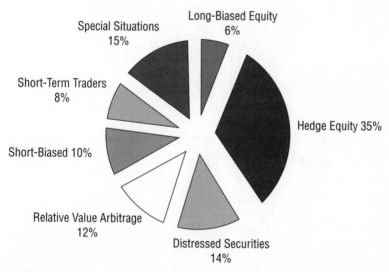

FIGURE 10.5 Fund of Funds: Diversified Strategies I

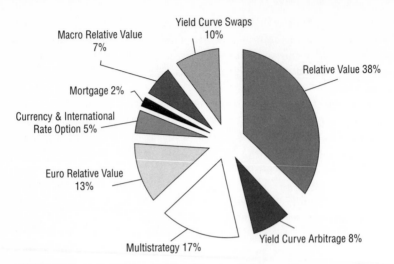

FIGURE 10.6 Fund of Funds: Fixed Income Arbitrage II

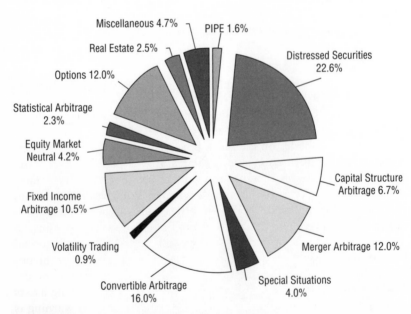

FIGURE 10.7 Fund of Funds: Diversified Strategies II

of sophistication play a critical role in differentiating and evaluating funds of funds.

Beyond such data, often little else is disclosed to potential investors, although funds of funds themselves have complained about lack of transparency from single-strategy hedge funds. In many instances it is an open question whether a fund of funds' classification of the strategy of a hedge fund in a particular category truly describes the manager's actual strategy. Sometimes a strategy's label seems to obscure rather than illuminate its purpose. The fixed income arbitrage category is a convenient box into which to deposit any hedge fund trading fixed income. While relative value can mean anything, equity market neutral has been used to include private investments in public entities (PIPE) funds, which are more akin to investment banking deals than stock picking prowess that traditional investors may be used to.

As has been discussed throughout this book, while it is difficult enough to discern the strategies of individual hedge funds, investors are expected to assess a fund of funds with little knowledge of the underlying hedge funds in the FoF portfolio. Indeed, it would be rare that the identities of the underlying managers are revealed. In this secretive atmosphere, one multibillion-dollar fund of funds stands out in that it freely discloses the identities of its managers to prospective investors, as well as arranging on occasion for the managers to meet with its clients. As the firm's senior partner put it, "I wouldn't invest in a black box and we didn't ask you to invest in a black box." If giving away supposed trade secrets is the key to success, this fund of funds has found it. Its 10-year return as of 2004 exceeded the HFR Diversified Index by some 5 percentage points while volatility was lower by 1 percent.

To put colorful shades on the black box, many FoFs fill their marketing material with information about their staffs' experience and statements about the processes they use to evaluate hedge funds and manage risks. However, little is available to tell where a FoF's reality ends and where its hopes for the future begin—in other words, where its practices have long been in place and where there are mere empty words. Thus, to evaluate a fund of funds, investors usually end up relying on its historical track record, any insight gleaned from the purported strategies of the underlying hedge funds, and judgment about the FoFs' management and capability of staff, mostly from how successful it has been in raising assets and the reputation of the senior partners. While the standard warning is "past results are not indicative of future performance," it is precisely past returns that investors end up relying on most to judge the future of a fund of funds.

PERFORMANCE OF FUNDS OF FUNDS

Fund of funds investors pay additional fees and are subject to additional lack of transparency and more severe liquidity restrictions. Have they got their money's worth? Several aspects of fund of funds fees are worth clarifying.

Fees on mutual funds are assessed on the gross returns of the underlying investments. FoFs' fees are calculated on the basis of the after-fee net returns of the underlying hedge funds. Thus, if a fund of funds has 50 percent in each of two hedge funds in its portfolio, and the two funds' returns are, respectively, +10 percent and –4 percent, both before incentive fees, the mutual fund model would show the FoF to have a gross return of 3 percent. In hedge funds, the winning fund would charge an incentive fee of 20 percent, thereby returning only 4 percent to the FoF. The losing fund, with a loss of –4 percent, would result in a loss of 2 percent to the FoF. The net result for the FoF's investment results would be a gain of 2 percent, before management and incentive fees at the FoF level.

Investors who invest directly with hedge funds would similarly pay incentive fees to winning funds. Investing through a fund of funds does not relieve investors of this fee burden. Likewise, investing through a retail platform like Merrill Lynch adds another fee layer on top of those charged by the hedge funds and FoFs.

The incentive fee charged by FoFs, however, does not seem to have any demonstrable relationship with their performances. That is, higher prices do not mean better. Research by Brown, Goetzmann, and Liang (2004)[9] has suggested FoFs that charge higher incentive fees have not produced higher returns than their lower-fee counterparts. Worse, it appears that higher-fee FoFs achieve lower risk-adjusted returns.[10] This means that the incentive fee of FoFs is "a deadweight that has the effect of simply reducing after-fee return."[11] The implication for FoF investors is, choose FoFs that do not have incentive fees, or whose fees are as low as possible, other considerations being equal.

Also, preliminary research has suggested that FoFs do not add alpha. Liang (2002)[12] studied the data on 4,464 hedge funds of Zurich Capital Markets. This hedge fund population included 2,357 hedge funds and 597 FoFs, both dead and live funds. The author found that in terms of raw returns, hedge funds outperformed FoFs in seven out of eight years between 1994 and 2001. In terms of the Sharpe ratio, hedge funds outperformed in five out of eight years. He concluded that "a fund-of-funds offers diversification but it comes with a cost: the fees may not justify the diversification effort."[13]

I reviewed the HFRI indexes on hedge funds and FoFs. For hedge funds, I used the HFRI Composite Fund Index, as the CSFB database does not have a category for funds of funds. For FoFs, I looked at four indexes:

the HFR Conservative, Diversified, Strategic, and Composite indexes. The data on these indexes are shown in Table 10.1.

The data in this table clearly do not suggest that funds of funds have outperformed the HFR Composite Index. In terms of returns, none of the four FoF indexes outpaced the Composite Index during the 1990 to 2004 period. Their Sharpe ratios are lower. Also, while every FoF category demonstrated negative skew and high kurtosis like the Composite Index, their returns were lower, signifying similar risks without corresponding payoffs.

If FoFs did not add value, is it perhaps because they could not select and access top-performing or difficult-to-access hedge funds? This is similar to a stock picker who cannot buy good stocks. The answer to this question, however, is not readily available, simply because FoFs rarely disclose the names of their hedge funds to investors. Nevertheless, a review of the correlations of the different HFR FoF indexes with the Composite Index, all at about 0.80, shows that the FoF indexes moved in virtual lockstep with the Composite Index, suggesting little observable alpha. Thus, although inferences as to the cause and effect can be made from risk and return data, in the absence of the managers' information, it is not easy to discern the sources of a fund of funds' performance, whether from picking the managers or from allocating funds to them; that is, from portfolio construction or from risk management. Perhaps the answer is a little bit of everything, but not enough to generate alpha.

TABLE 10.1 Performance: Funds of Funds and the HFR Composite Index, January 1990–May 2004

HFR Hedge Fund Index	Annualized Compounded ROR	Standard Deviation	Sharpe Ratio ($R_f = 5.0\%$)	Skew	Kurtosis	Correlation with Hedge Index
Hedge Fund Composite	14.51%	7.02%	1.28	−0.63	2.82	1.00
Conservative FoFs	8.87%	3.29%	1.12	−0.51	3.63	0.78
Diversified FoFs	9.31%	6.12%	0.69	−0.10	4.15	0.80
Strategic FoFs	13.43%	9.23%	0.89	−0.39	3.48	0.80
Composite FoFs	10.07%	5.71%	0.86	−0.26	4.20	0.82

Source: Hedge Fund Research.

However, as it often is the case with hedge fund data, indications of underperformance by funds of funds should be viewed with caution. The reason is that funds of funds discriminate with regard to hedge funds depending on their asset sizes; they tend to invest more with larger funds, and less with smaller funds. They also tend to shy away from new funds, which, if listed in a hedge fund index, would skew the index's return higher. Hedge fund index returns also may be overestimated because of survivorship and other biases. On the other hand, larger FoFs may have advantages over their smaller counterparts, with greater access to top hedge funds and ability to move assets around. These advantages should be reflected in FoF indexes' returns. Another complication in assessing the performance of funds of funds is that many of them tend to use specialized strategies; for example, fixed income–oriented strategies, such as fixed income arb and convertible arb. These strategies have underperformed long/short equity and global macro during the years of rising stock prices. Combining fixed income–oriented funds with higher return–oriented funds would tend to dampen the average rate of return of the mixed group.

On balance, when asset size of hedge funds is taken into account by way of comparing the HFR FoF indexes with the CSFB/Tremont Hedge Fund Index (which is asset-weighted) for the 1994 to May 2004 period, underperformance by funds of funds remains pronounced. During this period, annualized returns on the HFR Composite Index, at 11.1 percent, and the CSFB/Tremont Hedge Fund Index, at 10.4 percent, were not significantly different. However, the returns of the HFR FoF indexes were significantly lower, with Diversified being the worst at 6.3 percent while Conservative clocked in at 7.15 percent and Strategic at 7.3 percent, bringing the FoF Composite to 6.9 percent. Their Sharpe ratios, with the risk-free rate at 5 percent, were less than half of the HFR and CSFB/Tremont hedge indexes. While these statistics may not be entirely damning to funds of funds, they are not supportive of the argument that FoFs generate alpha from their unique ability to select and have access to top-performing hedge funds.

This conclusion does not come as a surprise to industry practitioners. As the asset management consulting firm Casey, Quirk & Acito observed in 2001, "To date, much of the perceived value of FOHF [fund of hedge funds] managers has been with sourcing/screening and with placement. That is to say, investors have counted on FOFH managers to identify and place money with attractive managers. Portfolio management has meant little more than diversification and monitoring little more than qualitative ongoing feedback."[14]

The practices of the FoFs in my sample (which by no means are scientifically representative) suggest that the state of the practice of the industry has changed little since those remarks were written. While some large FoFs have strived to put in place more effective portfolio and risk management processes, smaller firms with a few hundred million dollars, or less, of assets continue to operate on an ad hoc basis. Such firms in our sample continue to be dominated by the principal owners, who often come from client marketing backgrounds, while risk management is little more than conference calls with hedge fund managers once a month. No wonder the chief executive officer of a fund group lamented, "The fund of funds business is all about marketing."

This state of the practice partly stems from the structure of the hedge fund industry. Hedge funds are opaque and often do not disclose their holdings to investors. The amounts of leverage and their exposures to market factors change frequently during the month. This lack of information does much to reduce the effectiveness of risk monitoring at the individual hedge fund levels. Referring to the usefulness of risk monitoring services such as RiskMetrics, the manager of one FoF with several hundred million dollars under management said, "What good does it do for the portfolio as a whole?" if some hedge funds are willing to be completely transparent while others are not. He, like many others in our sample, relied on periodic conversations with hedge fund managers to gauge the prospects of his FoF's investments. Besides PerTrac, this FoF does little else in terms of quantitative analysis of hedge fund risks and exposures. This was the rule, not the exception. Some concepts such as risk budgeting have gained attention at some of the larger FoFs, but standard deviation remains the guiding risk measuring standard. Value at Risk remains a marketing tool, not used as a serious instrument for risk analysis. This state of affairs exists partly because the history of hedge funds is still short while advanced mathematical calculations such as the Cornish-Fisher conversion (which transforms nonnormality into normal distributions) requires at least 120 observations, or 10 years of history of monthly returns, to begin to have any meaning. At the same time, researchers and practitioners alike are still debating the appropriate risk measures and factors, as well as the return-generating processes of hedge funds.

In other words, the state of understanding of hedge funds is still evolving.

INVESTING WITH FUNDS OF FUNDS

Despite these limitations, funds of funds should continue to be an effective vehicle for investing in hedge funds. One important benefit is the opportunity for instant diversification even with small amounts of investments. In this regard, information on funds of funds is reasonably accessible. For example, a recent search on www.hedgeworld.com with the free membership turns up 48 funds of funds with at least three-year track records and 36 funds with five years or more of history. As shown in Table 10.2, of these funds, eight meet several important criteria: First, they are funds that are domiciled in the United States. Second, they have a three-year average return (as of January 2004) of at least 6 percent, and a five-year average from 6 percent to more than 15 percent. I look for funds that have the ability to generate an absolute return of 6 percent annually on a consistent basis. I also look for funds whose recent history is not too much out of line with the long-term track record. The reason is unusually strong recent results tilt the long-term track record up. Note that with the exception of fund number 7, the other funds tend to have one-year performance somewhat in line with their three- and five-year returns. On a preliminary basis, this short- and long-term consistency suggests statistically neutral skew and kurtosis. It can also be inferred that the management of these funds has produced consistent results through vastly varying market conditions in the past five years. These track records therefore warrant further consideration by investors.

Investors who have access to www.hedgefund.net and www.pertrac.com can obtain the names of additional funds of funds and can easily run an array of involved statistical analyses, including ranking these funds across various measures of performance and risk, calculating various risk statistics, and comparing their performances with traditional benchmarks and peer groups.

In selecting funds of funds, investors might keep in mind that while producing alpha is critical and economically worthwhile, access to and screening of hedge funds remain a hurdle that is difficult to overcome by

TABLE 10.2   Track Records of Selected Funds of Funds

Fund	Annualized Rates of Return		
	One-Year	Three-Year	Five-Year
1	7.44%	6.07%	8.26%
2	8.59	6.48	8.51
3	12.27	8.92	14.28
4	11.84	6.46	7.99
5	13.10	15.33	18.59
6	9.37	15.04	15.04
7	26.29	11.52	11.82
8	10.41	10.76	11.76

Source: HedgeWorld (www.hedgeworld.com).

most investors. The business has been and perhaps will always be a two-tier market. The first tier is the best-of-breed hedge funds, and the rest is everyone else. Access to the best and screening and monitoring of the rest will be the key drivers of the returns from hedge fund investing. To quote an observer, "Relationships also continue to play an essential role in matching quality performers with suitable investors. The best hedge funds often will accept additional funds with whom they have long relationships, while rejecting others. On their own, investors will find managers who will take their money. But these hedge funds are more likely to be newly established or mediocre performers. Although there will be success stories, new investors' lack of access to the best managers will be a disadvantage. In our view, this means that a bipolar industry is in the process of evolving. On one end are the quality hedge fund managers with an established clientele of small institutions, high net worth investors, and investment banks. They should continue to perform satisfactorily. On the other end of the spectrum are the uninitiated—new managers and new investors with great expectations. They are unlikely to fare as well."[15]

Not only the uninitiated but also experienced FoF managers can tumble as well. One FoF manager confessed that while leading the hedge fund unit of a well-known international investment bank some years ago he was an investor in the hedge fund Manhattan Investment Fund, which was accused of, among other things, inflating the amounts of assets under management. He said the fraud was not detected in spite of financial statements certified by leading public accounting firms. In fact, as charged by the Securities and Exchange Commission, beginning in September 1996, as the fund sustained losses that ultimately totaled more than $300 million, the fund's manager, Michael W. Berger, was reporting returns of between 12 and 27 percent annually.[16] By August 1999, Berger reported to investors that Manhattan Investment Fund had a net market value of more than $425 million when in reality it was never that large.

Another FoF manager with a couple of hundred million dollars allocated 13 percent of his fund with Beacon Hill and the entire investment was lost. Asked how this type of mistake can be avoided in the future, the manager's answer was, "We now limit the maximum to be 8 percent with any hedge fund." A prospective investor may not find sufficient comfort in knowing that his loss will be only smaller from this type of due diligence shortfall.

At the same time, access to good hedge funds is not always available to any fund of funds. Like hedge funds, funds of funds are a two-tiered business, those that have access to top hedge funds, and the rest.

Thus, while FoF investing is an effective strategy, choosing the right FoF is critical. First, an FoF must demonstrate an ability to perform due diligence on hedge funds. Its infrastructure and manifest capability for due diligence and risk monitoring are critical criteria for selection of funds of funds. The FoF whose manager had invested with Manhattan had a staff of three principals and a part-time assistant, while managing close to $200 million of assets for three different funds including a leveraged fund with some 50 underlying managers. Unfortunately, this type of shoestring operation was not unusual. In contrast, the director of a foundation active in hedge fund investing for its own account, with assets close to $2 billion, claimed his staff included lawyers and accountants who are dedicated exclusively to doing due diligence on the back-office operations of candidate funds.

Second, a critical service provided by FoFs is choosing the right hedge funds and having access to them. We have discussed access to hedge funds in general. Additionally, many funds of funds, even those with multibillion-dollar assets, do not invest with global macro and non-U.S. hedge funds even when they want to have exposures to international markets. This situation partly stems from the fact that these FoFs do not know about these funds, much less have any access to them, and do not dedicate any resources to do research and cultivate relationships with non-U.S. funds. Some large FoFs in my sample have not even heard of some well-known and respected European hedge funds. A common but clearly insufficient explanation from FoF managers is that U.S.-domiciled hedge funds have better-trained staffs who speak English, and more strictly observe risk management discipline.

Furthermore, some FoFs have been taking the easy way out by investing significant portions of their assets in multistrategy funds. One FoF has invested almost 50 percent of its approximately $75 million in assets with a couple of multistrategy funds, and the head of the firm wanted to make sure that this fact was known to clients as if this was a unique strength, not a shortcoming. While this case may be extreme, multistrategy funds are favorites of FoFs as they are a convenient way to obtain exposures to a variety of hedge fund strategies. However, this is also tantamount to FoFs delegating the monitoring and risk management functions to the multistrategy funds' managements, while collecting fees from investors to perform this function. Several FoF managers have remarked that investing with multistrategy funds is tantamount to a "leap of faith," because FoFs do not know how multistrategy funds allocate among different strategies, and what they are. As Myron S. Scholes, the Nobel laureate, observed, "The multistrategy funds are unlikely to have gathered the best talent available in all strategies. And, as psychologists claim, most organizations function better in complex environments when there is a separation of the decision makers from the information gatherers. The information gatherers become too involved with their own activities to make the best strategic decisions. The fund-of-funds advisors play an important role here in making appropriate allocation decisions."[17] Well, FoFs are not fulfilling this role when they invest excessively with multistrategy funds.

Another phenomenon that has recently become widespread is that some FoFs, failing to find attractive strategies and managers, have resorted to increasing their allocations to subprime lending hedge funds. As noted previously, these investments are often referred to as loan origination or private credit arbitrage. Selling illiquidity as alpha is clearly not what investors expect from funds of funds.

If FoFs perform the screening and access functions effectively and detect and avoid fraudulent practices in a timely fashion, they would well earn the 1 percent management fee. For the incentive fee, they would have to demonstrate superior investment performance. Toward this objective, they would need to develop "robust processes for portfolio construction and risk management as they do for identifying good managers and placing assets. In particular, risk management is emerging as the most distinguishing capability for sophisticated FOHF [fund of hedge funds] clients. Leading risk management capabilities have begun to include daily security-level analysis of each individual manager and the aggregate position of the entire FOHF. This analysis includes not only an integration of leading risk management packages but also proprietary modeling and data collection."[18]

It is evident from my sample of funds that FoFs with a few hundred million dollars under management have not made this type of resource commitment. Even FoFs that just passed the $1 billion threshold have only begun to think of these issues. No wonder it has become a rule of thumb that the critical mass of assets under management for FoFs is $1 billion. Below this barrier, FoFs have trouble attracting sophisticated institutional investors.

CONCLUSION

Funds of funds provide valuable services that many investors interested in investing with hedge funds would find hard to obtain: access to top hedge funds and diversification. For these services, funds of funds exact a price in the form of additional fees, reduced liquidity, and little transparency in terms of the hedge funds in their portfolios. However, there is scant evidence that the average fund of funds generates alpha or delivers the full range of services promised to investors, from access to difficult-to-access hedge funds to effective risk management.

CHAPTER 11

A Practical Guide to Investing in Hedge Funds

INFORMATION ON HEDGE FUNDS

This chapter's title is a misnomer. At best it is overly ambitious. The reality is that there is no shortcut in hedge fund investing. Hedge funds' strategies are often complex and sometimes exotic. They do not fully disclose what they do to generate returns. And they do not always return inquiries from prospective investors, or sometimes even their existing clients. They certainly do not advertise in flashy commercials like mutual funds.

It Pays to Look for Good Hedge Fund Managers

However, there are talented hedge fund managers, both emerging and long-established, who are capable of producing or have generated consistent and superior excess returns over time. They deserve to be sought out by investors, large or small. But for any number of reasons, they are choosy when it comes to accepting investors. One very successful manager recounted, "Someone else wanted to come back with $75 million, with meeting after meeting after meeting. I didn't want anything to do with those guys; it wouldn't work. We turned them down," and rightly so. For as a long/short strategy, this fund would not be suitable for investors who constantly watch the market indexes and become disappointed when the fund lags the market. Most mutual funds and traditional investment advisers would not be as discriminating. In the meantime, there are plenty of mediocre hedge funds, and on occasion, good managers who turn bad and scam artists who are ready to defraud unwary investors.

Every Portfolio Needs Protection

These cautionary tales notwithstanding, hedge funds are a strategy that should be part of the portfolios of any investors who are concerned with wealth preservation as opposed to getting rich, and those who have periodic spending commitments, such as (1) endowments and foundations that are committed to certain annual expenditures, (2) pension plans that seek a target rate of return to achieve reported earning stability, (3) wealthy families depending on steady investment returns to maintain their lifestyles, and (4) retirees who need regular income during retirement.

The term *strategy* is used for the specific purpose of distinguishing from hedge funds as investment vehicles. As a strategy, it is useful to think of hedge funds as a hedge or protection against downturns in the stock market as originally conceived by Alfred Winslow Jones to protect his portfolios from market declines such as the Crash of 1929. In this sense, every portfolio of long-only strategies needs hedge funds. Because the market does not go up forever, reducing the chances of large losses in market declines provides not only capital protection but also the ability to stay in the market when it comes back and resumes its long-term climb.

As investment vehicles, many hedge funds actually do provide hedges, while many others are no more than directional bets on the markets with potential for large losses, and yet others are better considered to be "alternative investments." "Hedges" funds are typically less volatile (lower standard deviation) than directional funds. As stand-alone investments they would not add incremental risks to existing portfolios of similar securities. For example, long/short equity or equity market neutral should not be incrementally riskier than the S&P 500. Directional funds, on the other hand, would add value if they generate alpha and have low or negative correlation with the investors' existing portfolios. However, "alternative" hedge funds often depend on illiquidity to generate returns or involve in specialized market niches such as PIPE.

Hedge funds can effectively serve as a diversification from traditional stock and bond portfolios. In addition to bonds, traditional equity investors seek diversification by way of allocating in other highly correlated assets such as international equities and small-cap stocks. Such a diversification only increases the portfolio risk. In order to reduce risks, diversification is effective only when the assets have low or negative correlation of returns. Hedge funds combine lower volatility and low correlations with the stock and bond markets and as such act as a moderator on the volatility of the overall portfolio.

Furthermore, as hedges, hedge funds—if managed by good managers—would reduce the potential for losses in severe and prolonged market declines, and at the same time generate excess long-term returns. To use the technical jargon, good "hedges" funds can be expected to produce higher Sharpe ratios at lower volatility of returns. If all hedge funds are capable of these results, all money could be invested with them. But it is not easy to find and have access to good hedge funds, and many good hedge funds are closed to new investors. It is therefore rewarding for investors to commit resources to search and select good hedge fund managers.

How much to invest in hedge funds is thus a question of how many good hedge funds can be found as well as how much diversification is optimal. Although it was shown previously that a 10 percent allocation would be the minimum for the benefits of hedge funds to be noticeable, the initial investment needs not be that large as there is value in starting small to gain familiarity and experience. As allocations to hedge funds grow larger, investors will have opportunities to learn about hedge fund investing firsthand, become more comfortable with the differences between hedge funds and long-only investments, and importantly develop relationships with a wide spectrum of hedge fund managers. However, as a diversification strategy, when allocations to hedge funds approach 50 percent, hedge funds begin to lose value as volatility of the overall portfolio (of stocks, bonds, and hedge funds) begins to rise after having steadily declined with increasing additional investments in hedge funds. The potential of large losses also increases at a faster pace.

Simplest Way Is to Invest with a Fund of Funds

The simplest way to invest in hedge funds is through a fund of hedge funds. It does cost an extra layer of fees, however, typically 1 percent plus incentive fees.

Funds of funds exact a price for providing a host of services that it is difficult for investors to perform on their own. Their basic functions are gaining access to and selection of hedge fund managers and as such allow investors instant diversification, even with fairly small amounts of investments. A good fund of funds should produce reasonable return and be able to avoid fraudulent artists like Manhattan Investment Fund and disasters such as Beacon Hill. Well-managed funds of funds can add value by selecting top-performing hedge funds that produce consistently strong returns regardless of the direction of the capital markets, as well as for managing portfolio risks and portfolio rebalancing from time to time. These tasks require professional skills and sure hands and therefore are deserving of the incentive fees if performed well.

Know the Fund of Funds and Its Hedge Funds

It is critical that investors understand how a fund of funds organizes and carries out these functions.

They need to analyze the asset allocation strategy and portfolio composition of the fund, how managers are selected, when and why investments are redeemed, the infrastructure, resources, management, and staff that the FoF has in place to execute these activities. Preferably the FoF would disclose the identities of the underlying managers prior to investment. Track record, though not predictive of future returns, can serve as a good validation for the FoF's strategy, risk management, and operation in past market upheavals. Remember that risk is persistent; risky funds will remain risky in the future. A volatile track record as compared to its peers, instances of unusual losses, investing with managers of suspect reputation, and/or using out-of-the-ordinary strategies—these are issues that should alert prudent investors.

A Place to Start Looking for Funds of Funds and Hedge Funds

Information on hedge funds has become increasingly available. Investors can access both funds of funds as well as (single-strategy) hedge funds at such web sites as www.hedgeworld.com, which can be free for accredited investors, or with fees ranging from a few hundred dollars to a few thousand at www.hedgefund.net, www.pertrac.com, and www.hedgefundresearch.com. There is also the *Directory of Fund of Hedge Funds*, an annual publication of the Alternative Asset Center. The 2004 edition has fairly detailed information, including locations, phone numbers, and e-mail addresses, on 750 funds of funds with assets of $120 billion, or more than half of the fund of hedge funds universe, and a listing of the 50 largest funds of funds. HedgeWorld .com also has published a directory of hedge funds called *HedgeWorld Annual Compendium* with performance data and contact information on 2,200 hedge funds managed by 1,300 managers. Although by no means complete, a starter list of viable FoFs can be accumulated from these sources. Additional information on hedge fund strategies can be found at the web sites of CSFB/Tremont, www.hedgeindex.com, and of EDHEC Risk and Asset Management Research Centre, www.edhec-risk.com.

The next step is to contact the funds of funds by e-mail. FoFs generally respond to serious investor inquiries, especially from those whose business affiliations are bona fide. Large and successful FoFs, however, usually require large minimum investments, often in excess of $1 million, though sometimes smaller initial amounts are accepted with the proviso that additional investments will be made to make up for the shortfall. Smaller funds of funds may require as little as $100,000. The amount of the required minimum, however, should not be a selection criterion. Investors would be better off walking away than investing with a mediocre FoF simply because it agrees to take less.

FoFs' Minimum Investments and Other Requirements

The minimum investment requirement is or should be among the least of issues that concern investors. The rule "know your managers" applies equally to FoFs as well as single-strategy hedge funds. Unlike buying and selling stocks, there is no market for hedge fund investments. Every investment is a private contract between the investor and the fund manager. As such, observation of the normal rules and etiquettes of personal and business relationships might help investors to pick up on signs about the fund managers that are not evident from contract and legal provisions.

As limited partners of the FoF, investors are expected to review and sign stacks of documents running into hundreds of pages. First, there is the fund's prospectus or offering memorandum wherein the strategy, potential risks, management profiles, and a host of legal disclosures are supposed to be disclosed to investors. Then there is the partnership agreement, which governs the relationship, obligations, and rights of the investors who are the limited partners, and the general partner who is the manager of the fund. Finally there is the subscription document, which is really the application to buy into the fund. Bank-sponsored FoFs may also require their banking clients to sign additional disclosure forms. Investors would do well to read these documents as carefully as possible, for the provisions are usually very broad and permit the fund managers a great deal of flexibility to deploy investor monies and restrict redemptions. Investors should not feel compelled to accept any of these provisions if they appear to be excessive or onerous, even though these documents are hard to change and as a result investors may have to walk away from funds with good track records. This is also the time to finalize negotiations on the terms, including any fee discounts and possibly more liberal liquidity provisions, including a shorter lockup period. Even large FoFs have been known to agree to these so-called side letters, whose provisions are applied only to designated investors. As part of this documentation and disclosure, investors will be expected to certify that they are accredited.

An accredited investor is (1) an individual who has made $200,000 a year in income for the past two years and has a reasonable expectation of doing so in the future, or together with a spouse has an income of $300,000 per year or net worth of $1 million, excluding homes and automobiles; (2) an entity such as a partnership, corporation, limited liability company, trust, employee benefit plan, or organization described in section 501(c)(3) of the Internal Revenue Code with total assets exceeding $5 million; or (3) a broker-dealer registered pursuant to Section 15 of the Securities Exchange Act of 1934, an insurance company as defined in Section 2(13) of the Securities Act of 1933, a registered investment company, a bank, or a similar U.S. institution acting in its individual or fiduciary capacity. Clearly investors who are able to meet the required minimum investments should have no trouble satisfying the accredited qualification.

If accepted, funds need to be wired before the end of the month for investments to start earning returns the following month. Subsequently, the investments cannot be withdrawn until after the lockup period, which usually lasts anywhere between three months to a year, has expired. For redemptions following the lockup period, a notice usually of 30 days is required. However, not all capital of an investor can be redeemed after the notice period as typically FoFs (and hedge funds) retain a portion of the requested redemptions until the fund's accounts are audited. If a fund of funds has a liquidity gate provision, which limits total withdrawals to a small percentage of the fund's assets, only a proportionate fraction of any investor's capital can be redeemed at any time if total redemptions from investors exceed the provisions of the liquidity gate. Supposedly this liquidity gate allows a fund of funds facing mass investor defections to manage the liquidation of the portfolio positions in an orderly manner. This flexibility is crucial if the investment positions are with hedge funds that have lengthy lockup and notice periods. However, some investors may find this liquidity gate clause objectionable if it severely interferes with their own liquidity requirements.

Not to Overdiversify

How many funds of funds are to be held in a portfolio? This question clearly depends on the amount of investment capital. A $10 million portfolio should have sufficient capital to invest in several funds of funds plus single-strategy hedge funds. Having more than one FoF reduces the selection risk, or the risk of choosing a bad fund. Thus, a very large institutional investor may need to invest with a greater number of funds of funds if it limits its investment with any FoF to a relatively small percentage of each fund's assets, say 10 percent. Also it helps to manage the investor's liquidity needs, as redemptions can be spaced out among more than one FoF.

However, a lineup of several funds of funds implies a fairly large number of managers, perhaps well in excess of 50, albeit they are under the umbrellas of the FoFs. This may not be efficient in the risk/return framework. Recall the discussion in Chapter 7 that diversification benefits become marginal while systemic risks increase as the number of hedge funds becomes large. When liquidity and selection risks are considered, the optimal number of managers probably is around 25 to 30. This level of manager diversification can be easily achieved with one or two funds of funds, assuming some degree of overlapping of managers.

Diversify with Single-Strategy Hedge Funds

In addition to or in lieu of funds of funds, an investor with sufficient capital may invest with single-strategy hedge funds. In this case, with due consideration for the liquidity and selection risks, the diversification benefits should be realized with 25 to 30 hedge funds. However, such a portfolio would require a substantial commitment of time and financial resources. In fact, with such a lineup of managers, there is really no shortcut from a full-fledged organization to do the appropriate amount of due diligence, portfolio construction, performance evaluation, and risk management.

Invest in Hedge Funds with "Hedges"

For investors who prefer to invest with only a few hedge funds, a few funds in the "hedges" category would serve well to diversify from concentration in traditional long-only stock and bond investments. "Hedges" funds use short selling as a fundamental strategy to hedge away their markets' systemic risks, unlike others that take ongoing beta risks by predominantly long or short strategies, or make directional bets either way, separately or simultaneously, with both long and short trades. A few well-chosen "hedges" funds in long/short equity, equity market neutral, convertible arbitrage, event driven, and multistrategy should provide the bulk of the diversification benefits. For diversification, these strategies have lower volatility and lower correlation with the stock market than any long-only equity strategy, be it large company or financial stocks, or hedge funds that are predominantly directional. As stand-alone investments, historically the CSFB/Tremont indexes in these categories have had smaller maximum drawdowns than the S&P 500. As discussed in Chapter 3, in years of stock market rallies, these indexes had provided quite respectable returns, in the double-digit percentage range. During the 2000 to 2002 bear market, they still produced positive results, or in a few instances, suffered only small losses. The poor performances of these indexes occurred in times of market crises, of which the summer of 1998 amid the Russian debt default and Long-Term Capital Management's near collapse was the worst. The rapid rise of interest rates in 1994 due to the Federal Reserve's aggressive monetary tightening was also an unfavorable period for these strategies. However, as history has it, these losses were short-lived and gains in subsequent months more than made up for the losses. Yet, it should be kept in mind that the track record of hedge funds as a group is fairly short and the future may not be as benign as the past.

Know Your Hedge Fund Managers

Whether a few or an extensive lineup of hedge funds, the cardinal rule in hedge fund investing is "know your manager." As parts of the overall profile, it is about the manager as an individual as much as about his strategy, about how he makes money for investors. While a manager's personal background and pedigree attest to his credibility, it is his investment strategy and experience in it that determine the performance and the results.

How Does a Hedge Fund Manager Make Money?

Many hedge funds' strategies are difficult to understand, even for experienced professionals. Nevertheless, investors should expect a fund manager to be able to explain in understandable terms how the fund generates returns, and whether the results are from following the market or from some specialized skills such as stock picking or credit analysis. Listening to a manager describing his strategy, his winners, and his mistakes goes a long way in detecting inconsistencies, as well as issues that he might be reluctant to discuss at length or regarding which he has only vague answers. Questions beget information, from what is said as much as what is not. In any case, a risky fund will remain risky. A fund that uses leverage must be viewed as riskier than a nonleveraged peer. And a fund that has a clearly defined process to manage risks tends to be more prepared to deal with adverse market conditions than a counterpart that does not. When it comes to risks, there is no room for denial or flip answers.

If It's Too Good, It's Probably Not True

As in any human endeavors, especially when large amounts of money are involved, the potential for frauds and poorly conceived ideas abounds in the hedge fund industry. In this respect, if something looks too good or too easy, it probably is not true. Writing options is a legitimate hedging strategy but naked option writing is not a free lunch and its risks need to be clearly understood. Illiquid securities can generate attractive returns for their risks, but investors need not invest with funds selling illiquidity as alpha and charging incentive fees.

Long-Term Investing with Lower Volatility

In the main, many hedge fund managers are talented individuals who have had long and successful investment careers, sometimes at the top of their peer groups. They provide investment strategies that do not assume markets go up forever and that seek to generate positive returns even in poor market conditions. Above all, their strategies are embedded with protection against market declines, which is more than can be said about long-only strategies.

Nevertheless, even the best can sometimes tumble or underperform when compared to a market index like the S&P 500 or Russell 2000. In retrospect, if a long/short equity fund lagged the stock market in 1999 but subsequently had enough short positions to protect itself during the ensuing bear market, its earlier underperformance should be congratulated. The point is, market indexes are not necessarily a good benchmark to judge hedge fund performance. While the capital markets overall set the boundaries for hedge funds' returns, a good hedge fund might lag market indexes in a strong stock market, yet still can generate superior long-term results with lower volatility by providing protection in poor market conditions.

This is the essence of a good long-term investment strategy.

Happy investing!

Notes

INTRODUCTION

1. *BusinessWeek*, September 17, 2001.
2. *Wall Street Journal*, October 7, 2002, p. C1.
3. *Financial Times*, July 13, 2004, p. 13.
4. As quoted in www.albournevillage.com, June 14, 2004.

CHAPTER 1   The Market Goes Up Forever?

1. Jeremy J. Siegel, *Stocks for the Long Run: The Definitive Guide to Financial Market Returns and Long-Term Investment Strategies*, 3rd ed. (New York: McGraw-Hill, 2002), pp. 3–5.
2. Ibid., p. 3.
3. Ibid., p. 4.
4. Ibid.
5. James K. Glassman and Kevin A. Hassett, *Dow 36,000: The New Strategy for Profiting from the Coming Rise in the Stock Market* (New York: Times Books, 1999).
6. Mark Bruno, "Foundations, Endowments Adopt Absolute Outlook," *Altnews*, October 23, 2003.
7. See, for example, Robert D. Arnott, "Editor's Corner: Sustainable Spending in a Lower-Return World," *Financial Analysts Journal*, September/October 2004, pp. 6–9. Also, Robert D. Arnott and Peter L. Bernstein, "What Risk Premium Is 'Normal'?" *Financial Analysts Journal*, March/April 2002, pp. 64–85, and Ira Carnahan, "Money & Investing: Should You Still Be a Bull," Forbes.com, April 19, 2004 (www.jeremysiegel.com/view_article.asp?p=330).
8. Greg Jensen and Jason Rotenberg, "Bubbling Again?," Bridgewater Associates, *Bridgewater Daily Observations*, July 15, 2003.
9. Dick Ramsden, in "Insights into the Yale Formula for Endowment Spending," (*Commonfund News*, September 5, 2003), explained the average approach used at Yale University as follows: "Institution has an approximately $100 million endowment in the year ending 6/30/03, spending was 4.5% or $4.5 million, CPI increased in the 12 months to 12/31/02 by 2.1%. The average of endowment market values for the four quarters ended 12/31/02 (3/31; 6/30; 9/30; 12/31) is $103,750,000, reflecting performance over the period and additions (gifts, bequests, etc.) to endowment. Based on the formula, the calculation of the amount to be spent in fiscal year 2004 is as follows: 70%

of $4.5 million (FY 2003 spending) equals $3,150,000—increased by 2.1% equals $3,216,150. Four-quarter average endowment market value ending 12/31/02 is $103,750,000. 30% times $103,750,000 times 4.5% spending rate equals $1,400,625. FY 2004 allowed spending is $3,216,150 plus $1,400,625 or $4,616,775, a 2.6% increase."

10. Stephanie Strom, "Fluctuating Market a Culprit As Foundation Grants Slip," *New York Times*, April 5, 2004, p. A19.

11. Ibid.

12. Richard E. Anderson, "Endowment Spending: The Problem Will Be with Us for a While," *Commonfund Commentary*, May 2003.

13. Ibid.

14. Ibid.

15. The Foundation Center, "Foundation Growth and Giving Estimates: 2003 Preview," *Foundations Today Series*, 2004 Edition.

16. Ibid.

17. Greg Winter, "College Endowments Make Happy Discovery: Black Ink," *New York Times*, February 20, 2004, p. A17.

18. Ibid. Remark attributed to Ralph A. Raffetto, managing director of endowments and foundations at the Bank of New York.

19. "Educational Endowments and Foundations Continue to Increase Alternative Investments to Enhance Returns in Challenging 2002 Financial Climate," Commonfund Institute, December 16, 2002.

20. Ibid.

21. Rich Blake, "Shifting into High Gear," *Institutional Investor*, March 2004, pp. 24–28.

22. Ibid., p. 26.

23. James P. Owen, *The Prudent Investor's Guide to Hedge Funds* (New York: John Wiley & Sons, 2000), p. 3.

24. Ibid.

25. Ibid., p. 7.

26. Commonfund, *CIO Commentary*, April 2003.

27. Treasury Inflation Protection Securities, or TIPS, are Treasury bonds whose interest rate is indexed to the inflation rate. Investors in such securities are protected against rising inflation.

28. Commonfund, *CIO Commentary*, April 2003.

29. See, for example, Robert P. Arnott, "Editor's Corner: Sustainable Spending in a Lower-Return World."

30. Siegel, *Stocks for the Long Run*, p. 18.

31. Mark Hulbert, "That Mirage in Foreign Harbors," *New York Times*, June 20, 2004, p. C1.

32. Harry Markowitz, "Portfolio Selection," *Journal of Finance* 7, No. 1, March 1952, pp. 77–91.

CHAPTER 2 It's the Risk, Not the Return

1. Mark Bruno, "Foundations, Endowments Adopt Absolute Outlook," *Altnews*, October 23, 2003.

2. *Wall Street Journal*, "Hedge Funds May Give Colleges Painful Lessons," October 7, 2002, p. C5.
3. Morgan Stanley Dean Witter, "Why Hedge Funds Make Sense?" November 2000.
4. Ibid.
5. Bing Liang, "Hedge Fund Performance: 1990–1999," *Financial Analysts Journal*, 57, No. 1, January/February 2001, p. 11–18.
6. Carl Ackermann, Richard McEnally, and David Ravenscraft. "The Performance of Hedge Funds: Risk, Return, and Incentives," *Journal of Finance 54*, No. 3, June 1999, pp. 833–874.
7. Greg N. Gregoriou and Fabrice Rouah, "Large versus Small Hedge Funds: Does Size Affect Performance?," *Journal of Alternative Investments*, Winter 2002, pp. 75–77.
8. Morgan Stanley, "Why Hedge Funds Make Sense?"
9. Ibid.
10. Liang, "Hedge Fund Performance: 1990–1999."
11. Bing Liang, "On the Performance of Hedge Funds," Case Western Reserve University, March 1999.
12. Ackermann, McEnally, Ravenscraft, "Performance of Hedge Funds."
13. Chris Brooks and Harry M. Kat, "The Statistical Properties of Hedge Fund Index Returns and Their Implications for Investors," *Journal of Alternative Investments*, Fall 2002, pp. 26–44.
14. Thomas Schneeweis and Georgi Georgiev, "The Benefits of Hedge Funds," Center for International Securities and Derivatives Markets, Isenberg School of Management, University of Massachusetts, June 19, 2002.
15. Gaurav S. Amin and Harry M. Kat, "Diversification and Yield Enhancement with Hedge Funds," Working Paper #0008 Cass Business School, City University, London, Alternative Investment Research Centre Working Paper Series, October 7, 2002.
16. "High-Performance Endowments Allocate More to Alternatives, Commonfund Finds," HedgeWorld, January 22, 2004 (www.hedgeworld.com).
17. "Endowment Hedge Fund Share Grows As University Spending Swamps Returns," HedgeWorld, January 20, 2004 (www.hedgeworld.com).
18. See Elroy Dimson, Paul Marsh, and Mike Staunton, "Irrational Optimism," *Financial Analysts Journal*, January/February 2004, pp. 15–25, citing Frank Fabozzi and Ronald Ryan, "The Pension Crisis Revealed," *Journal of Investing*, Fall 2003, pp. 43–48.
19. Ibid.

CHAPTER 3   Going for the Gold

1. "Macro Hedge Funds Return to Favour," *Financial Times*, February 9, 2004.
2. Ibid. In a review of the growth of the hedge fund industry, the Securities and Exchange Commission observed,

> *(Hennessee Group estimates that the 34 percent growth of hedge funds in 2003 was due to both performance (20 percent) and new*

capital (14 percent)). See also *Sanford C. Bernstein & Co.,* Hedge Fund Industry Update—One Year Later, The Song Remains The Same, *Bernstein Research Call (July 28, 2004) (hedge fund assets grew globally by approximately 31 percent in calendar year 2003 with aggregate assets reaching $870 billion in March 2004) ("Bernstein 2004 Report"). Hedge fund inflows have also continued to set records.* See *Chris Clair,* Hedge Fund Inflows Set Another Record, *HedgeWorld/Inside Edge, Aug. 16, 2004 (second quarter 2004 inflows of $43.3 billion bested the record set in the first quarter);* Too Much Money Chasing Too Few Real Stars, *Financial Times, July 22, 2004 (first quarter 2004 inflows were $38.2 billion, following record 2003 inflows of $72 billion).*

   Some estimate that hedge fund assets are already at or near $1 trillion. See Boom Or Bust? Banks And Hedge Funds, *The Economist (Oct. 9, 2004); Daniel Kadlec,* Will Hedge Funds Take A Dive?, *Time, Oct. 4, 2004; Amey Stone,* Hedge Funds Are Everyone's Problem, *BusinessWeek, Aug. 6, 2004.*

   As of the end of August 2004, equity mutual funds' assets were $3.8 trillion. At $870 billion, hedge funds' assets were equal to 22.9 percent of this figure. See *Investment Company Institute,* Trends in Mutual Fund Investing: August 2004, *News Release (available at http://www.ici.org, visited on Oct. 13, 2004).*

See Securities and Exchange Commission, "Registration under the Advisers Act of Certain Hedge Fund Advisers," Release No. IA-2333; File No. S7-30-04 (www.sec.gov/rules/final/ia-2333.htm#P85_18913).

3. Jeremy Smerd, "Net Assets in Hedge Funds Balloon to Record Numbers," Hedgefund.net, January 26, 2004.

4. Edhec-Risk, Better Not to Invest At All Than to Allocate Small Proportions," *Industry News,* March 11, 2004 (www.edhec-risk.com/latest_news/Alternative%20Investments/RISKArticle1079018925253948960/view).

5. Edhec-Risk, "Encouraging Record Inflow to Hedge Funds," *Industry News,* February 12, 2004 (www.edhec-risk.com/latest_news/Alternative%20Investments/RISKArticle1076590685685754711/view).

6. "U.S. Educational Endowments and Foundations See 'Light at the End of the Tunnel' with Moderate Improvement in Returns in Fiscal Year 2003," Press Release, Commonfund, January 21, 2004.

7. Edhec-Risk, "US Endowments Embrace Hedge Funds amidst Public Outcry," *Alternative Investments,* March 4, 2003 (www.edhec-risk.com/latest_news/Alternative%20Investments/RISKArticle1078402026609537344/view).

8. "Champagne Funds for Chardonnay Investors," *Business 2.0,* May 2003, pp. 132–134.

9. See Securities and Exchange Commission, "Registration under the Advisers Act of Certain Hedge Fund Advisers" (www.sec.gov/rules/final/ia-2333.htm #P88_21262). The Commission reviewed the enforcement action against those participating in mutual funds' market timing:

In the past year, we have sanctioned persons charged with late trading of mutual fund shares on behalf of groups of hedge funds, and mutual fund advisers or principals for permitting hedge funds' market timing. In the Matter of Invesco Funds Group, Inc., AIM Advisors, Inc., and AIM Distributors, Inc., *Investment Advisers Act Release No. 2311 (Oct. 8, 2004) (Commission found that mutual fund adviser entered into an undisclosed arrangement permitting hedge funds to market time the adviser's mutual funds in a manner inconsistent with the mutual funds' prospectuses);* SEC v. PIMCO Advisors Fund Management, LLC, *Investment Advisers Act Release No. 2292 (Sept. 13, 2004) (Commission found that mutual fund adviser entered into a market timing arrangement permitting over 100 mutual fund market timing transactions by hedge funds in exchange for hedge funds' investment in adviser's other investment vehicles; mutual fund adviser also provided hedge funds with material nonpublic portfolio information concerning four of the adviser's mutual funds);* In the Matter of Banc One Investment Advisors Corporation and Mark A. Beeson, *Investment Advisers Act Release No. 2254 (June 29, 2004) (Commission found that investment adviser permitted Canary hedge fund manager Edward Stern to time the adviser's mutual funds, contrary to the funds' prospectuses; helped arrange financing for the timing trades; failed to disclose the timing arrangements; and provided Stern with nonpublic portfolio information);* In the Matter of Pilgrim Baxter & Associates, Ltd., *Investment Advisers Act Release No. 2251 (June 21, 2004) (Commission found that mutual fund adviser permitted a hedge fund, in which one of its executives had a substantial financial interest, to engage in repeated and prolonged short-term trading of several mutual funds and that one of its executives provided material nonpublic portfolio information to a broker-dealer, which passed it on to its hedge fund customers);* In the Matter of Strong Capital Management, Inc., et al., *Investment Advisers Act Release No. 2239 (May 20, 2004) (Commission found that investment adviser disclosed material nonpublic information about mutual fund portfolio holdings to Canary hedge funds, and permitted Canary and the adviser's own chairman to engage in undisclosed market timing of mutual funds managed by adviser);* SEC v. Security Trust Co., N.A., *Litigation Release No. 18653 (Apr. 1, 2004) (consent to judgment by trust company charged with facilitating late trades and market timing by affiliated hedge funds over at least a three-year period);* In the Matter of Stephen B. Markovitz, *Administrative Proceedings Release No. 33-8298 (Oct. 2, 2003) (Commission found that Markovitz engaged in late trading on behalf of hedge funds).* See also In the Matter of Alliance Capital Management, L.P., *Investment Advisers Act Release No. 2205 (Dec. 18, 2003) (Commission found that investment adviser permitted known market timers, including Canary hedge funds, to market time its mutual funds, in exchange for the timers' investments in Alliance's investment vehicles);* In the Matter of James Patrick Connelly, Jr., *Investment Advisers Act Release No. 2183 (Oct. 16, 2003) (Commission found that vice chairman of mutual fund adviser permitted market timing by known market timer, including at least one hedge fund). We have also sanctioned mutual fund advisers for permitting certain investors to engage in undisclosed market timing of their funds; hedge funds were among the market timers in these cases.* In the Matter of RS Investment Management, *Investment Advisers Act Release No. 2310 (Oct. 6, 2004);* In the Matter of Janus Capital Management, LLC, *Investment Advisers Act Release No. 2277 (Aug. 18, 2004). In addition, we have sanctioned insurance companies for facilitating undisclosed market timing of mutual funds through variable annuity products marketed and sold to market timers including hedge funds.* In the Matter of CIHC, Inc., Conseco Services, LLC, and Conseco Equity Sales, Inc., *Investment Company Act Release No. 26526 (Aug. 9, 2004) and* In the Matter of Inviva, Inc. and Jefferson National Life Insurance Company, *Investment Company Act Release No. 26527 (Aug. 9, 2004).*

10. William F. Sharpe, "Capital Asset Prices: A Theory of Market Equilibrium under Conditions of Risk," *Journal of Finance* 19, No. 3, September 1964, pp. 425–442.

11. See Alan Dorsey et al., "Are Hedge Funds or Hedge Fund of Funds an Asset Class or a Strategy among Asset Classes?," CRA RogersCasey, White Paper, March 2003.

12. U.S. Securities and Exchange Commission, *Securities and Exchange Commission, Plaintiff, v. Rhino Advisors, Inc. and Thomas Badian, Defendants,* February 26, 2003 (www.sec.gov/litigation/complaints/comp18003.htm). As described in the SEC complaint, "Rhino's trading allowed [its brokerage client in whose behalf Rhino engaged in the trades which are the subject of the SEC's complaint] to profit from the scheme in at least two ways. First, the short sales locked in a sale price for [the company's] stock that was higher than the conversion price for the shares ultimately used to cover the open short positions. Second, Rhino's short sales increased the supply of [the company's] shares in the market and depressed the price. As a result of the depressed market price, [Rhino's brokerage client] converted the Debenture to a greater number of shares of [the company's] stock, which were already discounted to the market, and which it then used to cover its previous short sales made at higher prices." Also, see John D. Finnerty, "Short Selling, Death Spiral Convertibles, and the Profitability of Stock Manipulation," Fordham University, Working Paper, March 2005 (www.sec.gov/rules/petitions/4-500/jdfinnerty050505.pdf).

PART TWO   Evaluating and Selecting Hedge Funds

1. Mark Hulbert, "Behind Many Enticing Hedge Funds, Stale Prices," *New York Times*, June 20, 2004, p. D1.

CHAPTER 4 The Skewed Statistics of Hedge Fund Returns

1. *Wall Street Journal*, "Hedge Funds May Give Colleges Painful Lessons," October 7, 2002, p. C5.
2. Harry Markowitz, "Portfolio Selection," *Journal of Finance* 7, No. 1, 1952, pp. 77–91.
3. Chris Brooks and Harry M. Kat, "The Statistical Properties of Hedge Fund Index Returns and Their Implications for Investors," *Journal of Alternative Investments*, Fall 2002, pp. 26–44. Readers might note that analyses of historical hedge fund returns are heavily influenced by periodic upheavals in the global capital markets. Though unpredictable, such systematic events have shown to be recurring throughout history.
4. Ibid., p. 30.
5. Ibid.
6. A skew equal to +/–0.22 can be considered as zero. Kurtosis of a normal distribution is 3. Excess kurtosis is kurtosis of a value greater than 3. Excess kurtosis equal to +/–0.45 can be considered as zero.
7. William F. Sharpe, "Capital Asset Prices: A Theory of Market Equilibrium under Conditions of Risk," *Journal of Finance* 19, No. 3, September 1964, pp. 425–442.
8. Andrew W. Lo, "Risk Management for Hedge Funds: Introduction and Overview," November/December 2001. *Financial Analysts Journal* 57, No. 6, pp. 16–33.
9. Richard Spurgin, "How to Game Your Sharp Ratio," *Journal of Alternative Investments* 4, No. 3, 2001, pp. 38–46. Also, see Thomas Schneeweis, "Alpha, Alpha, Who Got the Alpha?," Working Paper, October 5, 1999.
10. Ibid.
11. François-Serge Lhabitant, "Derivatives in Portfolio Management: Why Beating the Market Is Easy," *Derivatives Quarterly*, Winter, November 2000 (www .edhec-risk.com/edhec_publications/RISKReview1055927251987929638/ attachments/EDHEC_WhyBeatingTheMarketIsEasy.pdf).
12. Walter Gehin, "Hedge Fund Performance," Edhec-Risk, August 2003 (www .edhec-risk.com/performance_and_style_analysis/EDHEC%20Publications/ RISKReview1070901068627242430/attachments/HEDGE%20FUND%20 PERFORMANCE.pdf).
13. Stephen J. Brown, William N. Goetzmann, and James M. Park, "Careers and Survival: Competition and Risk in the Hedge Fund and CTA Industry," *Journal of Finance* 56, 2001.
14. Bing Liang, "Hedge Fund Performance: 1990–1999," *Financial Analysts Journal* 57, No. 1, 2001.
15. Bing Liang, "Hedge Funds: The Living and the Dead," *Journal of Financial and Quantitative Analysis* 35, No. 3, September 2000. Survivorship bias of offshore funds may be higher, around 3 percent. See Stephen J. Brown, William N. Goetzmann, and Roger G. Ibbotson, "Offshore Hedge Funds: Survival and Performance 1989–1995," *Journal of Business*, No. 72, 1999, pp. 91–117.

16. Bing Liang, "Hedge Fund Performance: 1990–1999," *Financial Analysts Journal* 57, No. 1, 2001.
17. William Fung and David A. Hsieh, "Performance Characteristics of Hedge Funds and Commodity Funds: Natural versus Spurious Biases," Duke University Working Paper, May 2000 (http://faculty.fuqua.duke.edu/~dah7/fof.pdf).
18. See Gaurav S. Amin and Harry M. Kat, "Welcome to the Dark Side: Hedge Fund Attrition and Survivorship Bias 1994–2001," Working Paper, ISMA Center, University of Reading.
19. Laurent Favre and Andrew Singer, "The Difficulties of Measuring the Benefits of Hedge Funds," *Journal of Alternative Investments*, Summer 2002 (www.edhec-risk.com/edhec_publications/RISKReview1047569131698585459/attachments/The%20difficulties%20of%20measuring%20the%20benefits%20of%20HF2.pdf).
20. Harry M. Kat and Gaurav Amin, Diversification and Yield Enhancement with Hedge Funds, *Journal of Alternative Investments* 5, No. 3, 2002, pp. 50–58.
21. Ibid.
22. Gaurav S. Amin and Harry M. Kat, "Stocks, Bonds and Hedge Funds: Not a Free Lunch," ISMA Centre Discussion Papers in Finance 2002-11, April 29, 2002 (www.ismacentre.rdg.ac.uk/pdf/discussion/DP2002-11.pdf).
23. Vikas Agarwal and Narayan Y. Naik, "Does Gain-Loss Analysis Outperform Mean-Variance Analysis? Evidence from Portfolios of Hedge Funds and Passive Strategies," Working Paper, November 1999.

CHAPTER 5   Evaluating Hedge Fund Strategies

1. I adapt from the taxonomy scheme in Thomas Schneeweis and Richard Spurgin, "Hedge Funds: Portfolio Risk Diversifiers, Return Enhancers or Both?," Center for International Securities and Derivatives Markets (CISDM), Isenberg School of Management, University of Massachusetts, July 2000.
2. Andrew W. Lo, "Risk Management for Hedge Funds: Introduction and Overview," *Financial Analysts Journal* 57, No. 6, November/December 2001, pp. 16–33.
3. Greg Jensen and Jason Rosenberg, "Hedge Funds Selling Beta as Alpha," Bridgewater Associates Daily Observations, June 17, 2003.
4. Ibid.
5. William Fung and David A. Hsieh, "Event Risk and Risk Management of Global Yield Curve Exposure," *Journal of Fixed Income* 6, No. 2, 1996, pp. 37–48 (http://faculty.fuqua.duke.edu/~dah7/jfi1996.pdf).
6. David A. Hsieh and William Fung, "The Risk in Fixed Income Hedge Fund Styles," *Journal of Fixed Income* 12, No. 2, September 2002, pp. 6–27 (http://faculty.fuqua.duke.edu/~dah7/Fixedinc.pdf).
7. Ibid. The authors constructed a model to estimate the effect of credit spreads on fixed income arb funds: HFRI FI Arb return = 0.0096 – 5.37 times (Change in Credit Spread). Thus, 4.95% = 0.0096 – 5.37 * 1.10.
8. Ibid. The authors cited a loss of 6 percent by the HFR index, apparently an error.

9. In percentage terms:

$$\text{Percent long} = \frac{X_L}{X_L + X_S} \qquad \text{Percent short} = \frac{X_S}{X_L + X_S}$$

10. Hsieh and Fung, "Risk in Fixed Income Hedge Fund Styles."
11. Clifford Asness, Robert Krail, and John Liew, "Do Hedge Funds Hedge?" *Journal of Portfolio Management*, Fall 2001 (www.aqrcapital.com).
12. Ibid.
13. Ibid.
14. Ibid.
15. Alper Daglioglu and Bhaswar Gupta, "The Benefits of Hedge Funds," Center for International Securities and Derivatives Markets (CISDM), Isenberg School of Management, University of Massachusetts, March 2003.
16. Schneeweis and Spurgin, "Hedge Funds."

CHAPTER 6   Picking the Winners

1. Noel Amenc and Lionel Martellini, "The Alpha and Omega of Hedge Fund Performance," EDHEC Business School, Lille, February 27, 2003 (www .edhec-risk.com/edhec_publications/RISKReview1045562533936171352/ attachments/EDHEC_alphaomega.pdf).
2. M. J. Howell, "Fund Age and Performance," *Journal of Alternative Investments*, Fall 2001 (www.edhec-risk.com/site_edhecrisk/public/performance_ and_style_analysis/Research%20News/RISKReview1058528457431877640).
3. Greg N. Gregoriou, "Hedge Fund Survival Lifetimes," *Journal of Asset Management*, December 2002, pp. 237–252.
4. Morgan Stanley Dean Witter, "Why Hedge Funds Make Sense?" November 2000.
5. Martin M. Herzberg and Haim A. Mozes. "The Persistence of Hedge Fund Risk: Evidence and Implications for Investors," *Journal of Alternative Investments*, Fall 2003, pp. 22–42 (www.edhec-risk.com/site_edhecrisk/ public/performance_and_style_analysis/Research%20News/RISKReview 1070964705463940477).
6. Jeremy Smerd, "AU Feature: Emerging Managers Surface as Tomorrow's Leaders," Hedfund.net, June 14, 2004.
7. Morgan Stanley, "Why Hedge Funds Make Sense?"
8. Ardian Harri and B. Wade Brorsen, "Performance Persistence and the Source of Returns for Hedge Funds," Working Paper, July 2002 (http://go.okstate .edu/~brorsen/WP/hedge_funds_ardian.pdf).
9. Herzberg and Mozes, "Persistence of Hedge Fund Risk."
10. Ibid.
11. Ibid.
12. Amenc and Martellini, "Alpha and Omega."
13. Noel Amenc, S. El Bied, and Lionel Martellini, "Predictability in Hedge Fund Returns," *Financial Analysts Journal*, 59, No. 5, September–October 2003 pp. 32–46

14. Ibid.
15. Vikas Agarwal and Narayan Y. Naik, "Multi-Period Performance Analysis of Hedge Funds," *Journal of Quantitative and Financial Analysis* 35, No. 3, September 2000.
16. Morgan Stanley, "Why Hedge Funds Make Sense?"
17. Harry M. Kat and Faye Menexe, "Persistence in Hedge Fund Performance: The True Value of a Track Record," Alternative Investment Research Centre Working Paper #0007, September 2002.
18. Herzberg and Mozes, "Persistence of Hedge Fund Risk."
19. Ibid.
20. Ibid.
21. Amenc and Martellini, "Alpha and Omega."
22. Morgan Stanley, "Why Hedge Funds Make Sense?"
23. Daniel Capocci, Albert Corhay, and Georges Hubner, "Hedge Fund Performance and Persistence in Bull and Bear Markets," Working Paper, December 2003 (http://econwpa.wustl.edu/eps/fin/papers/0402/0402018.pdf).
24. Stuart Feffer and Christopher Kundro, "Understanding and Mitigating Operational Risk in Hedge Fund Investing," Capco White Paper, Capital Markets Company, March 2003.
25. Securities and Exchange Commission, Litigation Release No. 17230, November 13, 2001 (www.sec.gov/litigation/litreleases/lr17230.htm).
26. Bing Liang, "Hedge Fund Returns: Auditing and Accuracy," Draft, December 2002, Forthcoming in *Journal of Portfolio Management* (www.sec.gov/spotlight/hedgefunds/hedge-liang.htm).

CHAPTER 7   Constructing a Portfolio of Hedge Funds

1. See for example, Morgan Stanley Dean Witter, "Why Hedge Funds Make Sense?," November 2000.
2. Greenwich Associates, "The Alternative Balancing Act," December 2003.
3. R. McFall Lamm Jr., "Portfolios of Alternative Assets: Why Not 100% Hedge?" *Journal of Investing*, Winter 1999, pp. 87–97 (www.rjsinvestments.com/locked/general%20information%20on%20hedge%20funds/portfolios%20of%20alternative%20assets%20why%20not%20100%25%20hedge%20funds.pdf).
4. Ibid.
5. Gaurav S. Amin and Harry M. Kat, "Stocks, Bonds and Hedge Funds: Not a Free Lunch," ISMA Centre Discussion Papers in Finance 2002-11, April 29, 2002 (www.ismacentre.rdg.ac.uk/pdf/discussion/DP2002-11.pdf).
6. Ray Dalio, "An Open Letter to Investors: Post Modern Portfolio Theory—Engineering Targeted Returns and Risks," Bridgewater Associates, no date. Also available in modified version at www.bridgewaterassociates.com/pdf/PMPTAlpha2005.pdf).
7. Amin and Kat, "Stocks, Bonds and Hedge Funds."
8. Ibid.
9. Gaurav S. Amin and Harry M. Kat, "Hedge Fund Performance 1990–2000: Do the 'Money Machines' Really Add Value?," University of Reading, ISMA

Centre Discussion Papers in Finance 2001-05, September 6, 2001 (www.isma centre.rdg.ac.uk/pdf/discussion/DP2001-05.pdf).

10. François-Serge Lhabitant and Michelle Learned De Piante Vicin, "Finding the Sweet Spot of Hedge Fund Diversification," *Journal of Financial Transformation*, No. 10, April 2004 (www.edhec-risk.com/edhec_publications/RISK Review108305848680354686/attachments/Finding%20the%20Sweet%20 Spot%20of%20Hedge%20Fund%20Diversification.pdf). See also Barry A. Wintner, "How Many Hedge Funds Are Needed to Create a Diversified Fund of Funds?"(www.scandiumfunds.com/PDF/Diversification%20with%20hedge funds.pdf).

11. Gaurav Amin and Harry M. Kat, "Portfolios of Hedge Funds," Working Paper #0003, Alternative Investment Research Center Working Paper Series, Cass Business School, City University, July 11, 2002.

12. Ryan J. Davies, Harry M. Kat, and Sa Lu, "Single Strategy Funds of Hedge Funds," January 12, 2004 (www.edhec-risk.com/site_edhecrisk/public/ performance_and_style_analysis/Research%20News/RISKReview10754761 13566462783; full version www.edhec-risk.com/performance_and_style_ analysis/Research%20News/RISKReview1075476113566462783/attachments/ Single%20strategy%20funds%20of%20hedge%20funds.pdf).

13. Lamm, "Portfolios of Alternative Assets."

14. Noel Amenc and Lionel Martellini, "Portfolio Optimization and Hedge Fund Style Allocation Decisions," USC Marshall School of Business, Working Paper No. 02-4, March 2002. Also see Robert C. Merton, "On Estimating the Expected Return on the Market: An Exploratory Investigation," *Journal of Financial Economics* 8, December 1980, pp. 323–361.

15. Laurent Favre and Andreas Signer, "The Difficulties of Measuring the Benefits of Hedge Funds," *Journal of Alternative Investments*, Summer 2002.

16. R. McFall Lamm Jr. "Asymmetric Returns and Optimal Hedge Fund Portfolios," *Journal of Alternative Investments*, Fall 2003, pp. 9–21.

17. Ibid.

CHAPTER 8 Evaluating the Performance of Your Hedge Funds

1. In long-only investing, an alternative risk-adjusted measure is the Treynor ratio, which uses beta as the denominator instead of the standard deviation. It thus expresses the price per unit of systemic risk, instead of per unit of total risk as in the Sharpe ratio. Since beta is supposed to be small, except for predominantly directional strategies, total risk is a more relevant risk measure for hedge funds.

2. Ian McDonald, "Funds Adjust to Volatile Markets," *Wall Street Journal*, February 2, 2004, p. R1.

3. See for example, Martin J. Gruber, "Another Puzzle: The Growth in Actively Managed Mutual Funds," *Journal of Finance* 51, No. 3, July 1996, pp. 783–810.

4. See Greg Jensen and Jason Rotenberg, "Hedge Funds Selling Beta as Alpha," Bridgewater Associates Daily Observations, June 17, 2003.

5. David A. Hsieh and William Fung, "The Risk in Fixed Income Hedge Fund Styles," August 2002 (http://faculty.fuqua.duke.edu/~dah7/Fixedinc.pdf); *Journal of Fixed Income*, forthcoming.

6. Harry M. Kat and Joelle Miffre, "Performance Evaluation and Conditioning Information: The Case of Hedge Funds," Working Paper #0006, August 23, 2002.

CHAPTER 9   Buyers Beware

1. Roger Lowenstein, *When Genius Failed: The Rise and Fall of Long-Term Capital Management*, New York: Random House, 2000; Kevin Dowd, "Too Big to Fail?: Long-Term Capital Management and the Federal Reserve," *CATO Institute Briefing Paper No. 52*, September 23, 1999; and Philippe Jorion, "Risk Management Lessons from Long-Term Capital Management," *European Financial Management*, September 2000, pp. 277–300.

2. Stuart Feffer and Christopher Kundro, "Understanding and Mitigating Operational Risk in Hedge Fund Investing," Capco White Paper, The Capital Markets Company, March 2003.

3. George Crawford, "Must Prudent Investors Understand Hedge Fund Strategies," Fiduciary Foundation, July 2002 (www.fifo.org/Hedge_Fund.pdf).

4. U.S. Securities and Exchange Commission, *SEC v. Ashbury Capital Partners, L.P.*, Litigation Release No. 16770, October 17, 2000.

5. U.S. Securities and Exchange Commission, *SEC v. Burton G. Friedlander*, Litigation Release No. 18426, October 2003.

6. U.S. Securities and Exchange Commission, *SEC v. Higgins*, Litigation Release No. 17841, November 15, 2002.

7. U.S. Securities and Exchange Commission, *SEC v. Ryan J. Fontaine and Simpleton Holdings a/k/a Signature Investments Hedge Fund*, Litigation Release No. 17864, November 26, 2002 (www.sec.gov/litigation/litreleases/lr17864 .htm).

8. *SEC v. Beacon Hill Asset Management, L.L.C.* (November 15, 2002), as described in "Beacon Hill Principals Charged with Fraud, Case Expanded (Infovest21)," *Altnews*, June 17, 2004.

9. Stuart Feffer and Christopher Kundro, "Valuation Issues and Operational Risk in Hedge Funds," A Capco White Paper, The Capital Markets Company, December 2003.

10. Adam Bryan, "The Many Faces of Risk," *Journal of Financial Transformation* 5, August 2002.

11. David A. Hsieh and William Fung, "The Risk in Fixed Income Hedge Fund Styles," August 2002 (http://faculty.fuqua.duke.edu/~dah7/Fixedinc.pdf); *Journal of Fixed Income*, forthcoming.

12. Ibid.

13. Ibid., p. 25.

14. Richard Horwitz and Luis Rodriguez, "Merger Arbitrage Funds: Do They Deliver What They Promise?," Capital Market Risk Advisors.
15. Clifford Asness, Robert Krail, and John Liew, "Do Hedge Funds Hedge?," *Journal of Portfolio Management*, Fall 2001 (www.aqrcapital.com).
16. Andrew Lo, "Risk Management for Hedge Funds: Introduction and Overview," *Financial Analysts Journal* 57, No. 6, November 2002, p. 16.
17. Pascal Lambert and Peter Rose, "Risk Management for Hedge Funds—A Prime Broker's Perspective" (www.eubfn.com/arts/760_bearstearns.htm).
18. Amanda Cantrell, "Andor Replaces Manager of Poorly Performing Hedge Funds," *HedgeWorld*, December 17, 2003.
19. Bing Liang, "Hedge Fund Returns: Auditing and Accuracy," forthcoming in *Journal of Portfolio Management* (www.sec.gov/spotlight/hedgefunds/hedge-liang.htm).
20. Hsieh and Fung, "Risk in Fixed Income Hedge Fund Styles."

CHAPTER 10   Instant Diversification

1. Jeremy Smerd, "Net Assets in Hedge Funds Balloon to Record Numbers," HedgeFund.net, January 26, 2004.
2. Deborah Brewster, "Macro Hedge Funds Return to Favour," *Financial Times*, February 9, 2004.
3. Chidem Kurdas, "New Year: Fund of Funds Continue as Major Gateway into Industry," HedgeWorld.com, January 29, 2004.
4. Alexander M. Ineichen, "Fund of Hedge Funds: Industry Overview," *Journal of Wealth Management* 4, No. 4, Spring 2002, pp. 47–62 (www.blumont capital.com/downloads/articles/wp_fof_industry_0102.pdf).
5. Stephen J. Brown, William N. Goetzmann, and Bing Liang, "Fees on Fees in Funds of Funds," Yale International Center for Finance Working Paper No. 02-33, June 14, 2004 (http://papers.ssrn.com/sol3/papers.cfm?abstract_id= 335581).
6. Greg N. Gregoriou and Jean Pierre Gueyie, "Risk-Adjusted Performance of Funds of Hedge Funds Using a Modified Sharpe Ratio," *Journal of Wealth Management*, Winter 2003 (www.edhec-risk.com/site_edhecrisk/public/ performance_and_style_analysis/Research%20News/RISKReview10869312 59500349198).
7. Hilary Till, "The Capacity Implications of the Search for Alpha," *AIMA Journal*, June 2004 (www.aima.org/uploads/PremiaCap(2).pdf).
8. Greg Jensen and Jason Rotenberg, "Hedge Funds Selling Beta as Alpha," Bridgewater Associates Daily Observations, June 17, 2003.
9. Brown, Goetzmann, and Liang, "Fees on Fees."
10. Ibid.
11. Ibid.
12. Bing Liang, "Hedge Funds, Funds-of-Funds, and Commodity Trading Advisors," 2002 (www.mfainfo.org/images/pdf/Liang2002.pdf).
13. Ibid.

14. Casey, Quirk & Acito, "Fund of Hedge Funds: Rethinking Resource Requirements," September 2001 (www.cqallc.com/images/fohf_resource.pdf).
15. R. McFall Lamm Jr. and Tanya E. Ghaleb-Harter, "An Update on Hedge Fund Performance: Is a Bubble Developing?," *DB Absolute Return Strategies*, September 1, 2001 (www.mppf.org/DB_Hedge-Fund.pdf).
16. "SEC Charges Hedge Fund and Its Adviser with Fraud—Emergency Relief Ordered," Xagua Consulting Services, no date (www.xhedgefund.com/Manhattan%20Investment%20Fund.htm).
17. Myron S. Scholes, "The Future of Hedge Funds," *Journal of Financial Transformation* 10, April 2004, pp. 8–11.
18. Casey, Quirk & Acito, "Fund of Hedge Funds."

Bibliography

Acito, Christopher J., and F. Peter Fisher. "Fund of Hedge Funds: Rethinking Resource Requirements." *Journal of Alternative Investments* (Spring 2002).

Ackermann, Carl, Richard McEnally, and David Ravenscraft. "The Performance of Hedge Funds: Risk, Return, and Incentives." *Journal of Finance* 54, no. 3 (June 1999): 833–874.

Agarwal, Vikas, Naveen N. Daniel, and Narayan Y. Naik. "Flows, Performance, and Managerial Incentives in the Hedge Fund Industry." Working paper, September 2003.

Agarwal, Vikas, Naveen N. Daniel, and Narayan Y. Naik. "Role of Managerial Incentives, Flexibility, and Ability: Evidence from Performance and Money Flows." Working paper, April 5, 2005.

Agarwal, Vikas, and Narayan Y. Naik. "Does Gain-Loss Analysis Outperform Mean-Variance Analysis? Evidence from Portfolios of Hedge Funds and Passive Strategies." Working paper, November 1999.

Agarwal, Vikas, and Narayan Y. Naik. "Generalised Style Analaysis of Hedge Funds." *Journal of Asset Management* 1, no. 1 (2000): 93–109. www.gsu.edu/~fncvaa/genstyle.pdf.

Agarwal, Vikas, and Narayan Y. Naik. "Multi-Period Performance Persistence Analysis of Hedge Funds." *Journal of Financial and Quantitative Analysis* 35, no. 3 (September 2000): 327–342. www.gsu.edu/~fncvaa/Jfqapers.pdf.

Agarwal, Vikas, and Narayan Y. Naik. "On Taking the Alternative Route: Risks, Rewards, and Performance Persistence of Hedge Funds." *Journal of Alternative Investments* 2, no. 4 (Spring 2000): 6–23.

Agarwal, Vikas, and Narayan Y. Naik. "Performance Analysis of Hedge Funds with Option-Based and Buy-and-Hold Strategies." Working paper, August 2000.

Agarwal, Vikas, and Narayan Y. Naik. "Risks and Portfolio Decisions Involving Hedge Funds." *Review of Financial Studies* 7, no. 1 (Spring 2004): 63–98. http://facultyresearch.london.edu/docs/BSIGamma.pdf.

Amenc, Noël. "What Future for Alternative Indices?" Editorial, EDHEC-Risk and Asset Management Research Centre, June 7, 2004. www.edhec-risk.com/edito/What%20future%20for%20alternative%20indices.

Amenc, Noel, Sina El Bied, and Lionel Martellini. "Evidence of Predictability in Hedge Fund Returns." *Financial Analysts Journal* 59, no. 5 (September/October 2003): 32–46. www.edhec-risk.com/edhec_publications/RISKArticle103643215 6636469343/attachments/see%20full%20text%20(pdf).

Amenc, Noel, Philippe Malaise, Lionel Martellini, and Daphne Sfeir. "Evidence of Predictability in Bond Indices and Implications for Fixed-Income Tactical Style Allocation Decisions." Working paper, EDHEC Publications, October 2003. www.edhec-risk.com/edhec_publications/tsa%20bonds/attachments/tsa_bonds_10.pdf.

Amenc, Noel, and Lionel Martellini. "The Alpha and Omega of Hedge Fund Performance Measurement." Working paper, EDHEC Publications, February 2002. www.edhec-risk.com/site_edhecrisk/public/edhec_publications/RISK Review1045562533936171352; www.edhec-risk.com/edhec_publications/RISKReview1045562533936171352/attachments/EDHEC_alphaomega.pdf (Full version).

Amenc, Noel, and Lionel Martellini. "The Brave New World of Hedge Fund Indices." Working paper, EDHEC Publications, October 2002.

Amenc, Noel, and Lionel Martellini. "Portfolio Optimization and Hedge Fund Style Allocation Decisions." Working paper 02-4, USC Marshall School of Business, March 2002.

Amenc, Noel, Lionel Martellini, and Mathieu Vaissie. "Benefits and Risks of Alternative Investment Strategies." Working paper, EDHEC Publications, November 2002. www-rcf.usc.edu/~martelli/papers/brais.pdf; also www.edhec-risk.com/edhec_publications/RISKArticle1036426420978727721/attachments/full_text.pdf.

Amin, Gaurav S., and Harry M. Kat. "Diversification and Yield Enhancement with Hedge Funds." Working paper 0008, Cass Business School, City University, London, Alternative Investment Research Centre Working Paper Series, October 7, 2002.

Amin, Gaurav S., and Harry M. Kat. "Hedge Fund Performance 1990–2000: Do the 'Money Machines' Really Add Value?" University of Reading, ISMA Centre Discussion Papers in Finance 2001-05, September 6, 2001. www.ismacentre.rdg.ac.uk/pdf/discussion/DP2001–05.pdf.

Amin, Gaurav S., and Harry M. Kat. "Portfolios of Hedge Funds." Working paper 0003, Alternative Investment Research Centre Working Paper Series, Cass Business School, City University, July 11, 2002.

Amin, Gaurav S., and Harry M. Kat. "Stocks, Bonds and Hedge Funds: Not a Free Lunch." Working paper 0009, Cass Business School, City University, London, Alternative Investment Research Centre Working Paper Series (ISMA Centre Discussion Papers in Finance 2002-11) April 29, 2002. wwwismacentre.rdg.ac.uk/pdf/discussion/DP2002–11.pdf.

Amin, Gaurav S., and Harry M. Kat. "Welcome to the Dark Side: Hedge Fund Attrition and Survivorship Bias 1994–2001." Working paper, ISMA Centre, University of Reading.

Anderson, Richard E. "Endowment Spending: The Problem Will Be with Us for a While." Commonfund Commentary, May 2003. www.commonfund.org/Commonfund/Archive/CIO+Commentary/CIO_May_2003.htm.

Arnott, Robert D. "Editor's Corner: Sustainable Spending in a Lower-Return World." *Financial Analysts Journal* 60, no. 5 (September/October 2004): 6–9.

Asness, Clifford, Robert Krail, and John Liew. "Do Hedge Funds Hedge?" *Journal of Portfolio Management* (Fall 2001). www.aqrcapital.com/Do_Hedge_Funds _Hedge.htm.

Bares, P. A., R. Gibson, and S. Gyger. "Hedge Funds Allocation with Survival Uncertainty and Investment Constraints." Institute of Theoretical Physics, January 2002.

Blake, Rich. "Shifting into High Gear." *Institutional Investor* (March 2004): 24–28.

Boucher, Mark. *The Hedge Fund Edge: Maximum Profit/Minimum Risk Global Trend Trading Strategies.* New York: John Wiley & Sons, 1999.

Boyson, Nicole M. "Do Hedge Funds Exhibit Performance Persistence? A New Approach." October 2003. www.mgmt.purdue.edu/faculty/nboyson/persistence .pdf.

Brewster, Deborah. "Macro Hedge Funds Return to Favour." *Financial Times* (February 9, 2004).

Brooks, Chris, and Harry M. Kat. "The Statistical Properties of Hedge Fund Index Returns and Their Implications for Investors." *Journal of Alternative Investments* (Fall 2002): 26–44.

Brown, Stephen J., and William N. Goetzmann. "Hedge Funds with Styles." Working paper 00-29, Yale International Center for Finance, February 2001. www .absolutecapital.com.au/Research%20Articles/WILLIAM%20GOETZMANN .pdf.

Brown, Stephen J., William N. Goetzmann, and Roger G. Ibbotson. "Offshore Hedge Funds: Survival and Performance 1989–1995." *Journal of Business*, no. 72 (1999): 91–117.

Brown, Stephen J., William N. Goetzmann, and Bing Liang. "Fees on Fees in Funds of Funds." Working paper 02-33, Yale International Center for Finance, June 14, 2004. http://papers.ssrn.com/sol3/papers.cfm?abstract_id=335581.

Brown, Stephen J., William N. Goetzmann, and James M. Park. "Careers and Survival: Competition and Risk in the Hedge Fund and CTA Industry." *Journal of Finance* 56, no. 5 (October 2001).

Bruno, Mark. "Foundations, Endowments Adopt Absolute Outlook." *Altnews* (October 23, 2003).

Bryan, Adam. "The Many Faces of Risk." *Journal of Financial Transformation* 5 (August 2002). http://capco.com/journal.aspx?id=162.

Cantrell, Amanda. "Andor Replaces Manager of Poorly Performing Hedge Funds." HedgeWorld.com, December 17, 2003.

Capocci, Daniel, Albert Corhay, and Georges Hubner. "Hedge Fund Performance and Persistence in Bull and Bear Markets." Working paper, December 2004. http://econwpa.wustl.edu/eps/fin/papers/0402/0402018.pdf.

Capocci, Daniel, and Georges Hubner. "Analysis of Hedge Fund Performance." *Journal of Empirical Finance* 11, issue 1 (January 1, 2004): 55–89.

Casey, Quirk, and Acito. "Fund of Hedge Funds: Rethinking Resource Requirements." September 2001. www.cqallc.com/images/fohf_resource.pdf.

Chen, Peng, Barry Feldman, and Chandra Goda. "Portfolio with Hedge Funds and Other Alternatives." Working paper, July 2002. www.qwafafew.org/chicago/ papers/feldmanaugust2002.pdf.

Crawford, George. "Must Prudent Investors Understand Hedge Fund Strategies." Fiduciary Foundation, July 2002. www.fifo.org/hedge_fund.html.

Cvitanic, Jaksa, Ali Lazrak, Lionel Martellini, and Fernando Zapatero. "Optimal Allocation to Hedge Funds: An Empirical Analysis." Working paper, November 25, 2002. http://math.usc.edu/~cvitanic/PAPERS/funds.pdf.

Daglioglu, Alper, and Bhaswar Gupta. "The Benefits of Hedge Fund." Center for International Securities and Derivatives Markets, Isenberg School of Management, University of Massachusetts, March 2003.

Dalio, Ray. "An Open Letter to Investors: Post Modern Portfolio Theory—Engineering Targeted Returns and Risks." Bridgewater Associates, no date.

Davies, Ryan J., Harry M. Kat, and Sa Lu. "Fund of Hedge Funds Portfolio Selection: A Multiple Objective Approach." ICMA Centre, University of Reading, August 2005. http://papers.ssrn.com/sol3/papers.cfm?abstract_id=476862#Paper Download.

Davies, Ryan J., Harry M. Kat, and Sa Lu. "Single Strategy Funds of Hedge Funds." January 12, 2004. www.edhec-risk.com/site_edhecrisk/public/performance_and_style_analysis/Research%20News/RISKReview1075476113566462783.

Dimson, Elroy, Paul Marsh, and Mike Staunton. "Irrational Optimism." *Financial Analysts Journal* 60, no. 1 (January/February 2004): 15–25.

Dorsey, Alan, et al. "Are Hedge Funds or Hedge Fund of Funds an Asset Class or a Strategy among Asset Classes?" CRA RogersCasey, White paper, March 2003. www.crarogerscasey.com/contents/research/wp/HedgeFund2003.pdf.

Dowd, Kevin. "Too Big to Fail?—Long Term Capital Management and the Federal Reserve." CATO Institute Briefing Paper 52, September 23, 1999.

EDHEC-Risk. "Better Not to Invest at All Than to Allocate Small Proportions." March 11, 2004. www.edhec-risk.com/latest_news/Alternative%20Investments/RISKArticle1079018925253948960/view.

EDHEC-Risk. "Encouraging Record Inflow to Hedge Funds." Industry News, February 12, 2004. www.edhec-risk.com/latest_news/Alternative%20Investments/RISKArticle1076590685685754711/view.

EDHEC-Risk. "HNWIs Follow Lead of Institutional Investors, Says Survey." Business Analysis, March 11, 2004. www.edhec-risk.com/latest_news/Business%20_Strategy_Issues/RISKArticle1079008031833549385/view.

EDHEC-Risk. "Overview of Funds of Hedge Funds." June 11, 2004. www.edhec-risk.com/latest_news/Alternative%20Investments/RISKArticle108696058105388082/view.

EDHEC-Risk. "UBS Warburg Predicts a Paradigm Change in the Asset Management Industry." June 23, 2003. www.edhec-risk.com/latest_news/Alternative%20Investments/RISKArticle1056550629853402023/view.

EDHEC-Risk. "US Endowments Embrace Hedge Funds Amidst Public Outcry." March 4, 2004. www.edhec-risk.com/latest_news/Alternative%20Investments/RISKArticle1078402026609537344/view.

Fabozzi, Frank, and Ronald Ryan. "The Pension Crisis Revealed." *Journal of Investing* (Fall 2003): 43–48.

Favre, Laurent, and Jose-Antonio Galeano. "An Analysis of Hedge Fund Performance Using Loess Fit Regression." *Journal of Alternative Investments* (Spring 2002).

Favre, Laurent, and Jose-Antonio Galeano. "Mean-Modified Value-at-Risk Optimization with Hedge Funds." *Journal of Alternative Investments* (Fall 2002).www .edhec-risk.com/multistyle_multiclass/extreme_risk_allocation/review _current_research/RISKReview1063703886009117706/research_view.pt#ref 2002.

Favre, Laurent, and Andreas Signer. "The Difficulties of Measuring the Benefits of Hedge Funds." *Journal of Alternative Investments* (Summer 2002). www .edhec-risk.com/edhec_publications/RISKReview1047569131698585459/ attachments/The%20difficulties%20of%20measuring%20the%20benefits %20of%20HF2.pdf.

Feffer, Stuart, and Christopher Kundro. "Understanding and Mitigating Operational Risk in Hedge Fund Investing." A Capco White Paper, The Capital Markets Company, March 2003.

Feffer, Stuart, and Christopher Kundro. "Valuation Issues and Operational Risk in Hedge Funds." A Capco White Paper, The Capital Markets Company, December 2003.

The Foundation Center. "Foundation Growth and Giving Estimates: 2003 Preview." *Foundations Today Series*, 2004 Edition.

Fried, Carla. "Champagne Funds for Chardonnay Investors." *Business 2.0* (May 2003): 132–134.

Fung, Hung-Gay, Xiaoqing Eleanor Xu, and Jot Yau. "Do Hedge Fund Managers Display Skill?" *Journal of Alternative Investments* (Spring 2004). www .edhec-risk.com/site_edhecrisk/public/performance_and_style_analysis/ Research%20News/RISKReview1083919325433484813.

Fung, William, and David A. Hsieh. "Empirical Characteristics of Dynamic Trading Strategies: The Case of Hedge Funds." *Review of Financial Studies* 10, no. 2 (Summer 1997): 275–302. www.duke.edu/~dah7/rfs1997.pdf.

Fung, William, and David A. Hsieh. "Event Risk and Risk Management of Global Yield Curve Exposure." *Journal of Fixed Income* 6, no. 2 (1996): 37–48. http://faculty.fuqua.duke.edu/~dah7/jfi1996.pdf.

Fung, William, and David A. Hsieh. "Is Mean-Variance Analysis Applicable to Hedge Funds?" November 1997. http://faculty.fuqua.duke.edu/~dah7/m-v.pdf.

Fung, William, and David A. Hsieh. "Performance Attribution and Style Analysis: From Mutual Funds to Hedge Funds." February 1998. www.london.edu/ hedgefunds/Hedge_Fund_Centre/Published_Papers/style.pdf.

Fung, William, and David A. Hsieh. "Performance Characteristics of Hedge Funds and Commodity Funds: Natural versus Spurious Biases." Working paper, Duke University, May 2000. http://faculty.fuqua.duke.edu/~dah7/fof.pdf.

Fung, William, and David A. Hsieh. "A Primer on Hedge Funds." *Journal of Empirical Finance* (August 1999): 390–431. http://faculty.fuqua.duke.edu/~dah7/ primer.pdf.

Fung, William, and David A. Hsieh. "The Risk from Hedge Fund Strategies: Theory and Evidence from Trend Followers." *Review of Financial Studies* 14, no. 2 (Summer 2001): 313–341. www.turtletrader.com/hsieh_fung_final_paper.pdf.

Gehin, Walter. "Hedge Fund Performance." EDHEC Risk and Asset Management Research Center, August 2003. www.edhec-risk.com/performance_and_style_analysis/EDHEC%20Publications/RISKReview1070901068627242430/attachments/ HEDGE%20FUND%20PERFORMANCE.pdf.

Glassman, James K., and Kevin A. Hassett. *Dow 36,000: The New Strategy for Profiting from the Coming Rise in the Stock Market.* New York: Times Books, 1999.

Greenwich Associates. "The Alternative Balancing Act." December 2003.

Gregoriou, Greg N. "Hedge Fund Survival Lifetimes." *Journal of Asset Management* (December 2002): 237–252.

Gregoriou, Greg N., and Jean Pierre Gueyle. "Risk-Adjusted Performance of Funds of Hedge Funds Using a Modified Sharpe Ratio." *Journal of Wealth Management* (Winter 2003). www.edhec-risk.com/site_edhecrisk/public/performance_and_style_analysis/Research%20News/RISKReview1086931259500349198.

Gregoriou, Greg N., and Fabrice Rouah. "Large versus Small Hedge Funds: Does Size Affect Performance?" *Journal of Alternative Investment* (Winter 2002). www.edhec-risk.com/site_edhecrisk/public/performance_and_style_analysis/Research%20News/RISKReview1045663319007340143 (Summary).

Gruber, Martin J. "Another Puzzle: The Growth in Actively Managed Mutual Funds." *Journal of Finance* 51, no. 3 (July 1996): 783–810.

Gupta, Bhaswar, Baruk Cerrahoglu, and Alper Daglioglu. "Hedge Fund Strategy Performance: Using Conditional Approaches." *Journal of Alternative Investments* (Fall 2003).

Harri, Ardian, and B. Wade Brorsen. "Performance Persistence and the Source of Returns for Hedge Funds." Working paper, July 2002. http://go.okstate.edu/~brorsen/WP/hedge_funds_ardian.pdf.

Herzberg, Martin M., and Haim A. Mozes. "The Persistence of Hedge Fund Risk: Evidence and Implications for Investors." *Journal of Alternative Investments* (Fall 2003): 22–42. www.edhec-risk.com/site_edhecrisk/public/performance_and_style_analysis/Research%20News/RISKReview1070964705463940477.

"High-Performance Endowments Allocate More to Alternatives, Commonfund Finds." HedgeWorld.com, Thursday, January 22, 2004.

Horwitz, Richard, and Luis Rodriguez. "Merger Arbitrage Funds: Do They Deliver What They Promise." Capital Market Risk Advisors, no date.

Howell, M. J. "Fund Age and Performance." *Journal of Alternative Investments* (Fall 2001). www.edhec-risk.com/site_edhecrisk/public/performance_and_style_analysis/Research%20News/RISKReview1058528457431877640.

Hsieh, David A., and William Fung. "The Risk in Fixed Income Hedge Fund Styles." *Journal of Fixed Income* 12, no. 2 (September 2002): 6–27. http://faculty.fuqua.duke.edu/~dah7/Fixedinc.pdf.

Hulbert, Mark. "Behind Many Enticing Hedge Funds, Stale Prices." *New York Times* (June 20, 2004): D1.

Hulbert, Mark. "That Mirage in Foreign Harbors." *New York Times* (June 20, 2004): C1.

Hutton, Lyn. "CIO Commentary." Commonfund, April 2003. www.commonfund.org/commonfund/archive/cio+commentary/cio_april_2003.

Ineichen, Alexander M. *Absolute Returns: The Risk and Opportunities of Hedge Fund Investing.* New York: John Wiley & Sons, 2003.

Ineichen, Alexander M. "The Alpha in Fund of Hedge Funds: Do Fund of Hedge Funds Managers Add Value?" *Journal of Wealth Management* 5, no. 1 (Summer 2002): 8–25. www.blumontcapital.com/downloads/articles/wp_fof_alpha _0202.pdf.

Ineichen, Alexander M. "Fund of Hedge Funds: Industry Overview." *Journal of Wealth Management* 4, no. 4 (Spring): 47–62. www.blumontcapital.com/ downloads/articles/wp_fof_industry_0102.pdf.

Jaeger, Lars. "Hedge Fund Indices: A New Way to Invest in Absolute Return Strategies." *AIMA Journal* (June 2004). www.edhec-risk.com/site_edhecrisk/public/ research_news/choice/RISKReview1089704613542419134.

Jaeger, Robert A. *All about Hedge Funds: The Easy Way to Get Started.* New York: McGraw-Hill, 2003.

Jensen, Greg, and Jason Rotenberg. "Bubbling Again?" *Bridgewater Daily Observations*, Bridgewater Associates, July 15, 2003.

Jensen, Greg, and Jason Rotenberg. "Hedge Funds Selling Beta as Alpha." *Bridgewater Daily Observations*, Bridgewater Associates, June 17, 2003.

Jones, Charles P., and Jack W. Wilson. "The Changing Nature of Stock and Bond Volatility." *Financial Analysts Journal* (January/February 2004): 100–112.

Jorion, Philippe. "Risk Management Lessons from Long-Term Capital Management." *European Financial Management* (September 2000): 277–300.

Kat, Harry M. "In Search of the Optimal Fund of Hedge Funds." ISMA Centre Discussion Papers in Finance 2002-24, University of Reading, UK, October 25, 2002. www.ismacentre.rdg.ac.uk/pdf/discussion/DP2002–24.pdf.

Kat, Harry M., and Faye Menexe. "Persistence in Hedge Fund Performance: The True Value of a Track Record." Working paper 0007, Alternative Investment Research Centre, September 2002. www.business.city.ac.uk/airc/pdf/WP0007.pdf.

Kat, Harry M., and Joelle Miffre. "Performance Evaluation and Conditioning Information: The Case of Hedge Funds." Working paper 0006, August 23, 2002. www.business.city.ac.uk/airc/pdf/WP0006.pdf.

Kazemi, Hossein, Thomas Schneeweis, and B. Gupta. "Omega as a Performance Measure." June 2003. www.edhec-risk.com/multistyle_multiclass/extreme _risk_allocation/review_current_research/RISKReview1063631261806712604; http://cisdm.som.umass.edu/research/pdffiles/omega.pdf.

Kazemi, Hossein B., Thomas Schneeweis, and George Martin. "Understanding Hedge Fund Performance: Research Issues Revisited—Part I." *Journal of Alternative Investments* (Winter 2002): 6–22.

Kazemi, Hossein, Thomas Schneeweis, and Dulari Pancholi. "Performance Persistence for Mutual Funds: Academic Evidence." Center for International Securities and Derivatives Markets, Isenberg School of Management, University of Massachusetts, May 2003.

Keating, Con, and William F. Shadwick. "A Universal Performance Measure." Finance Development Centre, London, May 2002.

Koh, F., W. T. H. Koh, and M. Teo. "Asian Hedge Funds: Return Persistence, Style, and Fund Characteristics." Working paper, Singapore Management University,

June 2003. www.edhec-risk.com/site_edhecrisk/public/performance_and_style _analysis/Research%20News/RISKReview105937613803255031.

Kundro, Christopher, and Stuart Feffer. "Valuation Issues and Operational Risk in Hedge Funds." A Capco White Paper, The Capital Markets Company, December 2003.

Kurdas, Chidem. "New Year: Fund of Funds Continue as Major Gateway into Industry." HedgeWorld.com, January 29, 2004.

Lambert, Pascal, and Peter Rose. "Risk Management for Hedge Funds—A Prime Broker's Perspective." www.eubfn.com/arts/760_bearstearns.htm.

Lamm, R. McFall, Jr. "Asymmetric Returns and Optimal Hedge Fund Portfolios." *Journal of Alternative Investments* (Fall 2003): 9–21. www.gloriamundi.org/ picsresources/hfl.pdf.

Lamm, R. McFall, Jr. "Portfolios of Alternative Assets: Why Not 100% Hedge?" *Journal of Investing* (Winter 1999): 87–97. www.rjsinvestments.com/locked/ general%20information%20on%20hedge%20funds/portfolios%20of%20 alternative%20assets%20why%20not%20100%25%20hedge%20funds.pdf.

Lamm, R. McFall, Jr., and Tanya E. Ghaleb-Harter. "An Update on Hedge Fund Performance: Is a Bubble Developing?" *DB Absolute Return Strategies* (September 1, 2001). www.mppf.org/DB_Hedge-Fund.pdf.

Lavinio, Stefano. *The Hedge Fund Handbook: A Definitive Guide for Analyzing and Evaluating Alternative Investments.* New York: McGraw-Hill, 2000.

Lhabitant, François-Serge. "Derivatives in Portfolio Management: Why Beating the Market Is Easy." *Derivatives Quarterly* (Winter 2000). www.edhec-risk.com/ edhec_publications/RISKReview1055927251987929638/attachments/EDHEC _WhyBeatingTheMarketIsEasy.pdf.

Lhabitant, François-Serge. "Evaluating Hedge Fund Investments: The Role of Pure Style Indices." EDHEC Risk and Asset Management Research Center, December 2003. www.edhec-risk.com/edhec_publications/RISKReview10830609295 73713739/attachments/Barry%20HF%20VaR1%2009.02.04.pdf.

Lhabitant, François-Serge. *Hedge Funds: Myths and Limits.* Chichester: John Wiley & Sons, 2002.

Lhabitant, François-Serge, and Michelle Learned. "Hedge Fund Diversification: How Much Is Enough?" *Journal of Alternative Investments* (Winter 2002): 23–49.

Lhabitant, François-Serge, and Michelle Learned De Piante Vicin. "Finding the Sweet Spot of Hedge Fund Diversification." *Journal of Financial Transformation*, no. 10 (April 2004). www.edhec-risk.com/edhec_publications/RISK Review108305848680354686; www.edhec-risk.com/edhec_publications/RISK Review108305848680354686/attachments/Finding%20the%20Sweet%20 Spot%20of%20Hedge%20Fund%20Diversification.pdf.

Liang, Bing. "Hedge Fund Performance: 1990–1999." *Financial Analysts Journal* 57, no. 1 (January/February 2001): 11–18.

Liang, Bing. "Hedge Fund Returns: Auditing and Accuracy." Draft, December 2002. www.sec.gov/spotlight/hedgefunds/hedge-liang.htm.

Liang, Bing. "Hedge Funds, Funds-of-Funds, and Commodity Trading Advisors."

Case Western Reserve University, September 2002. www.mfainfo.org/images/pdf/Liang2002.pdf.

Liang, Bing. "Hedge Funds: The Living and the Dead." *Journal of Financial and Quantitative Analysis* 35, no. 3 (September 2000).

Liang, Bing. "On the Performance of Alternative Investments: CTAs, Hedge Funds, and Funds of Funds." Isenberg School of Management, University of Massachusetts, November 2003.

Liang, Bing. "On the Performance of Hedge Funds." March 1999. www.shoval.com/thelibrary/On%20the%20Performance%20of%20Hedge%20Funds%20%28Liang%29.pdf.

Lo, Andrew W. "Risk Management for Hedge Funds: Introduction and Overview." *Financial Analysts Journal* 57, no. 6 (November/December 2001): 16–33.

Lowenstein, Roger. *When Genius Failed: The Rise and Fall of Long-Term Capital Management.* New York: Random House, 2000.

Mahdavi, Mahnaz. "Risk-Adjusted Return When Returns Are Not Normally Distributed: Adjusted Sharpe Ratio." *Journal of Alternative Investments* (Spring 2004). www.edhec-risk.com/site_edhecrisk/public/research_news/choice/RISK Review1091700867335347667.

Markowitz, Harry. "Portfolio Selection." *Journal of Finance* 7, no. 1 (March 1952): 77–91.

McCrary, Stuart A. *How to Create and Manage a Hedge Fund: A Professional's Guide.* New York: John Wiley & Sons, 2002.

McDonald, Ian. "Funds Adjust to Volatile Markets." *Wall Street Journal* (February 2, 2004): R1.

Merton, Robert C. "On Estimating the Expected Return on the Market: An Exploratory Investigation." *Journal of Financial Economics* 8: 323–362.

Morgan Stanley Dean Witter. "Why Hedge Funds Make Sense?" November 2000.

Morgan Stanley Dean Witter. "Hedge Funds—Strategy and Portfolio Insights." December 2001.

New, Davis. "Hedge Fund Data." *Research Notes*, Wurts & Associates, March 2001. www.wurts.com/pdf/Hedge%20Funds.pdf.

Nicholas, Joseph G. *Investing in Hedge Funds: Strategies for the New Marketplace.* Princeton, NJ: Bloomberg Press, 1999.

Nicholas, Joseph G. *Market Neutral Investing: Long/Short Hedge Fund Strategies.* Princeton: Bloomberg Press, 2000.

Owen, James P. *The Prudent Investor's Guide to Hedge Funds: Profiting from Uncertainty and Volatility.* New York: John Wiley & Sons, 2000.

Philips, Thomas K., Emmanuel Yashchin, and David M. Stein. "Using Statistical Process Control to Monitor Active Managers." *Journal of Portfolio Management* (Fall 2003).

Posthuma, Nolke, and Peiter Jelle van der Sluis. "A Reality Check on Hedge Fund Returns." Working paper, July 2003. http://papers.ssrn.com/sol3/papers.cfm?abstract-id=438840#PaperDownload.

Rahl, Leslie, and Luis Rodriguez. "Is Closed Really Better." Capital Market Risk Advisors, no date.

Ramsden, Dick. "Insights into the Yale Formula for Endowment Spending." *Commonfund News* (September 5, 2003). www.commonfund.org/Commonfund/Archive/News/Yale_formula.htm.

Ranaldo, Angelo, and Laurent Favre. "How to Price Hedge Funds: From Two- to Four-Moment CAPM." Working paper, October 2003. www.edhec-risk.com/edhec_publications/RISKReview1067927350703560269/attachments/The%20working%20paper6.pdf.

Rockafellar, R. T., and S. Uryasev. "Conditional Value-at-Risk for General Loss Distributions." *Journal of Banking and Finance* (July 2002). www.edhec-risk.com/site_edhecrisk/public/multistyle_multiclass/Research%20News/RISK Review1077198205585710082.

Rosenberg, Mark James, P. Tomeo, and Sam Y. Chung. "Hedge Fund-of-Funds Asset Allocation Using a Convergent and Divergent Strategy Approach." *Journal of Alternative Investments* (Summer 2004). www.ssga.com/library/resh/Hedge_Fund_of_Fund_AA_Convergent_4.30.04CCRI1089396575.pdf.

Ross, Leola B., and George Oberhofer. "What the 'Indexes' Don't Tell You about Hedge Funds." Working paper, March 2002. http://papers.ssrn.com/sol3/papers.cfm?abstract-id=314868#PaperDownload.

Schneeweis, Thomas. "Alpha, Alpha, Who's Got the Alpha?" Working paper, October 5, 1999.

Schneeweis, Thomas. "Dealing with Myths of Hedge Fund Investment." *Journal of Alternative Investments* (Winter 1998).

Schneeweis, Thomas, and Georgi Georgiev. "The Benefits of Hedge Funds." CISDM/School of Management, June 19, 2002.

Schneeweis, Thomas, and Richard Spurgin. "Hedge Funds: Portfolio Risk Diversifiers, Return Enhancers or Both?" CISDM/Isenberg School of Management, University of Massachusetts, July 2000.

Scholes, Myron S. "The Future of Hedge Funds." *Journal of Financial Transformation* 10 (April 2004): 8–11. www.capco.com/uploadedFiles/Members/Journal/Vol10/j10art01.pdf; www.capco.com/pdf/j10art01.pdf.

Scholz, Hendrik, and Marco Wilkens. "Interpreting Sharpe Ratio—The Market Climate Bias." Working paper, June 2004. http://papers.ssrn.com/sol3/papers.cfm?abstract_id=524842#PaperDownload.

Sharpe, William F. "Capital Asset Prices: A Theory of Market Equilibrium under Conditions of Risk." *Journal of Finance* 19, no. 3 (September 1964): 425–442.

Smerd, Jeremy. "AU Feature: Emerging Managers Surface as Tomorrow's Leaders." Hedgefund.net, June 14, 2004.

Smerd, Jeremy. "Net Assets in Hedge Funds Balloon to Record Numbers." Hedgefund.net, January 26, 2004.

Spurgin, Richard. "How to Game Your Sharp Ratio." *Journal of Alternative Investments* (Winter 2001): 38–46.

Strachman, Daniel A. *Getting Started in Hedge Funds.* 2nd ed. Hoboken, NJ: John Wiley & Sons, 2005.

Till, Hilary. "The Capacity Implications of the Search for Alpha." *AIMA Journal* (June 2004). www.aima.org/uploads/PremiaCap(2).pdf.

Till, Hilary. "Risk Measurement of Investments in the Satellite Ring of a Core-Satellite Portfolio: Traditional versus Alternative Approaches." Premia Risk Consultancy Inc., Chicago. Also in Geoff Hirt and J. Clay Singleton (eds.), *The Core-Satellite Approach to Portfolio Management.* New York: McGraw-Hill, 2004.

"U.S. Educational Endowments and Foundations See 'Light at the End of the Tunnel' with Moderate Improvement in Returns in Fiscal Year 2003." Press release, Commonfund, January 21, 2004.

U.S. Securities and Exchange Commission. "Registration under the Advisers Act of Certain Hedge Fund Advisers." Release No. IA-2333; File No. S7-30-04. www.sec.gov/rules/final/ia-2333.htm#P85_18913.

U.S. Securities and Exchange Commission. *SEC v. Ashbury Capital Partners, L.P.* Litigation Release No. 16770, October 17, 2000. See SEC web site.

U.S. Securities and Exchange Commission. *SEC v. Beacon Hill Asset Management, L.L.C.* (November 15, 2002), as described in "Beacon Hill Principals Charged with Fraud, Case Expanded (Infovest21)." *Altnews* (June 17, 2004). See also www.sec.gov/litigation/litreleases/lr17841.htm.

U.S. Securities and Exchange Commission. *SEC v. Burton G. Friedlander.* Litigation Release No. 18426, October 2003. See SEC web site.

U.S. Securities and Exchange Commission. *SEC v. Higgins.* Litigation Release No. 17841, November 15, 2002. See SEC web site.

U.S. Securities and Exchange Commission. *SEC v. Michael W. Berger.* Litigation Release No. 17230, November 13, 2001. www.sec.gov/litigation/litreleases/lr17230.htm.

U.S. Securities and Exchange Commission. *SEC v. Ryan J. Fontaine and Simpleton Holdings a/k/a Signature Investments Hedge Fund.* Litigation Release No. 17864, November 26, 2002. www.sec.gov/litigation/litreleases/lr17864.htm.

Vaissie, Mathieu. "A Detailed Analysis of the Construction Methods and Management Principles of Hedge Fund Indices." EDHEC Risk and Asset Management Research Centre, December 2003.

Winter, Greg. "College Endowments Make Happy Discovery: Black Ink." *New York Times* (February 20, 2004): A17.

Wintner, Barry A. "How Many Hedge Funds Are Needed to Create a Diversified Fund of Funds?" March 2001. www.scandiumfunds.com/PDF/Diversification%20with%20hedgefunds.pdf.

Yang, Taewon, and Ben Branch. "Merger Arbitrage: Evidence of Profitability." no date. http://cisdm.som.umass.edu/research/pdffiles/article2taiwonandbranch.pdf.

Zuckerman, Gregory. "Hedge Funds May Give Colleges Painful Lessons." *Wall Street Journal* (October 7, 2002): C5.

Index